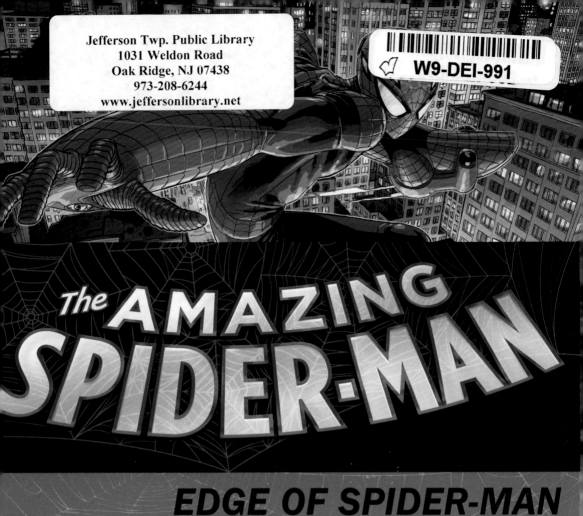

The AMAZING SPIDER-MAN

EDGE OF SPIDER-MAN

#1 — SPIDER-MAN NOIR
WRITERS: **DAVID HINE**
WITH **FABRICE SAPOLSKY**
ARTIST/COVER: **RICHARD ISANOVE**

#2 — GWEN STACY: SPIDER-WOMAN
WRITER: **JASON LATOUR**
ARTIST/COVER: **ROBBI RODRIGUEZ**
COLOR ARTIST: **RICO RENZI**

#3 — AARON AIKMAN: THE SPIDER-MAN
WRITER/ARTIST/COVER: **DUSTIN WEAVER**

#4 — "I WALKED WITH A SPIDER!"
WRITER: **CLAY MCLEOD CHAPMAN**
ARTIST: **ELIA BONETTI**
COLOR ARTIST: **VERONICA GANDINI**
COVER ART: **GARRY BROWN**

#5 — SP//DR
WRITER: **GERARD WAY**
ARTIST/COVER: **JAKE WYATT**
COLOR ARTIST: **IAN HERRING**

LETTERER: **VC'S CLAYTON COWLES**
ASSISTANT EDITOR: **DEVIN LEWIS**
SENIOR EDITORS: **NICK LOWE** WITH **ELLIE PYLE**

SPIDER-MAN CREATED BY STAN LEE & STEVE DITKO

Collection Editor: **Jennifer Grünwald**
Assistant Editor: **Sarah Brunstad**
Associate Managing Editor: **Alex Starbuck**
Editor, Special Projects: **Mark D. Beazley**
Senior Editor, Special Projects: **Jeff Youngquist**
SVP Print, Sales & Marketing: **David Gabriel**

Editor in Chief: **Axel Alonso**
Chief Creative Officer: **Joe Quesada**
Publisher: **Dan Buckley**
Executive Producer: **Alan Fine**

ZING SPIDER-MAN: EDGE OF SPIDER-VERSE. Contains material originally published in magazine form as EDGE OF SPIDER-VERSE #1-5. First printing 2015. ISBN# 978-0-7851-9728-7. Published by MARVEL
LDWIDE, INC., a subsidiary of MARVEL ENTERTAINMENT, LLC. OFFICE OF PUBLICATION: 135 West 50th Street, New York, NY 10020. Copyright © 2015 MARVEL No similarity between any of the names, characters,
ons, and/or institutions in this magazine with those of any living or dead person or institution is intended, and any such similarity which may exist is purely coincidental. **Printed in Canada.** ALAN FINE, President,
el Entertainment; DAN BUCKLEY, President, TV, Publishing and Brand Management; JOE QUESADA, Chief Creative Officer; TOM BREVOORT, SVP of Publishing; DAVID BOGART, SVP of Operations & Procurement,
shing; C.B. CEBULSKI, SVP of Creator & Content Development; DAVID GABRIEL, SVP Print, Sales & Marketing; JIM O'KEEFE, VP of Operations & Logistics; DAN CARR, Executive Director of Publishing Technology; SUSAN
SPI, Editorial Operations Manager; ALEX MORALES, Publishing Operations Manager; STAN LEE, Chairman Emeritus. For information regarding advertising in Marvel Comics or on Marvel.com, please contact Niza Disla
tor of Marvel Partnerships, at ndisla@marvel.com. For Marvel subscription inquiries, please call 800-217-9158. **Manufactured between 3/6/2015 and 4/13/2015 by SOLISCO PRINTERS, SCOTT, QC, CANADA.**

8 7 6 5 4 3 2 1

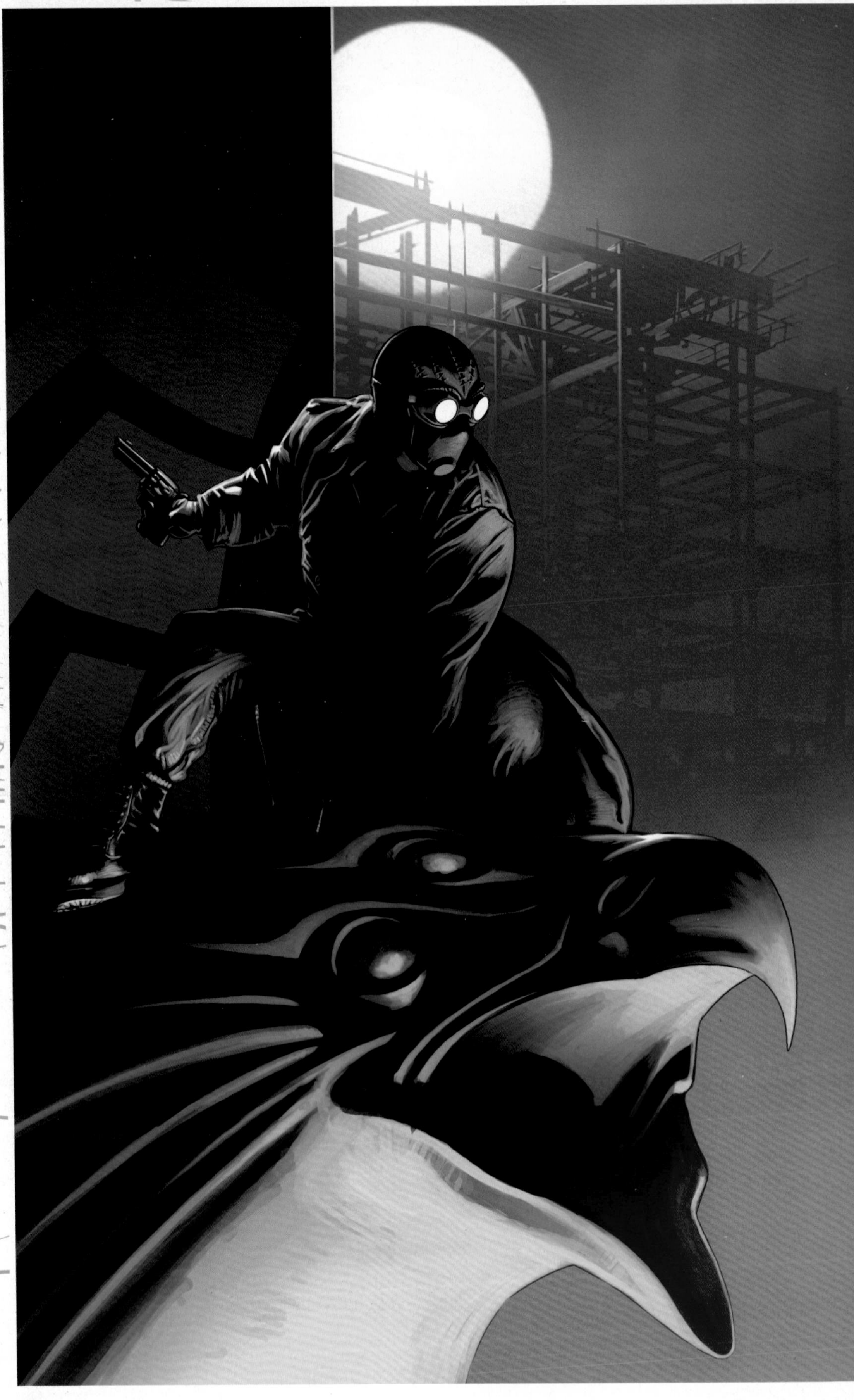

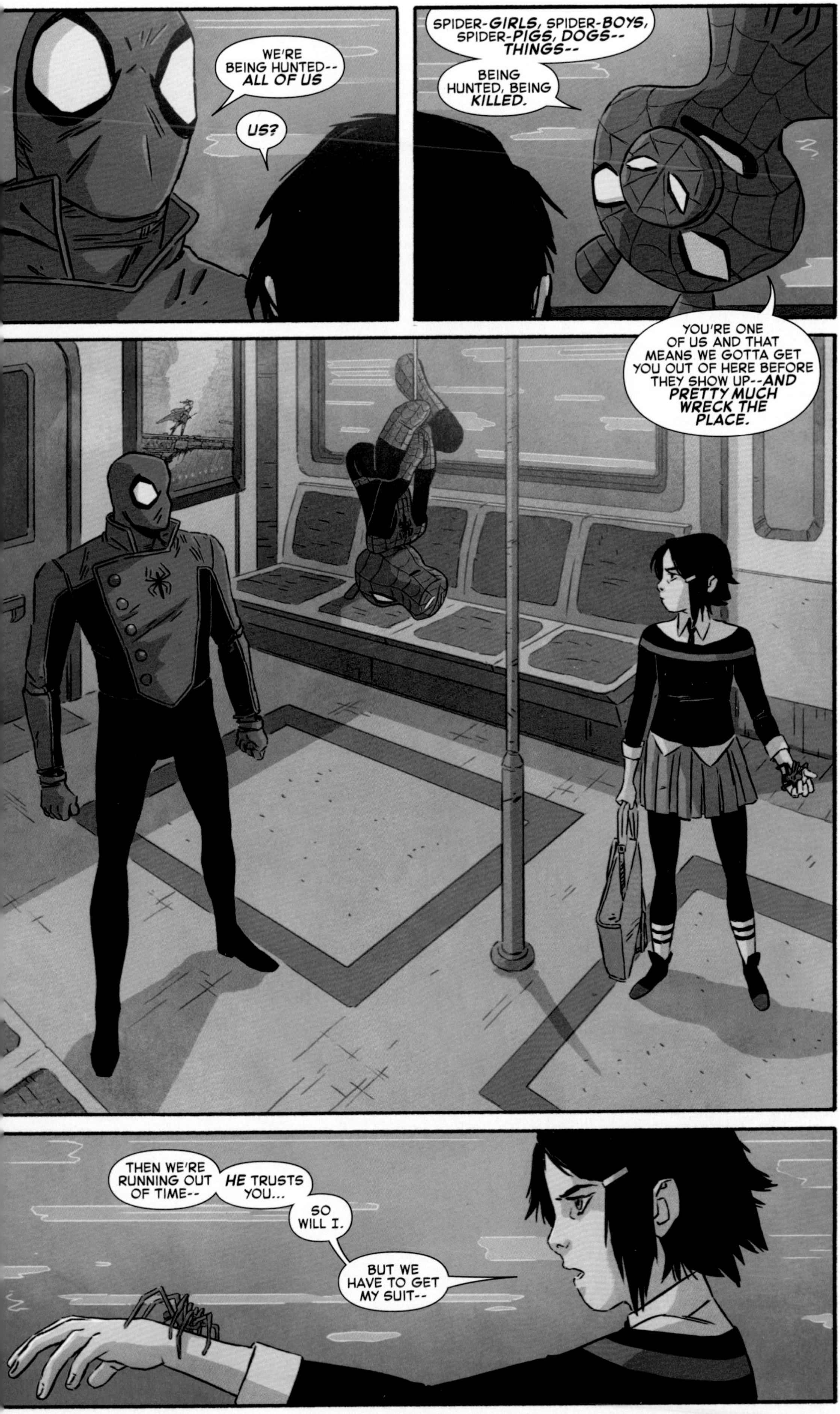

WE'RE BEING HUNTED-- ALL OF US
US?
SPIDER-GIRLS, SPIDER-BOYS, SPIDER-PIGS, DOGS-- THINGS--
BEING HUNTED, BEING KILLED.
YOU'RE ONE OF US AND THAT MEANS WE GOTTA GET YOU OUT OF HERE BEFORE THEY SHOW UP--AND PRETTY MUCH WRECK THE PLACE.
THEN WE'RE RUNNING OUT OF TIME--
HE TRUSTS YOU...
SO WILL I.
BUT WE HAVE TO GET MY SUIT--

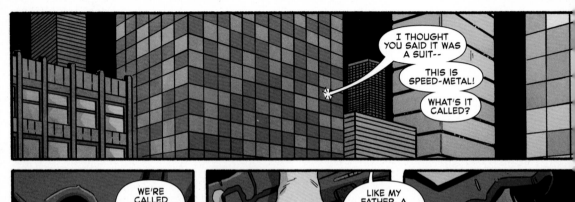

I THOUGHT YOU SAID IT WAS A SUIT--

THIS IS SPEED-METAL!

WHAT'S IT CALLED?

WE'RE CALLED SP//dr AND WE PROTECT THE CITY.

LIKE MY FATHER, A SOLDIER--WHO DIED IN SERVICE OF HIS PEOPLE--

--WE WILL BE THIS, UNTIL TERMINAL FAILURE--

THAT'S FAIRLY HARD-CORE.

GATE'S OPEN--WE GOTTA SWING...

DOES THAT THING MAKE A LOT OF NOISE?

YEAH...

...THE GOOD KIND.

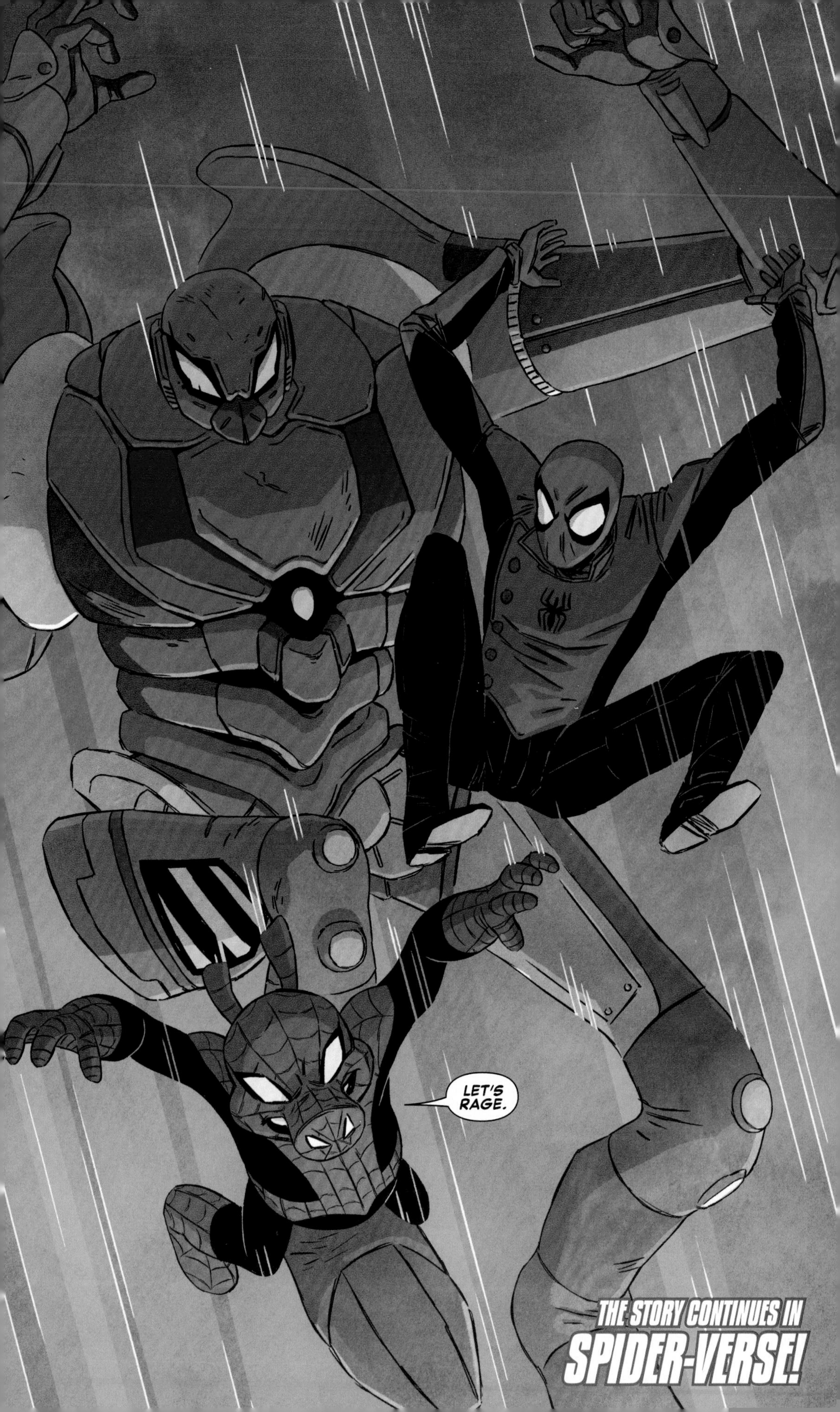
LET'S RAGE.
THE STORY CONTINUES IN SPIDER-VERSE!

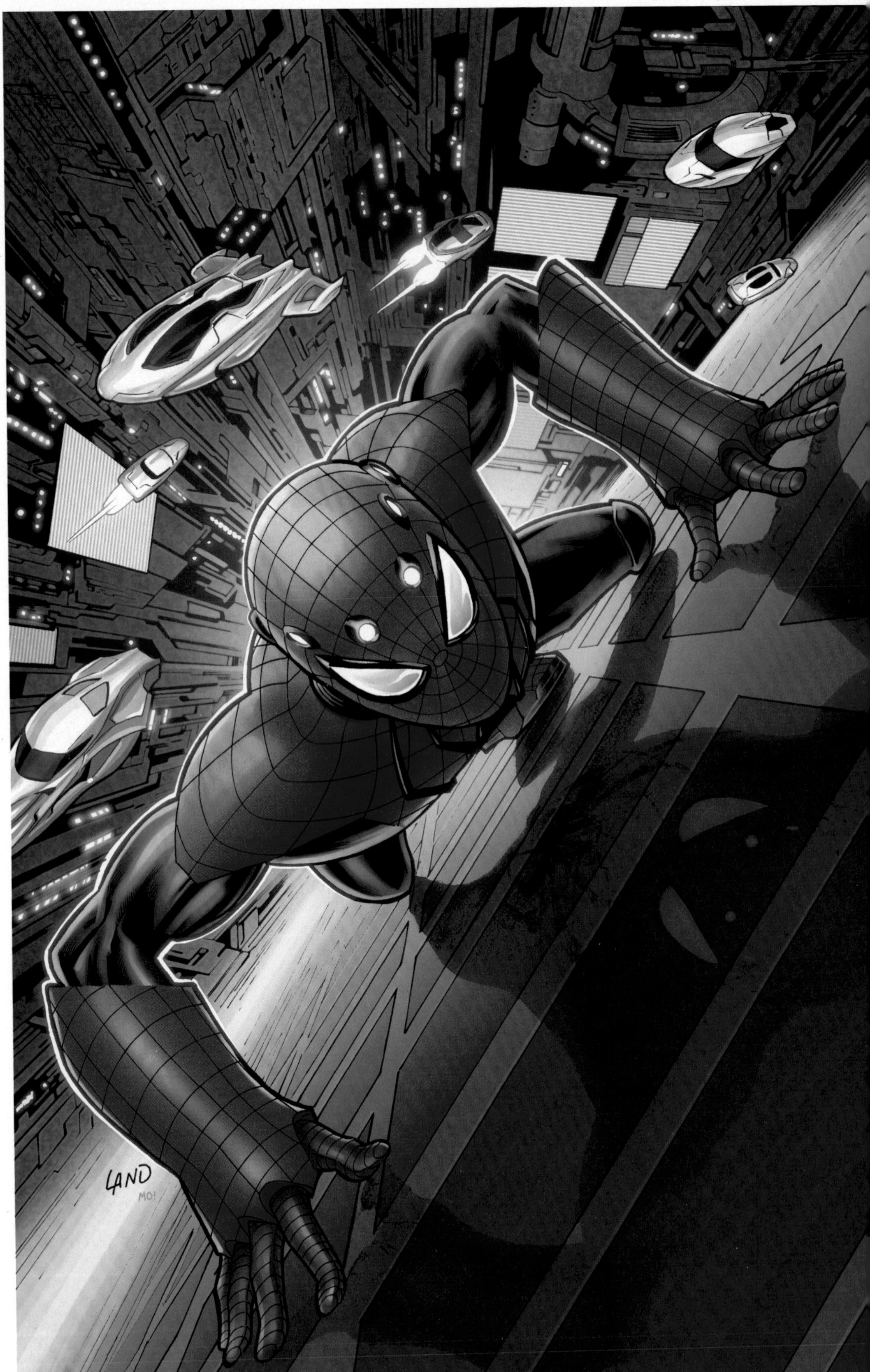
LAND
MO!

#3 VARIANT BY GREG LAND & MORRY HOLLOWELL

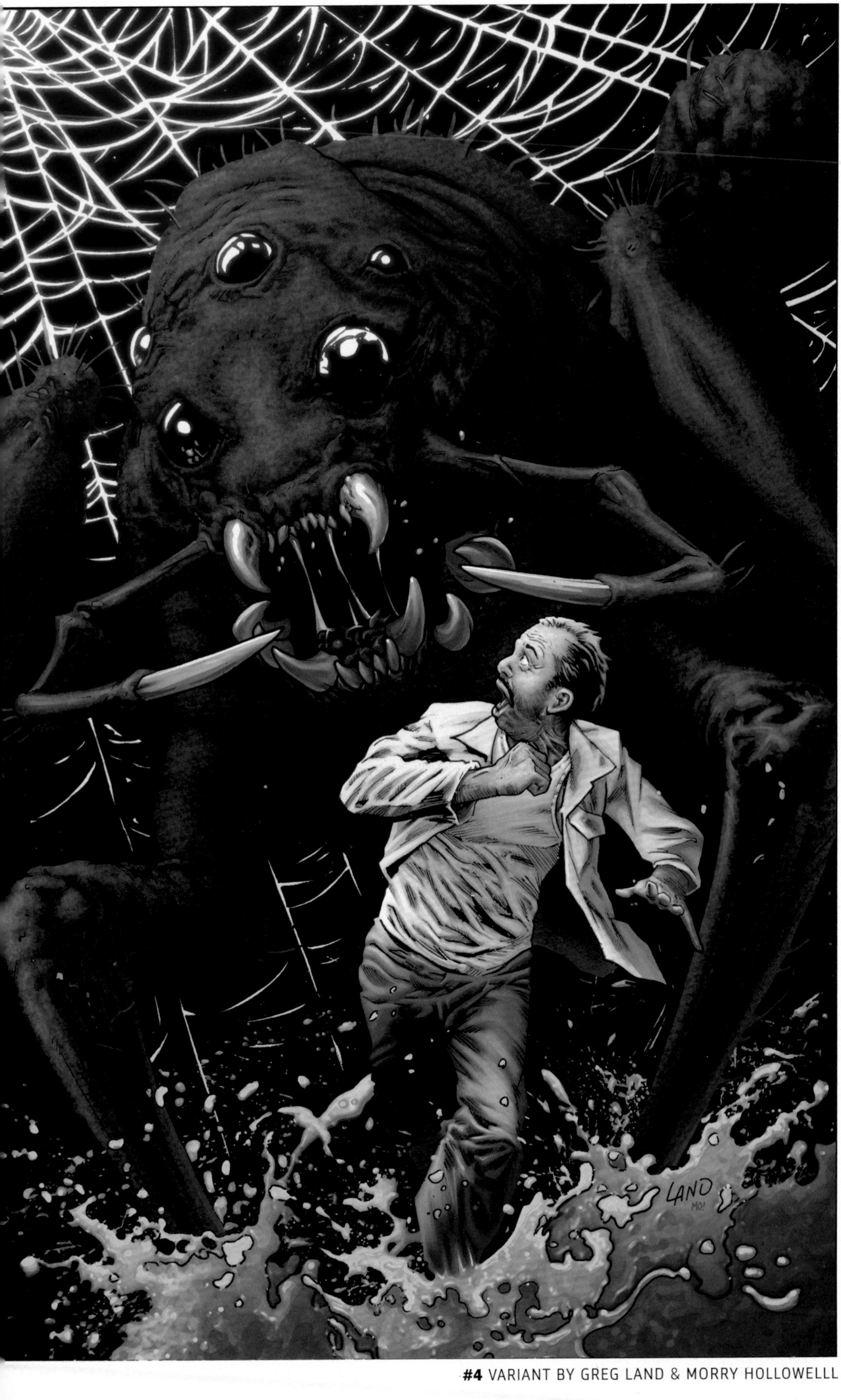
LAND
MO!

#4 VARIANT BY GREG LAND & MORRY HOLLOWELLL

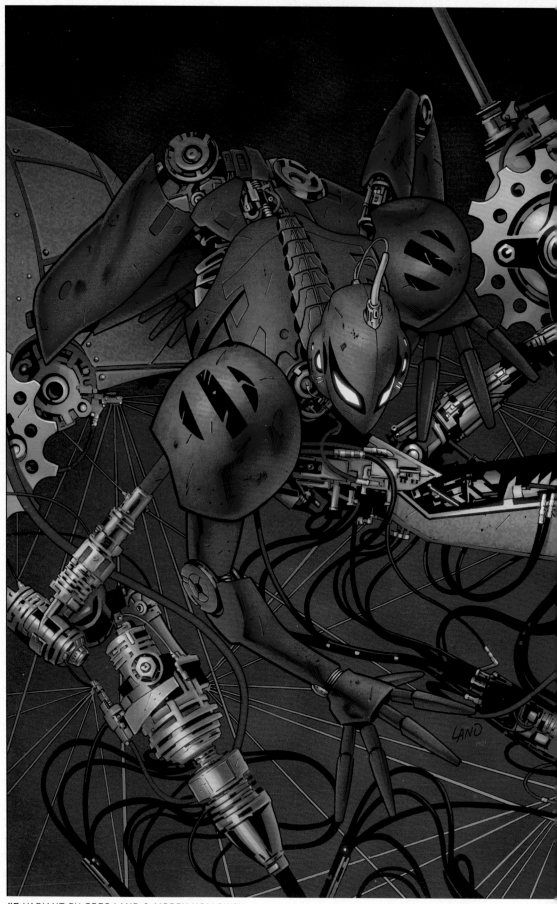

#5 VARIANT BY GREG LAND & MORRY HOLLOWELL

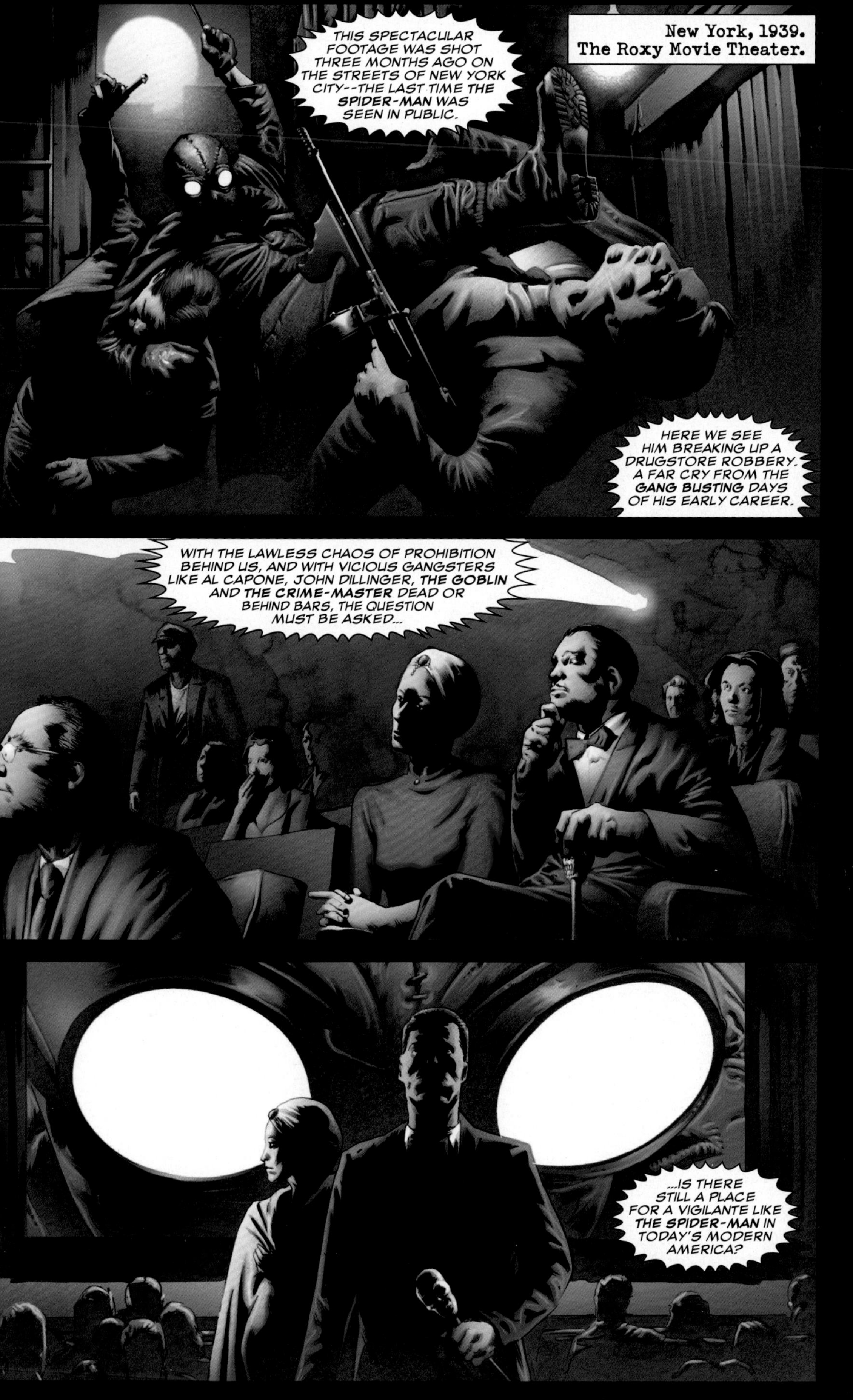
New York, 1939.
The Roxy Movie Theater.
THIS SPECTACULAR FOOTAGE WAS SHOT THREE MONTHS AGO ON THE STREETS OF NEW YORK CITY--THE LAST TIME THE SPIDER-MAN WAS SEEN IN PUBLIC.
HERE WE SEE HIM BREAKING UP A DRUGSTORE ROBBERY. A FAR CRY FROM THE GANG BUSTING DAYS OF HIS EARLY CAREER.
WITH THE LAWLESS CHAOS OF PROHIBITION BEHIND US, AND WITH VICIOUS GANGSTERS LIKE AL CAPONE, JOHN DILLINGER, THE GOBLIN AND THE CRIME-MASTER DEAD OR BEHIND BARS, THE QUESTION MUST BE ASKED...
...IS THERE STILL A PLACE FOR A VIGILANTE LIKE THE SPIDER-MAN IN TODAY'S MODERN AMERICA?

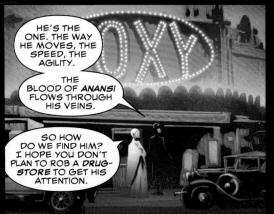

HE'S THE ONE. THE WAY HE MOVES, THE SPEED, THE AGILITY.

THE BLOOD OF *ANANSI* FLOWS THROUGH HIS VEINS.

SO HOW DO WE FIND HIM? I HOPE YOU DON'T PLAN TO ROB A *DRUG-STORE* TO GET HIS ATTENTION.

I'LL THINK OF SOMETHING. I CERTAINLY HAVE NO INTENTION OF SPENDING THE REST OF MY LIFE ENTERTAINING THE GREAT UNWASHED FROM A PUBLIC STAGE.

THE MAGNIFICENT MYSTERIO

APPEARING AT THE NEW YORK WORLD'S FAIR

LOOK, PA. *MYSTERIO THE MAGICIAN.*

HE CAN MAKE AN ELEPHANT *DISAPPEAR.*

YEAH?

CAN WE GO SEE HIM, PA? *CAN WE?*

I AIN'T GOT THE DOUGH TO WASTE ON SOME TWO-BIT CONJUROR.

HOW ABOUT THE *JUNGLELAND?* THEY'VE GOT A *THOUSAND* MONKEYS.

FRANK BUCK'S JUNGLELAND

A THOUSAND MONKEYS? NOW THAT'S *SOMETHING.* THAT I'D PAY TO SEE.

PASSED OVER FOR A *MONKEY?*

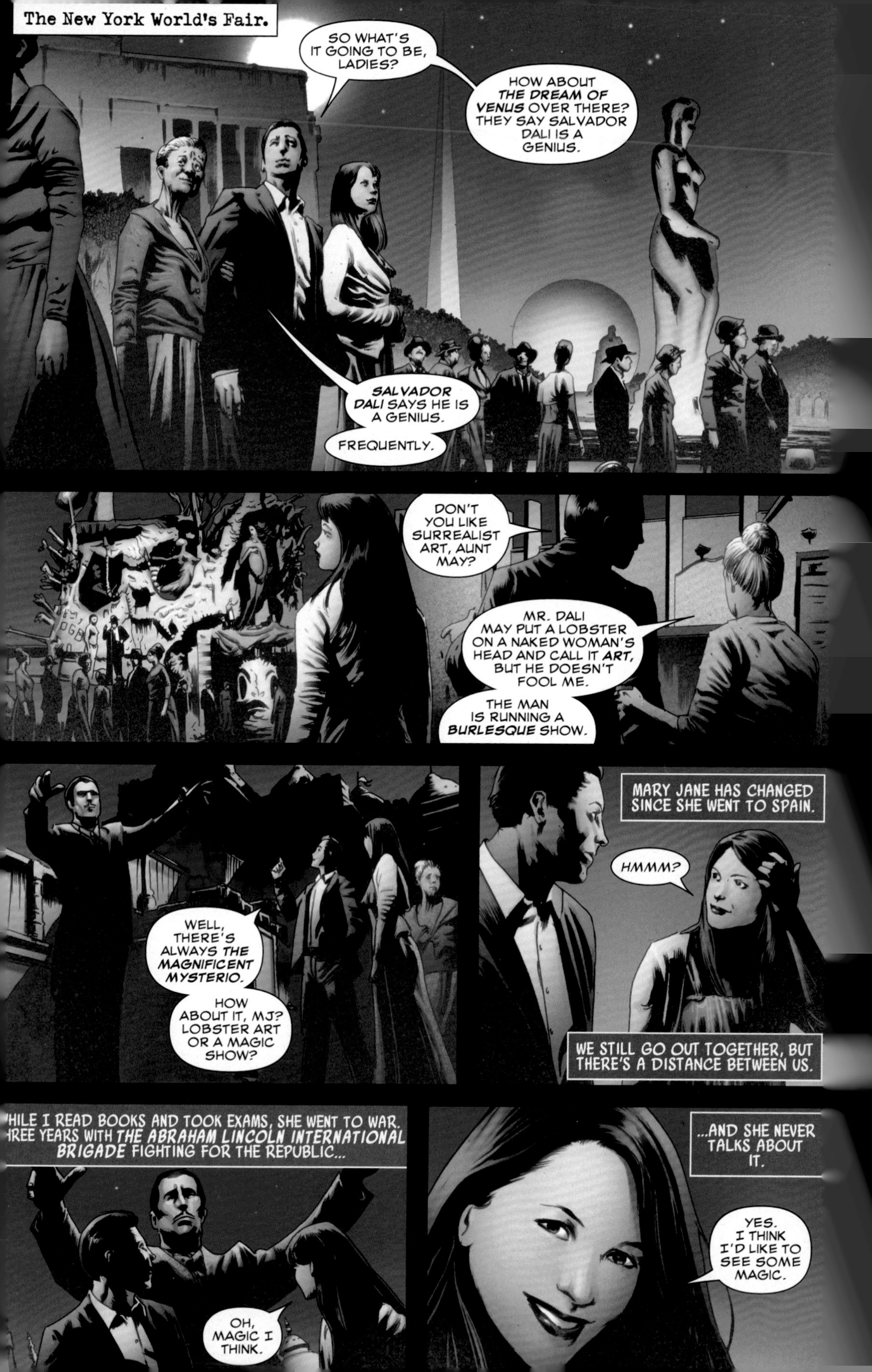

The New York World's Fair.
SO WHAT'S IT GOING TO BE, LADIES?
HOW ABOUT THE DREAM OF VENUS OVER THERE? THEY SAY SALVADOR DALI IS A GENIUS.
SALVADOR DALI SAYS HE IS A GENIUS.
FREQUENTLY.
DON'T YOU LIKE SURREALIST ART, AUNT MAY?
MR. DALI MAY PUT A LOBSTER ON A NAKED WOMAN'S HEAD AND CALL IT ART, BUT HE DOESN'T FOOL ME.
THE MAN IS RUNNING A BURLESQUE SHOW.
WELL, THERE'S ALWAYS THE MAGNIFICENT MYSTERIO.
HOW ABOUT IT, MJ? LOBSTER ART OR A MAGIC SHOW?
MARY JANE HAS CHANGED SINCE SHE WENT TO SPAIN.
HMMM?
WE STILL GO OUT TOGETHER, BUT THERE'S A DISTANCE BETWEEN US.
HILE I READ BOOKS AND TOOK EXAMS, SHE WENT TO WAR. HREE YEARS WITH THE ABRAHAM LINCOLN INTERNATIONAL BRIGADE FIGHTING FOR THE REPUBLIC...
OH, MAGIC I THINK.
...AND SHE NEVER TALKS ABOUT IT.
YES. I THINK I'D LIKE TO SEE SOME MAGIC.

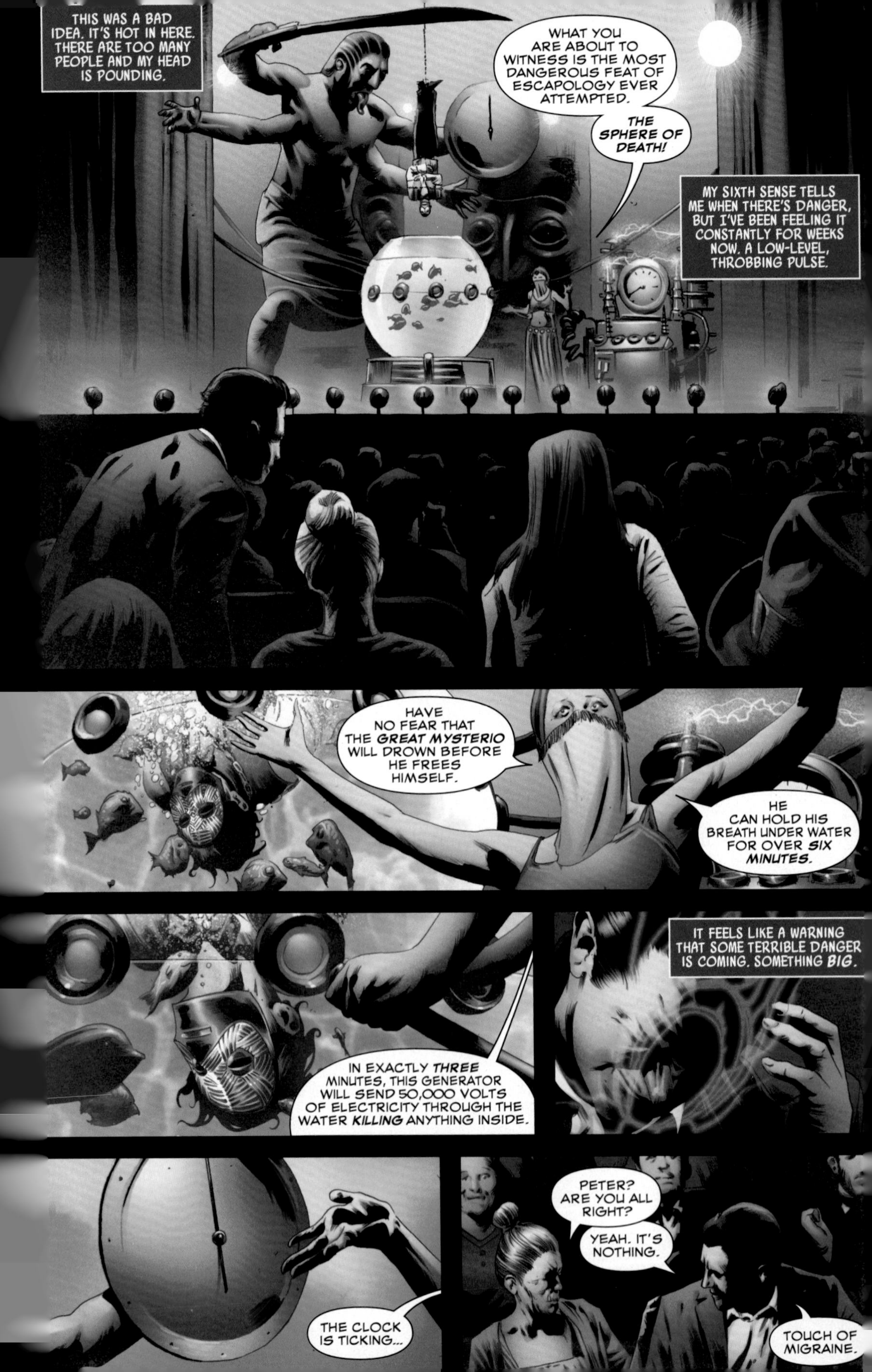
THIS WAS A BAD IDEA. IT'S HOT IN HERE. THERE ARE TOO MANY PEOPLE AND MY HEAD IS POUNDING.
WHAT YOU ARE ABOUT TO WITNESS IS THE MOST DANGEROUS FEAT OF ESCAPOLOGY EVER ATTEMPTED.
THE SPHERE OF DEATH!
MY SIXTH SENSE TELLS ME WHEN THERE'S DANGER, BUT I'VE BEEN FEELING IT CONSTANTLY FOR WEEKS NOW. A LOW-LEVEL, THROBBING PULSE.
HAVE NO FEAR THAT THE GREAT MYSTERIO WILL DROWN BEFORE HE FREES HIMSELF.
HE CAN HOLD HIS BREATH UNDER WATER FOR OVER SIX MINUTES.
IN EXACTLY THREE MINUTES, THIS GENERATOR WILL SEND 50,000 VOLTS OF ELECTRICITY THROUGH THE WATER KILLING ANYTHING INSIDE.
IT FEELS LIKE A WARNING THAT SOME TERRIBLE DANGER IS COMING. SOMETHING BIG.
THE CLOCK IS TICKING...
PETER? ARE YOU ALL RIGHT?
YEAH. IT'S NOTHING.
TOUCH OF MIGRAINE.

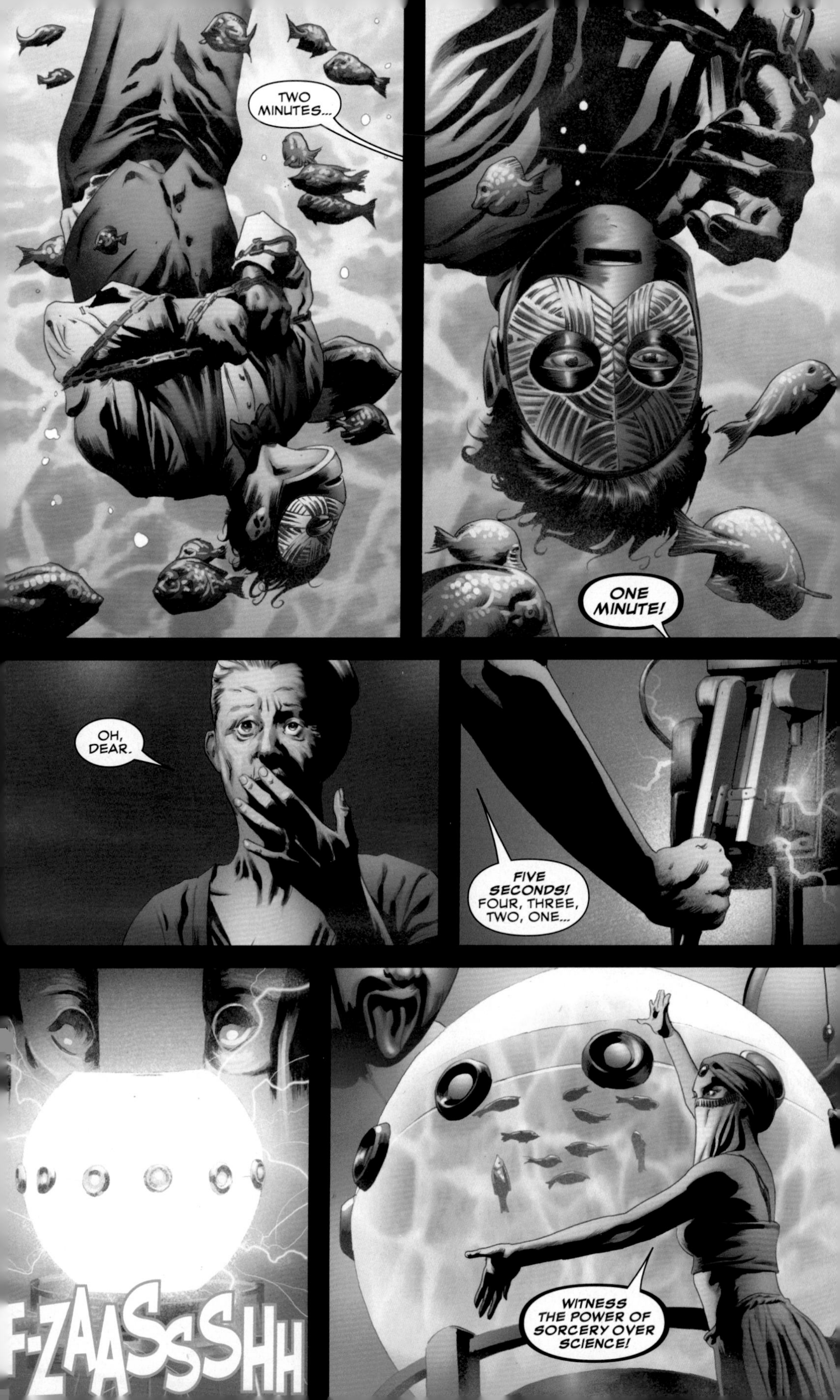
TWO MINUTES...
ONE MINUTE!
OH, DEAR.
FIVE SECONDS! FOUR, THREE, TWO, ONE...
F-ZAASSSHH
WITNESS THE POWER OF SORCERY OVER SCIENCE!

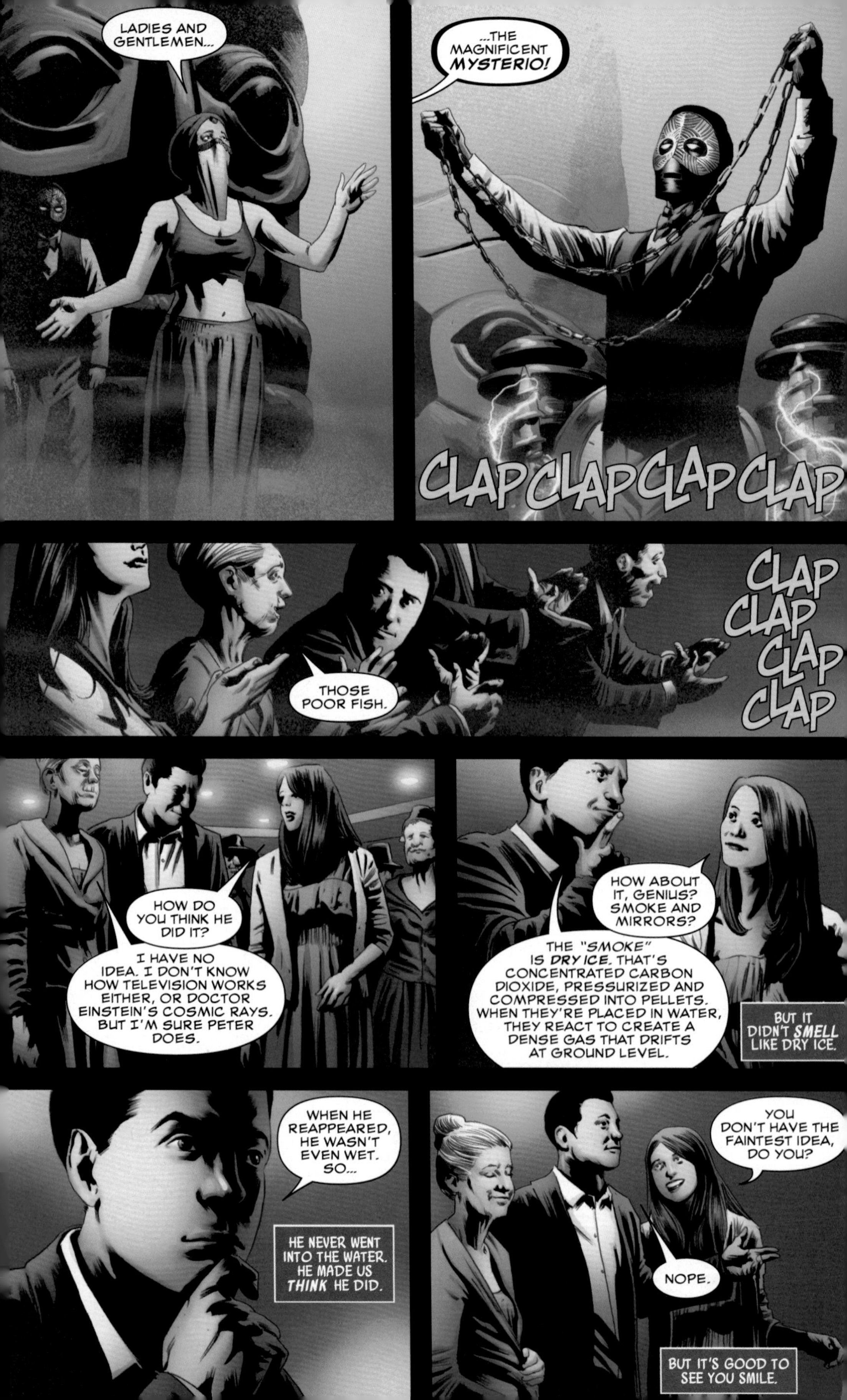

LADIES AND GENTLEMEN...
...THE MAGNIFICENT MYSTERIO!
CLAP CLAP CLAP CLAP
CLAP CLAP CLAP CLAP
THOSE POOR FISH.
HOW DO YOU THINK HE DID IT?
I HAVE NO IDEA. I DON'T KNOW HOW TELEVISION WORKS EITHER, OR DOCTOR EINSTEIN'S COSMIC RAYS. BUT I'M SURE PETER DOES.
HOW ABOUT IT, GENIUS? SMOKE AND MIRRORS?
THE "SMOKE" IS DRY ICE. THAT'S CONCENTRATED CARBON DIOXIDE, PRESSURIZED AND COMPRESSED INTO PELLETS. WHEN THEY'RE PLACED IN WATER, THEY REACT TO CREATE A DENSE GAS THAT DRIFTS AT GROUND LEVEL.
BUT IT DIDN'T SMELL LIKE DRY ICE.
WHEN HE REAPPEARED, HE WASN'T EVEN WET. SO...
HE NEVER WENT INTO THE WATER. HE MADE US THINK HE DID.
YOU DON'T HAVE THE FAINTEST IDEA, DO YOU?
NOPE.
BUT IT'S GOOD TO SEE YOU SMILE.

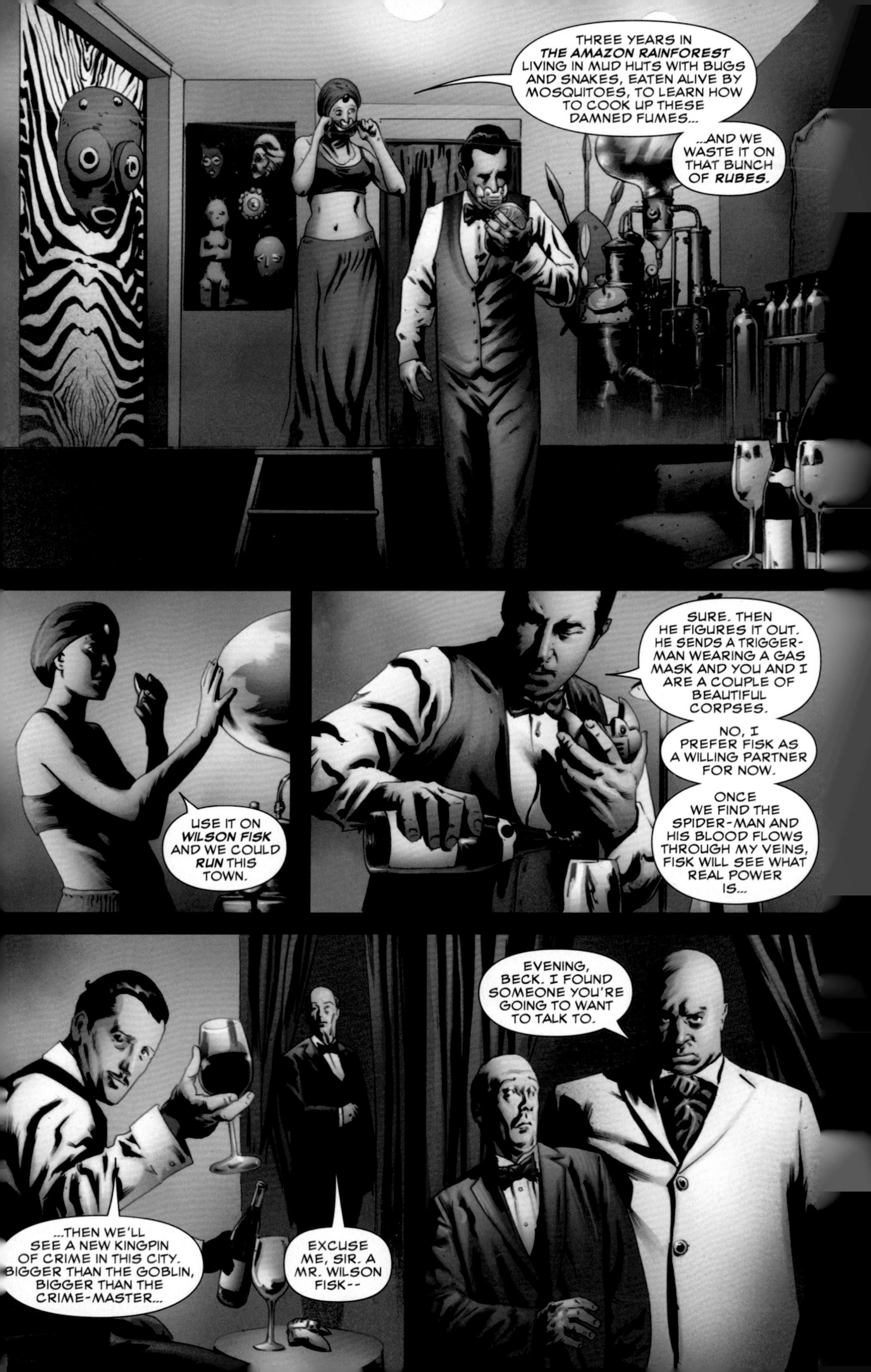
THREE YEARS IN THE AMAZON RAINFOREST LIVING IN MUD HUTS WITH BUGS AND SNAKES, EATEN ALIVE BY MOSQUITOES, TO LEARN HOW TO COOK UP THESE DAMNED FUMES...
...AND WE WASTE IT ON THAT BUNCH OF RUBES.
USE IT ON WILSON FISK AND WE COULD RUN THIS TOWN.
SURE. THEN HE FIGURES IT OUT. HE SENDS A TRIGGER-MAN WEARING A GAS MASK AND YOU AND I ARE A COUPLE OF BEAUTIFUL CORPSES.
NO, I PREFER FISK AS A WILLING PARTNER FOR NOW.
ONCE WE FIND THE SPIDER-MAN AND HIS BLOOD FLOWS THROUGH MY VEINS, FISK WILL SEE WHAT REAL POWER IS...
...THEN WE'LL SEE A NEW KINGPIN OF CRIME IN THIS CITY. BIGGER THAN THE GOBLIN, BIGGER THAN THE CRIME-MASTER...
EXCUSE ME, SIR. A MR. WILSON FISK--
EVENING, BECK. I FOUND SOMEONE YOU'RE GOING TO WANT TO TALK TO.

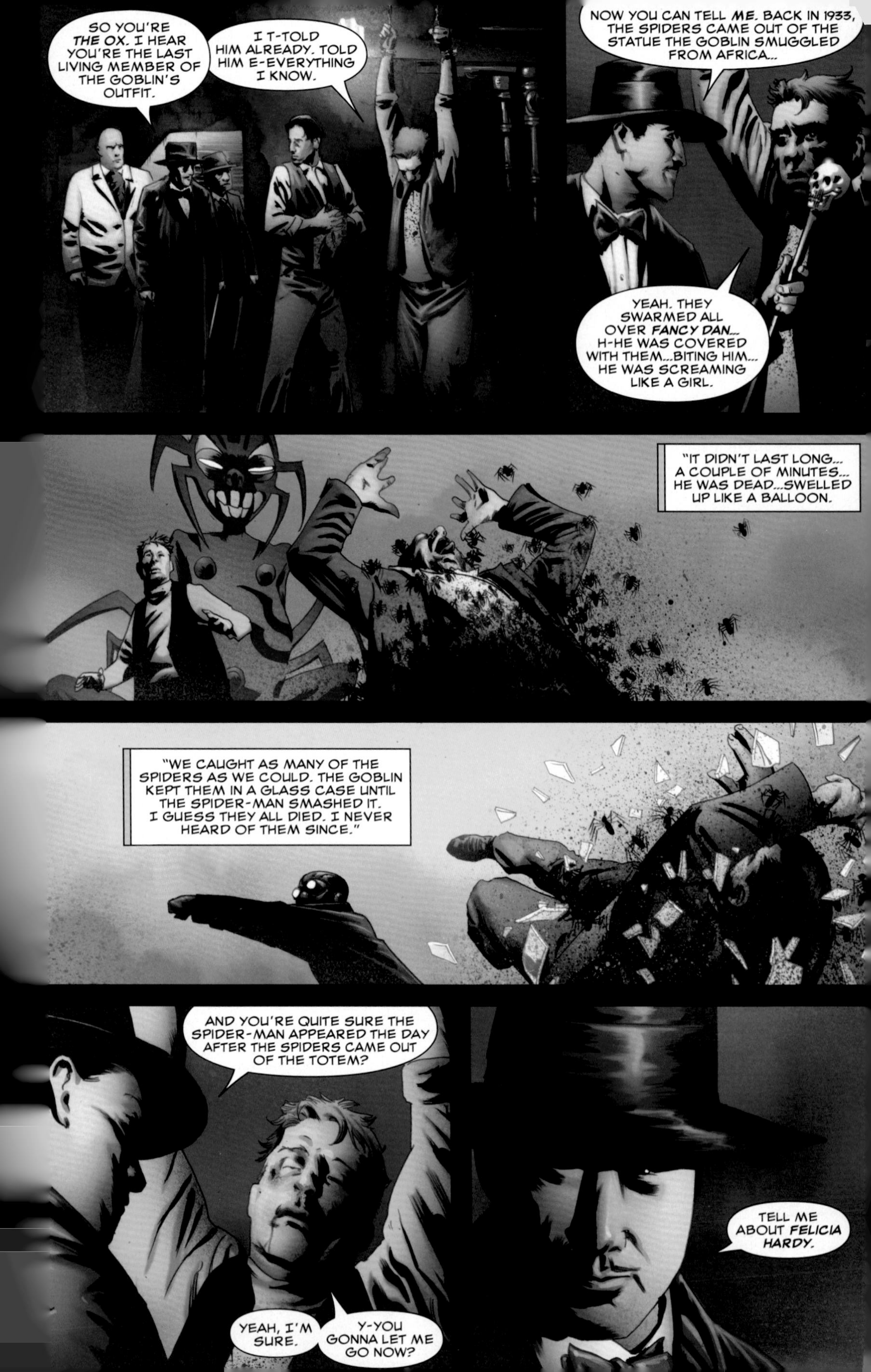
SO YOU'RE THE OX. I HEAR YOU'RE THE LAST LIVING MEMBER OF THE GOBLIN'S OUTFIT.
I T-TOLD HIM ALREADY. TOLD HIM E-EVERYTHING I KNOW.
NOW YOU CAN TELL ME. BACK IN 1933, THE SPIDERS CAME OUT OF THE STATUE THE GOBLIN SMUGGLED FROM AFRICA...
YEAH. THEY SWARMED ALL OVER FANCY DAN... H-HE WAS COVERED WITH THEM...BITING HIM... HE WAS SCREAMING LIKE A GIRL.
"IT DIDN'T LAST LONG... A COUPLE OF MINUTES... HE WAS DEAD...SWELLED UP LIKE A BALLOON.
"WE CAUGHT AS MANY OF THE SPIDERS AS WE COULD. THE GOBLIN KEPT THEM IN A GLASS CASE UNTIL THE SPIDER-MAN SMASHED IT. I GUESS THEY ALL DIED. I NEVER HEARD OF THEM SINCE."
AND YOU'RE QUITE SURE THE SPIDER-MAN APPEARED THE DAY AFTER THE SPIDERS CAME OUT OF THE TOTEM?
YEAH, I'M SURE.
Y-YOU GONNA LET ME GO NOW?
TELL ME ABOUT FELICIA HARDY.

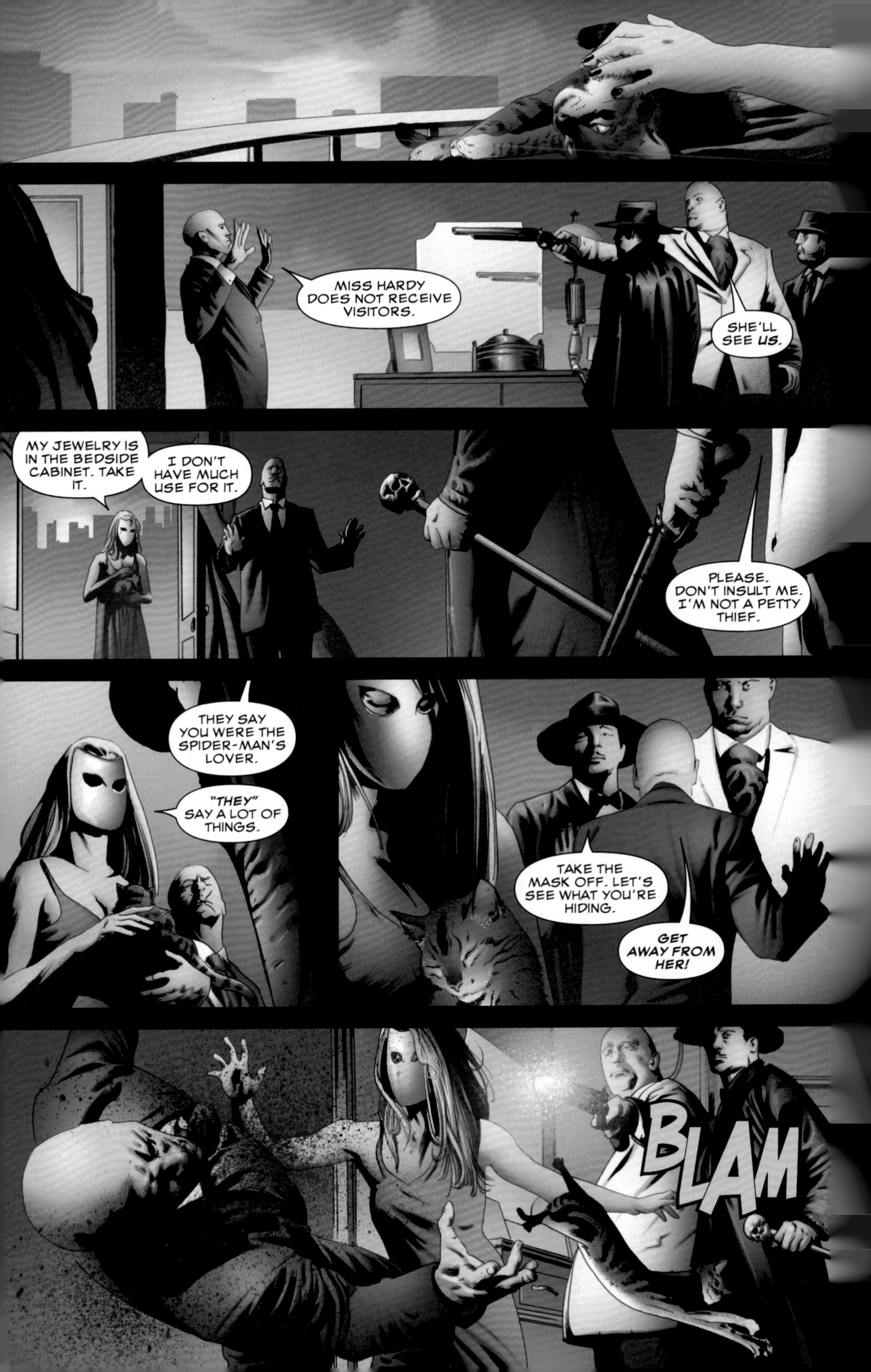
MISS HARDY DOES NOT RECEIVE VISITORS.
SHE'LL SEE *US*.
MY JEWELRY IS IN THE BEDSIDE CABINET. TAKE IT.
I DON'T HAVE MUCH USE FOR IT.
PLEASE. DON'T INSULT ME. I'M NOT A PETTY THIEF.
THEY SAY YOU WERE THE SPIDER-MAN'S LOVER.
"THEY" SAY A LOT OF THINGS.
TAKE THE MASK OFF. LET'S SEE WHAT YOU'RE HIDING.
GET AWAY FROM HER!
BLAM

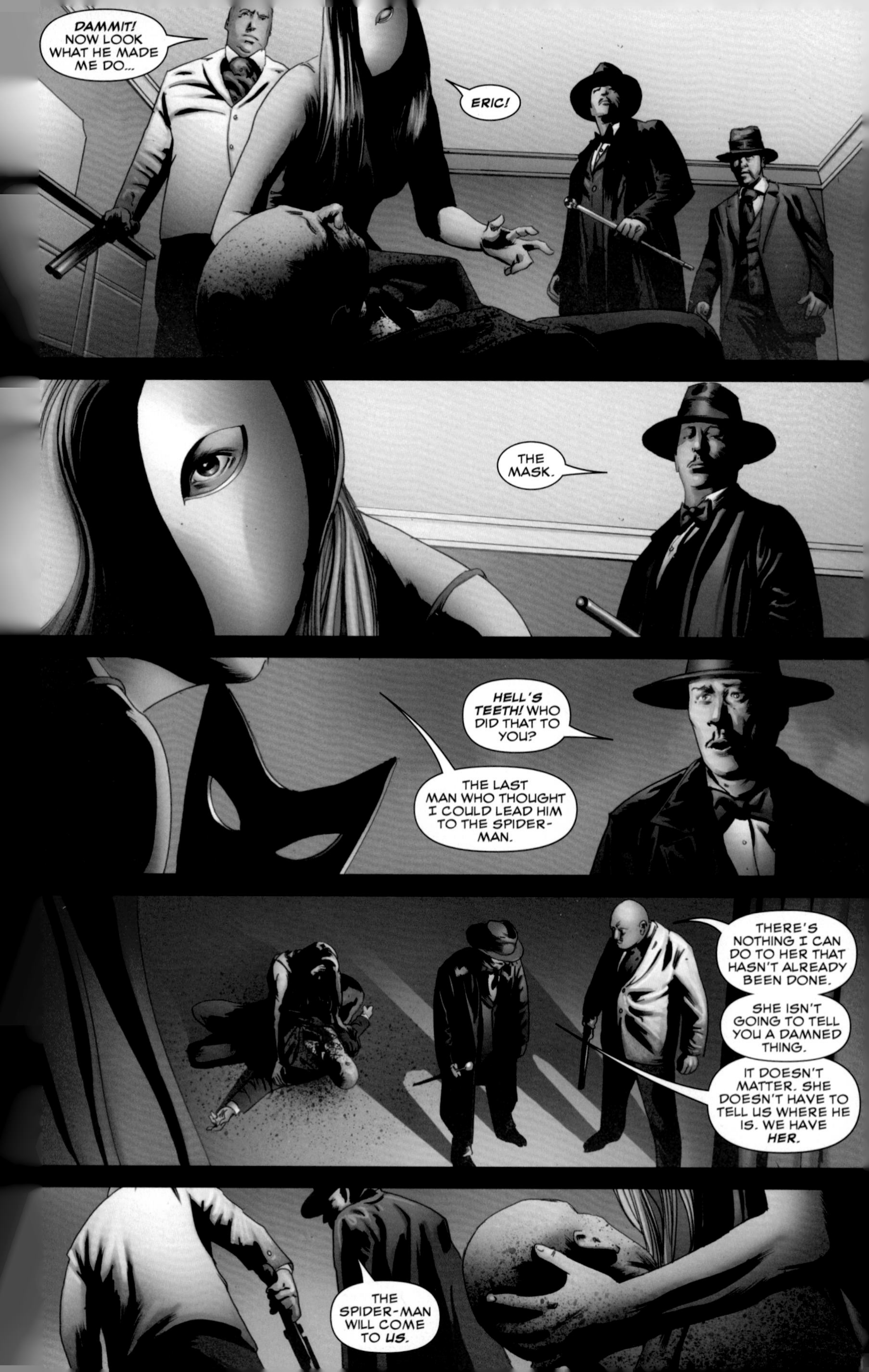
DAMMIT! NOW LOOK WHAT HE MADE ME DO...
ERIC!
THE MASK.
HELL'S TEETH! WHO DID THAT TO YOU?
THE LAST MAN WHO THOUGHT I COULD LEAD HIM TO THE SPIDER-MAN.
THERE'S NOTHING I CAN DO TO HER THAT HASN'T ALREADY BEEN DONE.
SHE ISN'T GOING TO TELL YOU A DAMNED THING.
IT DOESN'T MATTER. SHE DOESN'T HAVE TO TELL US WHERE HE IS. WE HAVE HER.
THE SPIDER-MAN WILL COME TO US.

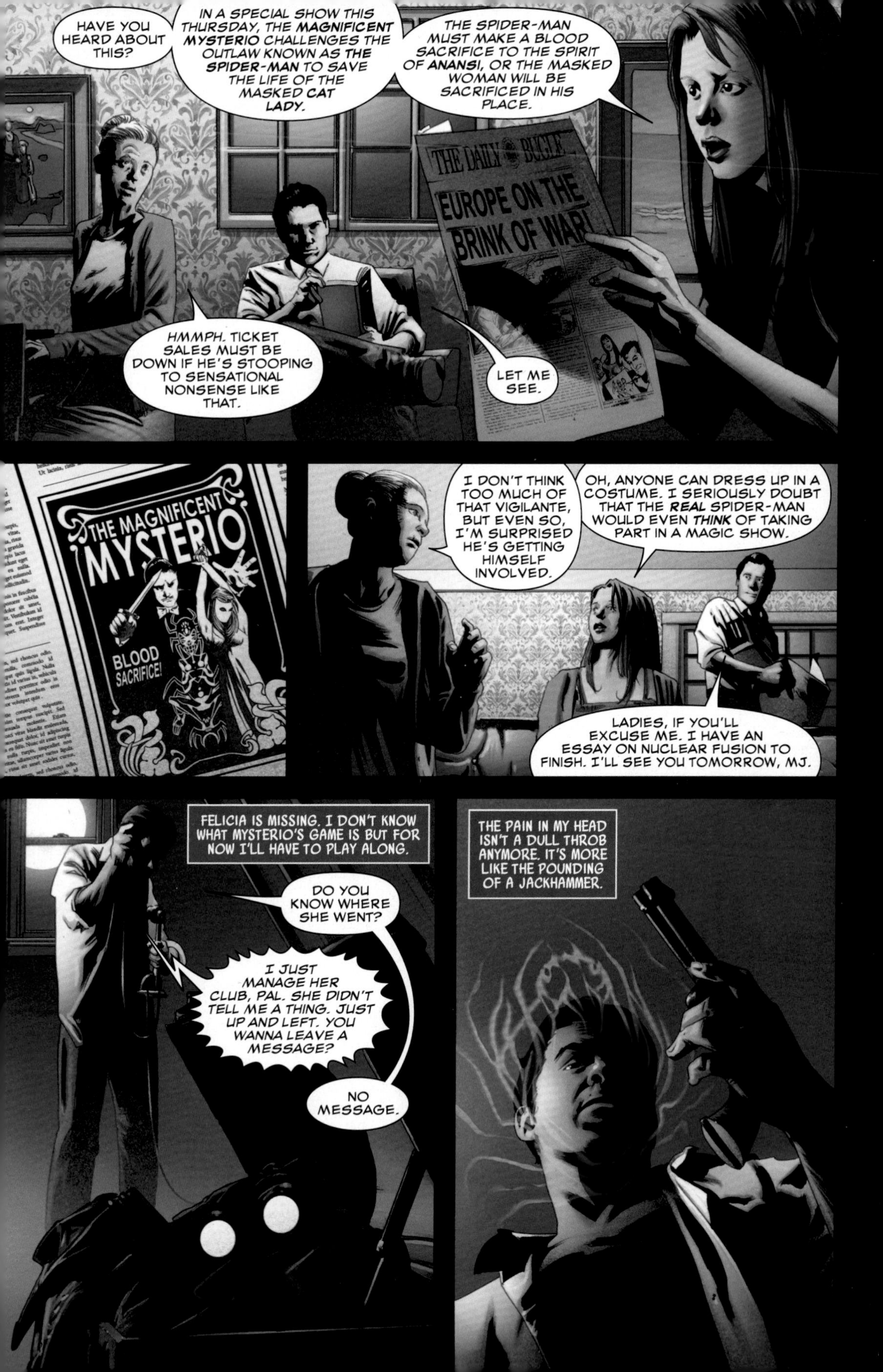
HAVE YOU HEARD ABOUT THIS?
IN A SPECIAL SHOW THIS THURSDAY, THE MAGNIFICENT MYSTERIO CHALLENGES THE OUTLAW KNOWN AS THE SPIDER-MAN TO SAVE THE LIFE OF THE MASKED CAT LADY.
THE SPIDER-MAN MUST MAKE A BLOOD SACRIFICE TO THE SPIRIT OF ANANSI, OR THE MASKED WOMAN WILL BE SACRIFICED IN HIS PLACE.
THE DAILY BUGLE
EUROPE ON THE BRINK OF WAR!
HMMPH. TICKET SALES MUST BE DOWN IF HE'S STOOPING TO SENSATIONAL NONSENSE LIKE THAT.
LET ME SEE.
THE MAGNIFICENT MYSTERIO
BLOOD SACRIFICE!
I DON'T THINK TOO MUCH OF THAT VIGILANTE, BUT EVEN SO, I'M SURPRISED HE'S GETTING HIMSELF INVOLVED.
OH, ANYONE CAN DRESS UP IN A COSTUME. I SERIOUSLY DOUBT THAT THE REAL SPIDER-MAN WOULD EVEN THINK OF TAKING PART IN A MAGIC SHOW.
LADIES, IF YOU'LL EXCUSE ME. I HAVE AN ESSAY ON NUCLEAR FUSION TO FINISH. I'LL SEE YOU TOMORROW, MJ.
FELICIA IS MISSING. I DON'T KNOW WHAT MYSTERIO'S GAME IS BUT FOR NOW I'LL HAVE TO PLAY ALONG.
DO YOU KNOW WHERE SHE WENT?
I JUST MANAGE HER CLUB, PAL. SHE DIDN'T TELL ME A THING. JUST UP AND LEFT. YOU WANNA LEAVE A MESSAGE?
NO MESSAGE.
THE PAIN IN MY HEAD ISN'T A DULL THROB ANYMORE. IT'S MORE LIKE THE POUNDING OF A JACKHAMMER.

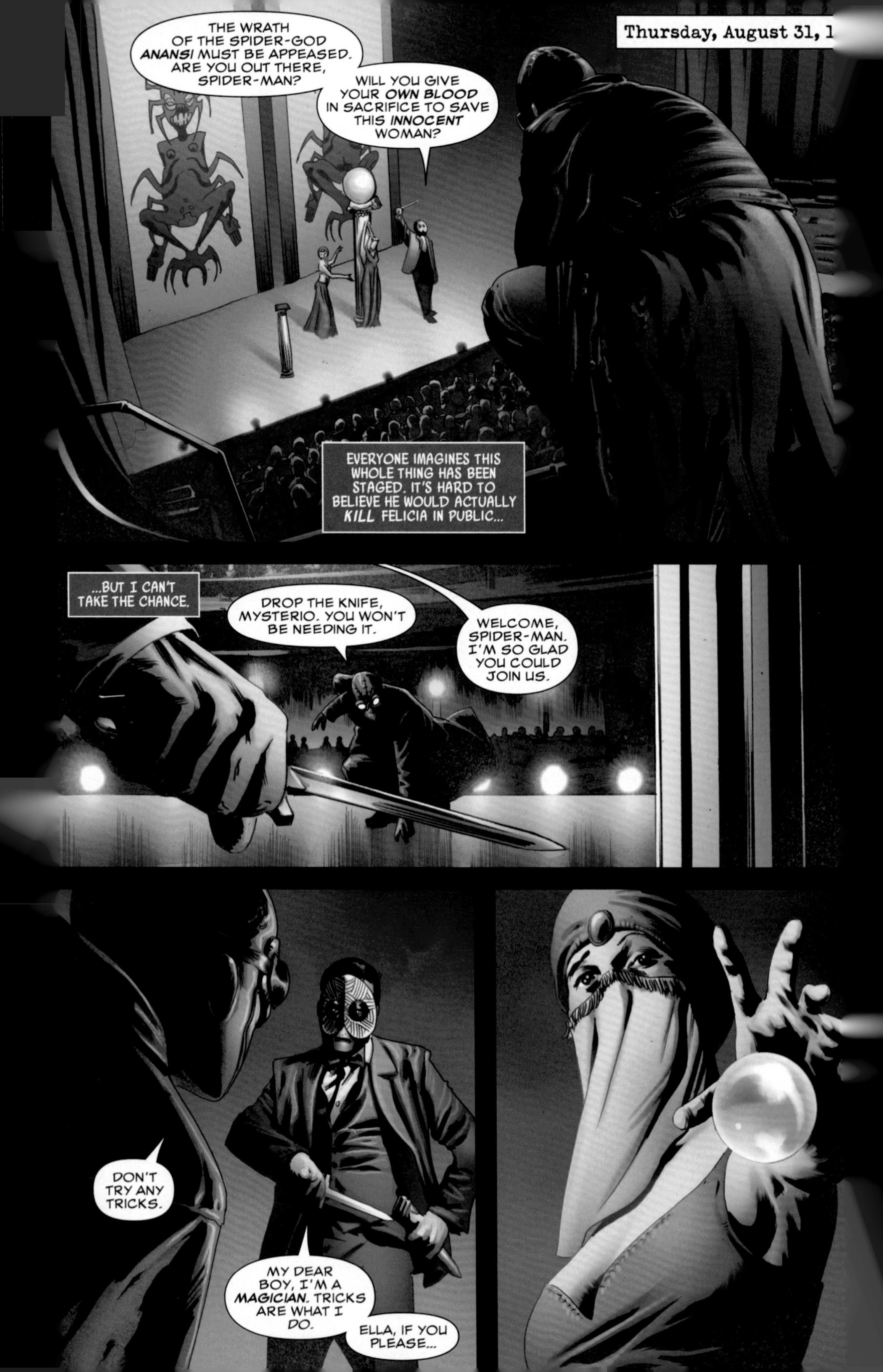

Thursday, August 31, 1
THE WRATH OF THE SPIDER-GOD ANANSI MUST BE APPEASED. ARE YOU OUT THERE, SPIDER-MAN?
WILL YOU GIVE YOUR OWN BLOOD IN SACRIFICE TO SAVE THIS INNOCENT WOMAN?
EVERYONE IMAGINES THIS WHOLE THING HAS BEEN STAGED. IT'S HARD TO BELIEVE HE WOULD ACTUALLY KILL FELICIA IN PUBLIC...
...BUT I CAN'T TAKE THE CHANCE.
DROP THE KNIFE, MYSTERIO. YOU WON'T BE NEEDING IT.
WELCOME, SPIDER-MAN. I'M SO GLAD YOU COULD JOIN US.
DON'T TRY ANY TRICKS.
MY DEAR BOY, I'M A MAGICIAN. TRICKS ARE WHAT I DO.
ELLA, IF YOU PLEASE...

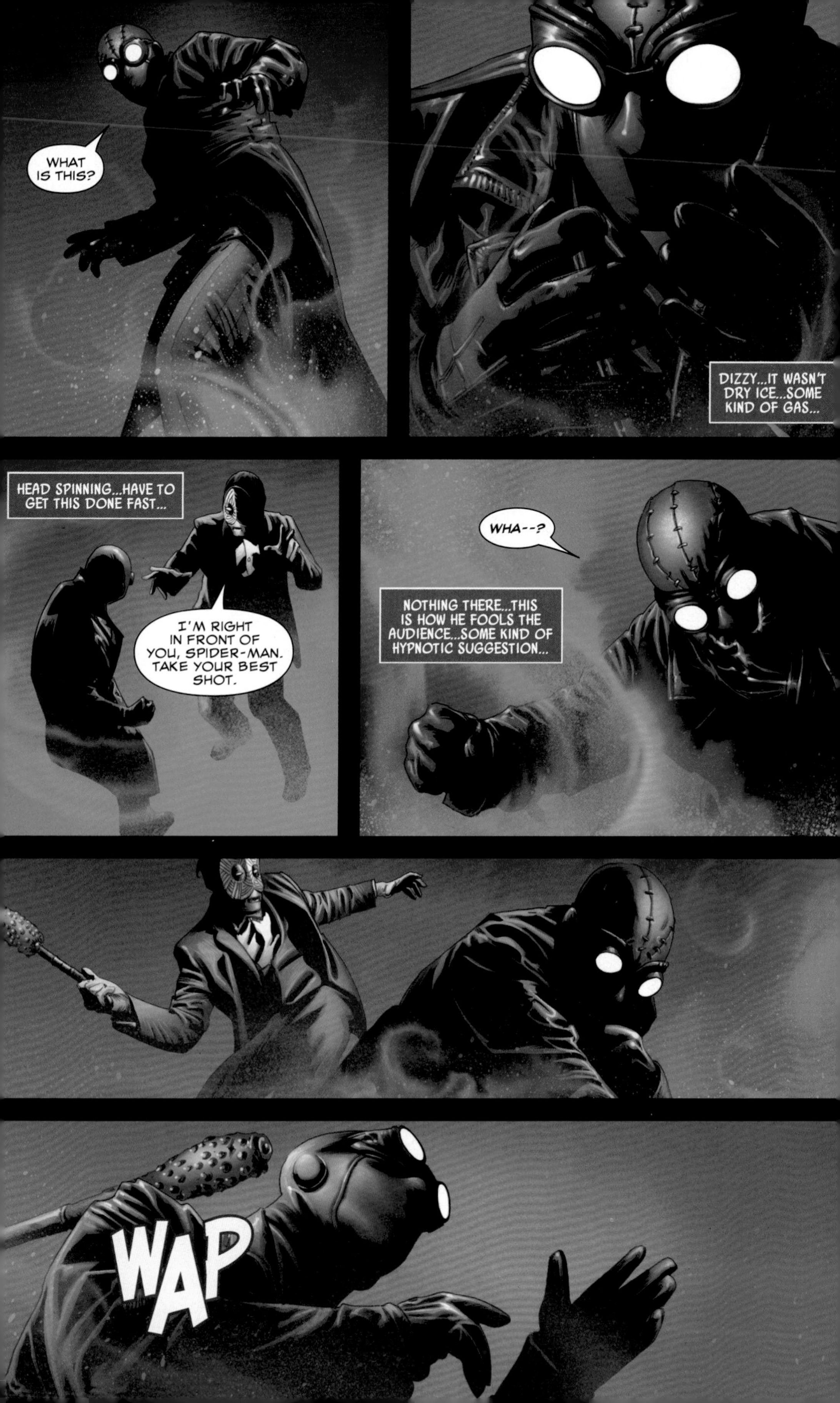
WHAT IS THIS?
DIZZY...IT WASN'T DRY ICE...SOME KIND OF GAS...
HEAD SPINNING...HAVE TO GET THIS DONE FAST...
I'M RIGHT IN FRONT OF YOU, SPIDER-MAN. TAKE YOUR BEST SHOT.
WHA--?
NOTHING THERE...THIS IS HOW HE FOOLS THE AUDIENCE...SOME KIND OF HYPNOTIC SUGGESTION...
WAP

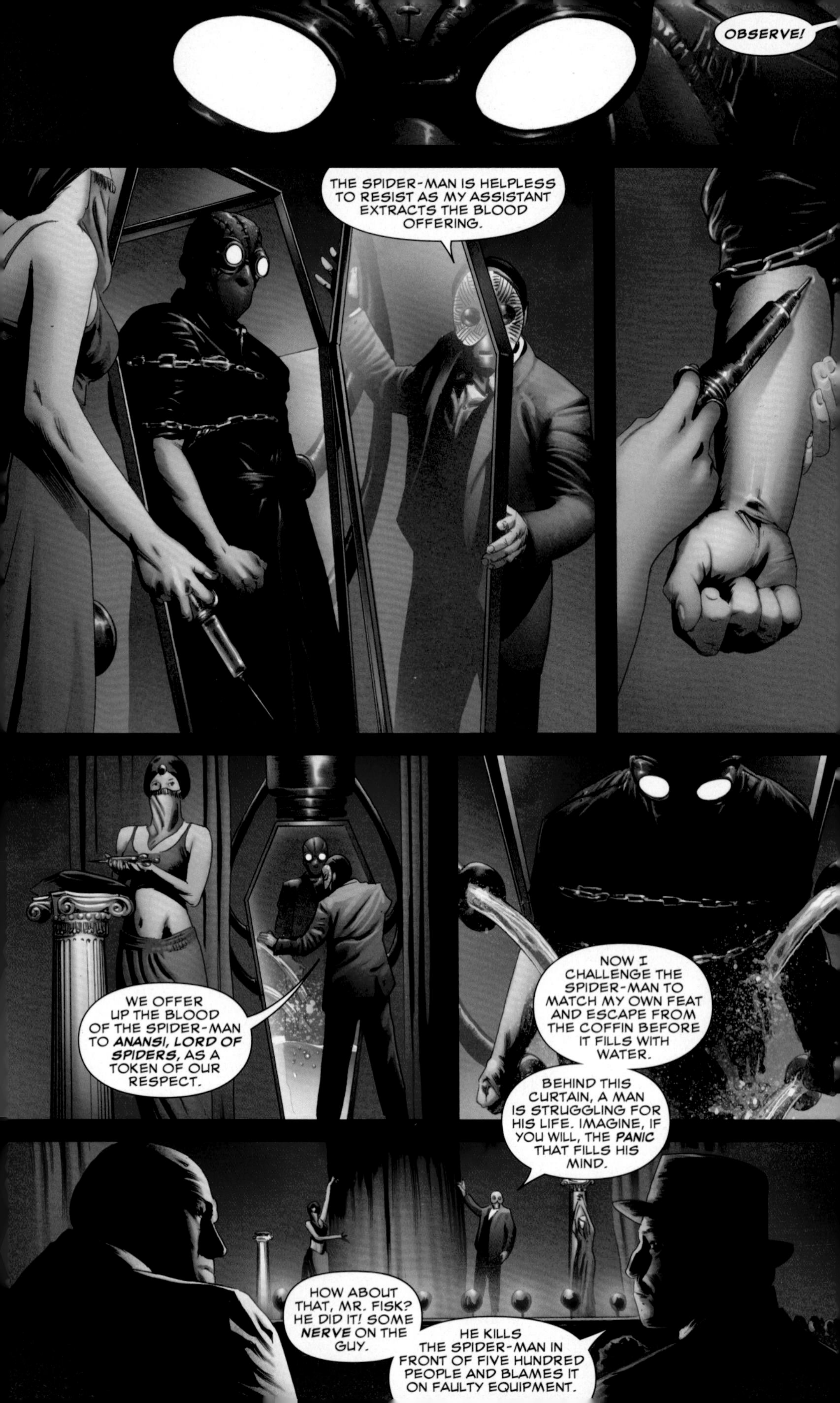
OBSERVE!
THE SPIDER-MAN IS HELPLESS TO RESIST AS MY ASSISTANT EXTRACTS THE BLOOD OFFERING.
WE OFFER UP THE BLOOD OF THE SPIDER-MAN TO ANANSI, LORD OF SPIDERS, AS A TOKEN OF OUR RESPECT.
NOW I CHALLENGE THE SPIDER-MAN TO MATCH MY OWN FEAT AND ESCAPE FROM THE COFFIN BEFORE IT FILLS WITH WATER.
BEHIND THIS CURTAIN, A MAN IS STRUGGLING FOR HIS LIFE. IMAGINE, IF YOU WILL, THE PANIC THAT FILLS HIS MIND.
HOW ABOUT THAT, MR. FISK? HE DID IT! SOME NERVE ON THE GUY.
HE KILLS THE SPIDER-MAN IN FRONT OF FIVE HUNDRED PEOPLE AND BLAMES IT ON FAULTY EQUIPMENT.

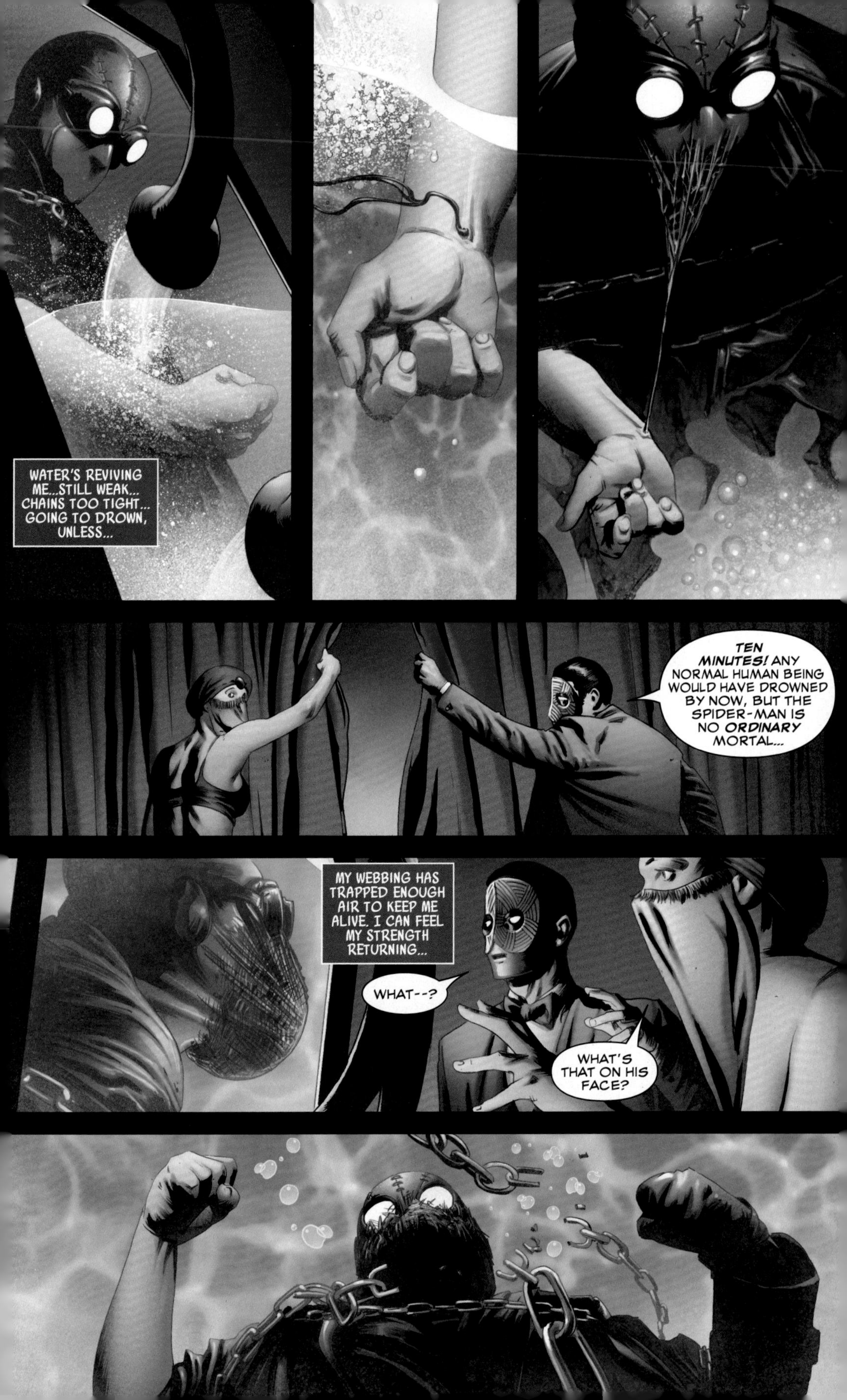

WATER'S REVIVING ME...STILL WEAK... CHAINS TOO TIGHT... GOING TO DROWN, UNLESS...
TEN MINUTES! ANY NORMAL HUMAN BEING WOULD HAVE DROWNED BY NOW, BUT THE SPIDER-MAN IS NO ORDINARY MORTAL...
MY WEBBING HAS TRAPPED ENOUGH AIR TO KEEP ME ALIVE. I CAN FEEL MY STRENGTH RETURNING...
WHAT--?
WHAT'S THAT ON HIS FACE?

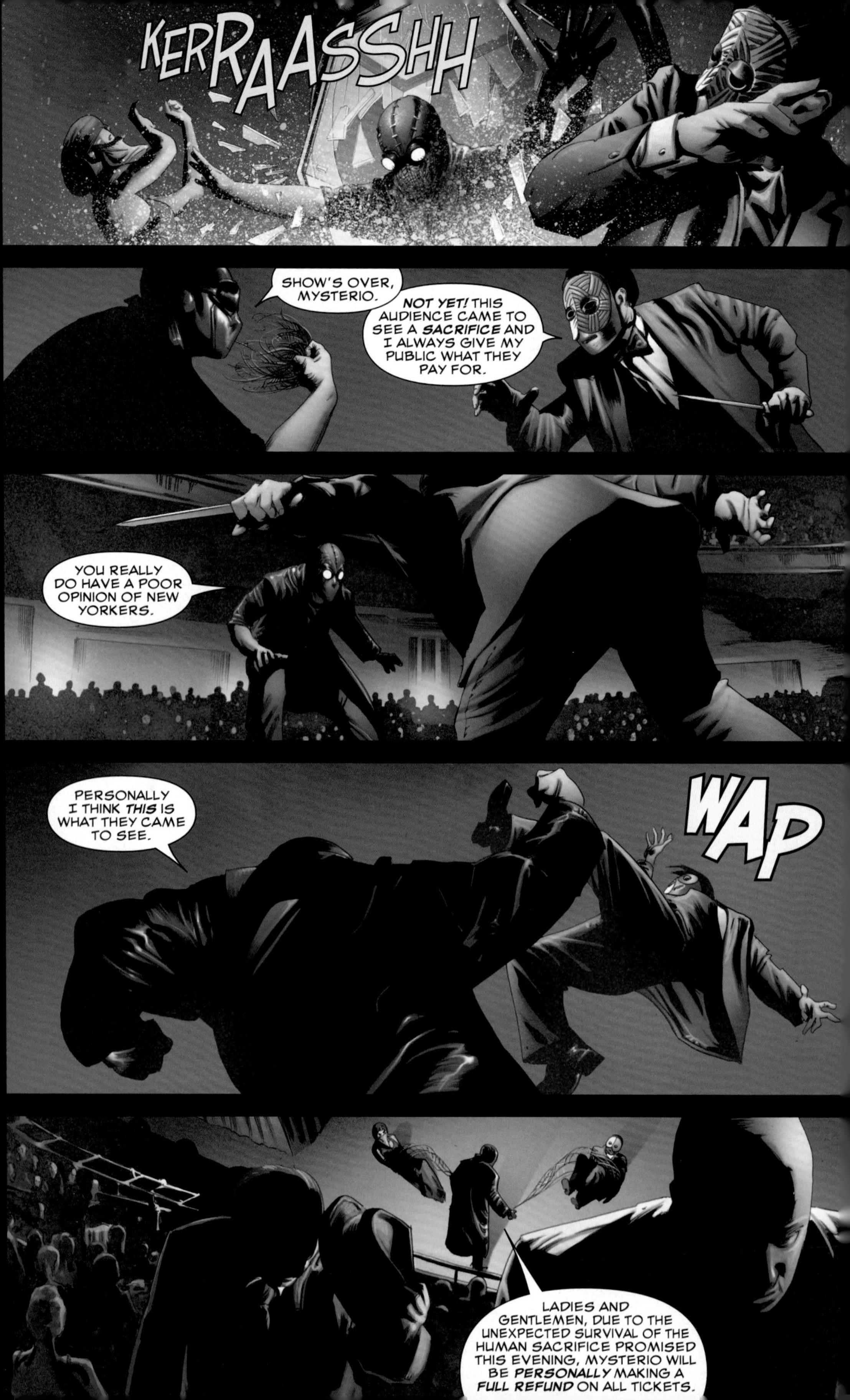
KERRAASSHH
SHOW'S OVER, MYSTERIO.
NOT YET! THIS AUDIENCE CAME TO SEE A SACRIFICE AND I ALWAYS GIVE MY PUBLIC WHAT THEY PAY FOR.
YOU REALLY DO HAVE A POOR OPINION OF NEW YORKERS.
PERSONALLY I THINK THIS IS WHAT THEY CAME TO SEE.
WAP
LADIES AND GENTLEMEN, DUE TO THE UNEXPECTED SURVIVAL OF THE HUMAN SACRIFICE PROMISED THIS EVENING, MYSTERIO WILL BE PERSONALLY MAKING A FULL REFUND ON ALL TICKETS.

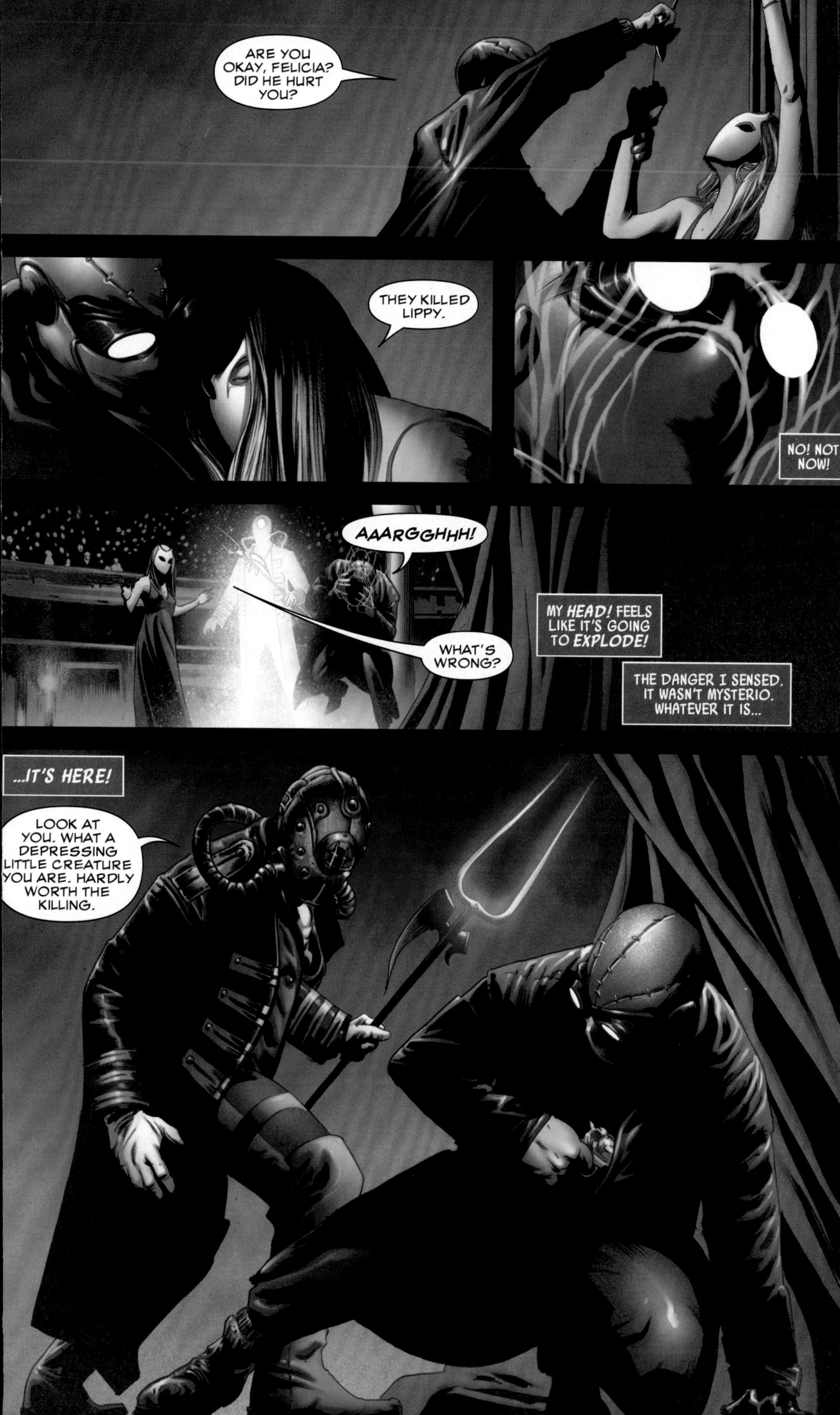
ARE YOU OKAY, FELICIA? DID HE HURT YOU?
THEY KILLED LIPPY.
NO! NOT NOW!
AAARGGHHH!
WHAT'S WRONG?
MY HEAD! FEELS LIKE IT'S GOING TO EXPLODE!
THE DANGER I SENSED. IT WASN'T MYSTERIO. WHATEVER IT IS...
...IT'S HERE!
LOOK AT YOU. WHAT A DEPRESSING LITTLE CREATURE YOU ARE. HARDLY WORTH THE KILLING.

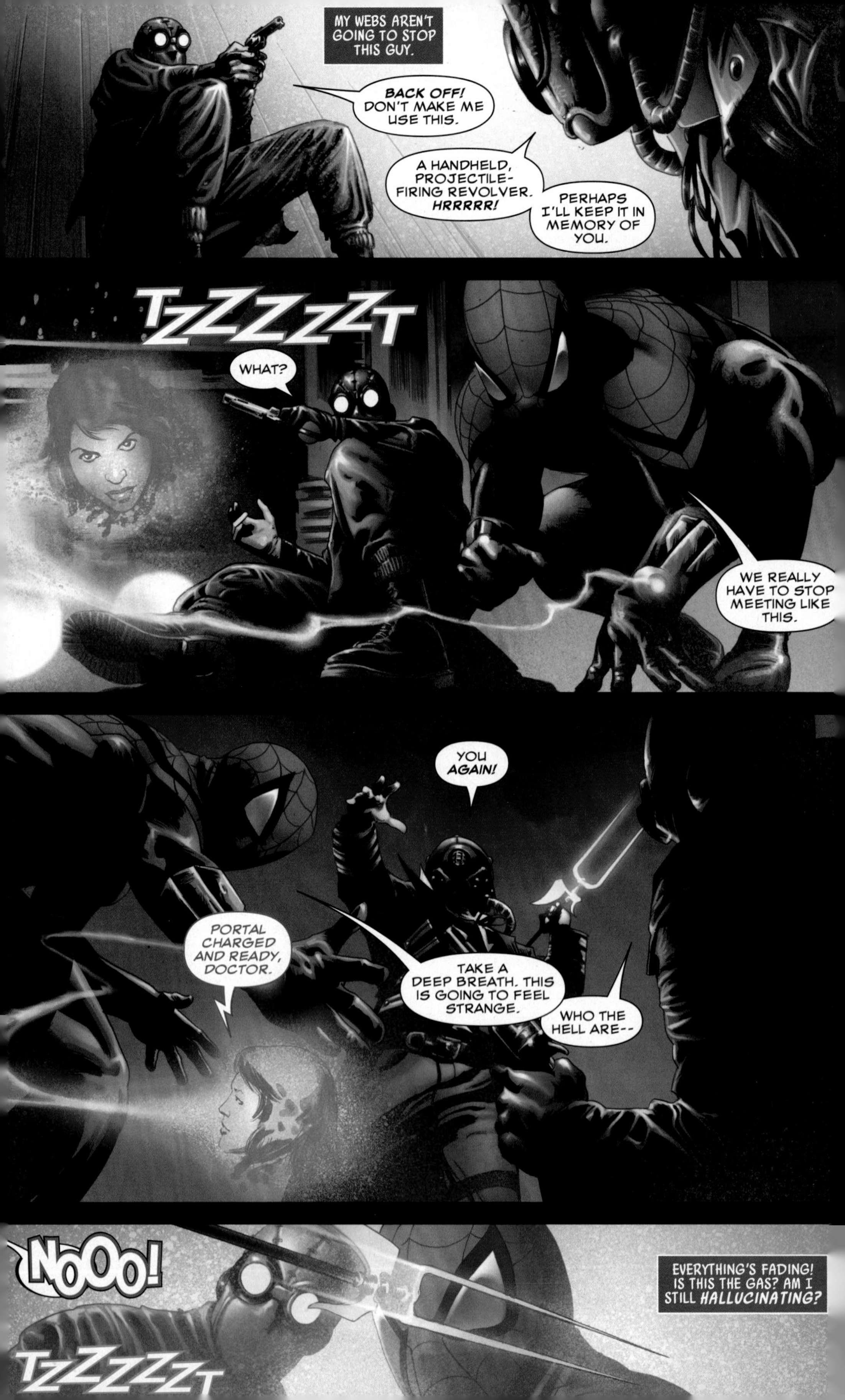
MY WEBS AREN'T GOING TO STOP THIS GUY.
BACK OFF! DON'T MAKE ME USE THIS.
A HANDHELD, PROJECTILE-FIRING REVOLVER. HRRRRR!
PERHAPS I'LL KEEP IT IN MEMORY OF YOU.
TZZZZZZT
WHAT?
WE REALLY HAVE TO STOP MEETING LIKE THIS.
YOU AGAIN!
PORTAL CHARGED AND READY, DOCTOR.
TAKE A DEEP BREATH. THIS IS GOING TO FEEL STRANGE.
WHO THE HELL ARE--
NOOO!
EVERYTHING'S FADING! IS THIS THE GAS? AM I STILL HALLUCINATING?
TZZZZZZT

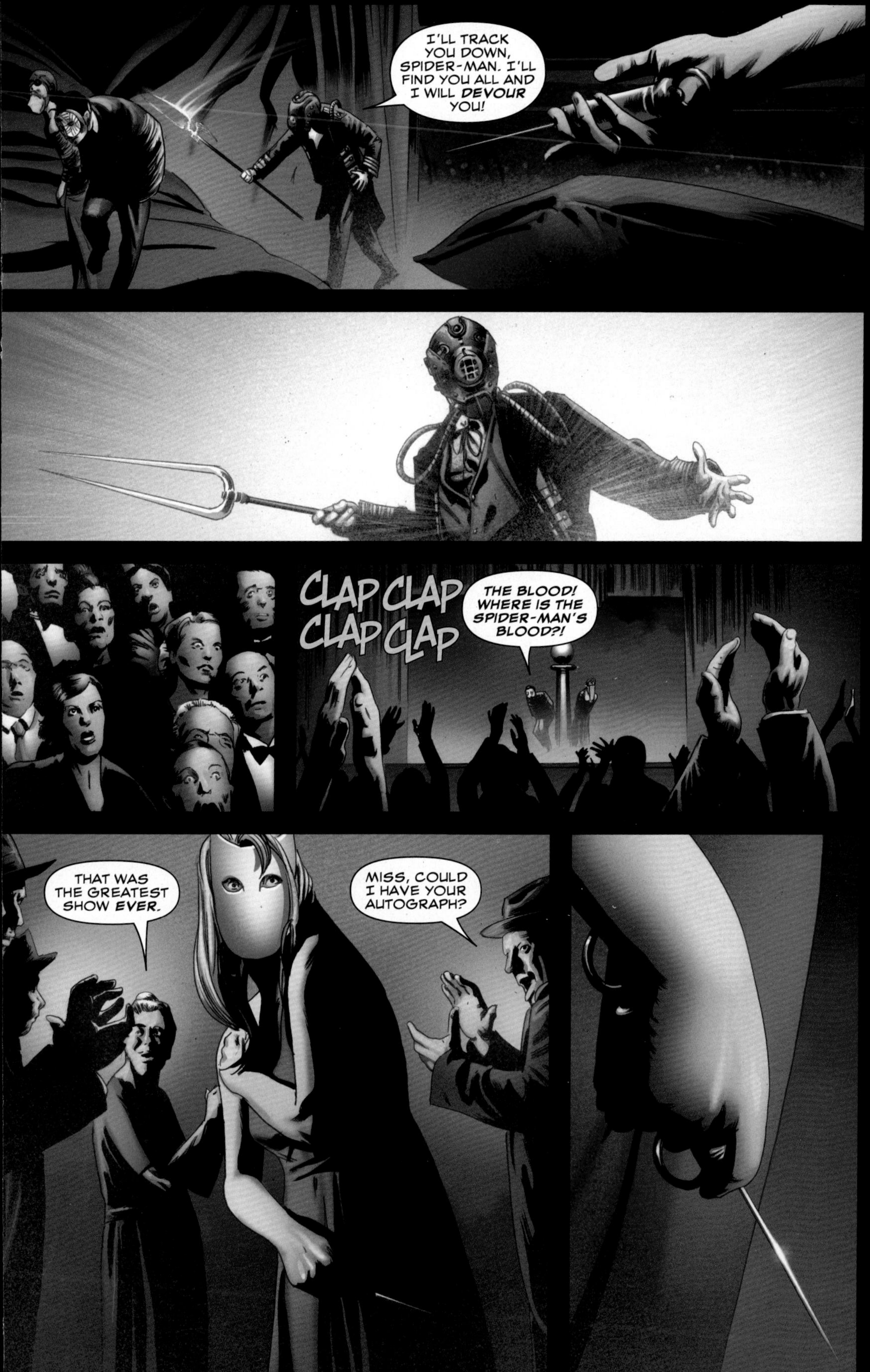
I'LL TRACK YOU DOWN, SPIDER-MAN. I'LL FIND YOU ALL AND I WILL **DEVOUR** YOU!
CLAP CLAP CLAP CLAP
THE BLOOD! WHERE IS THE SPIDER-MAN'S BLOOD?!
THAT WAS THE GREATEST SHOW **EVER**.
MISS, COULD I HAVE YOUR AUTOGRAPH?

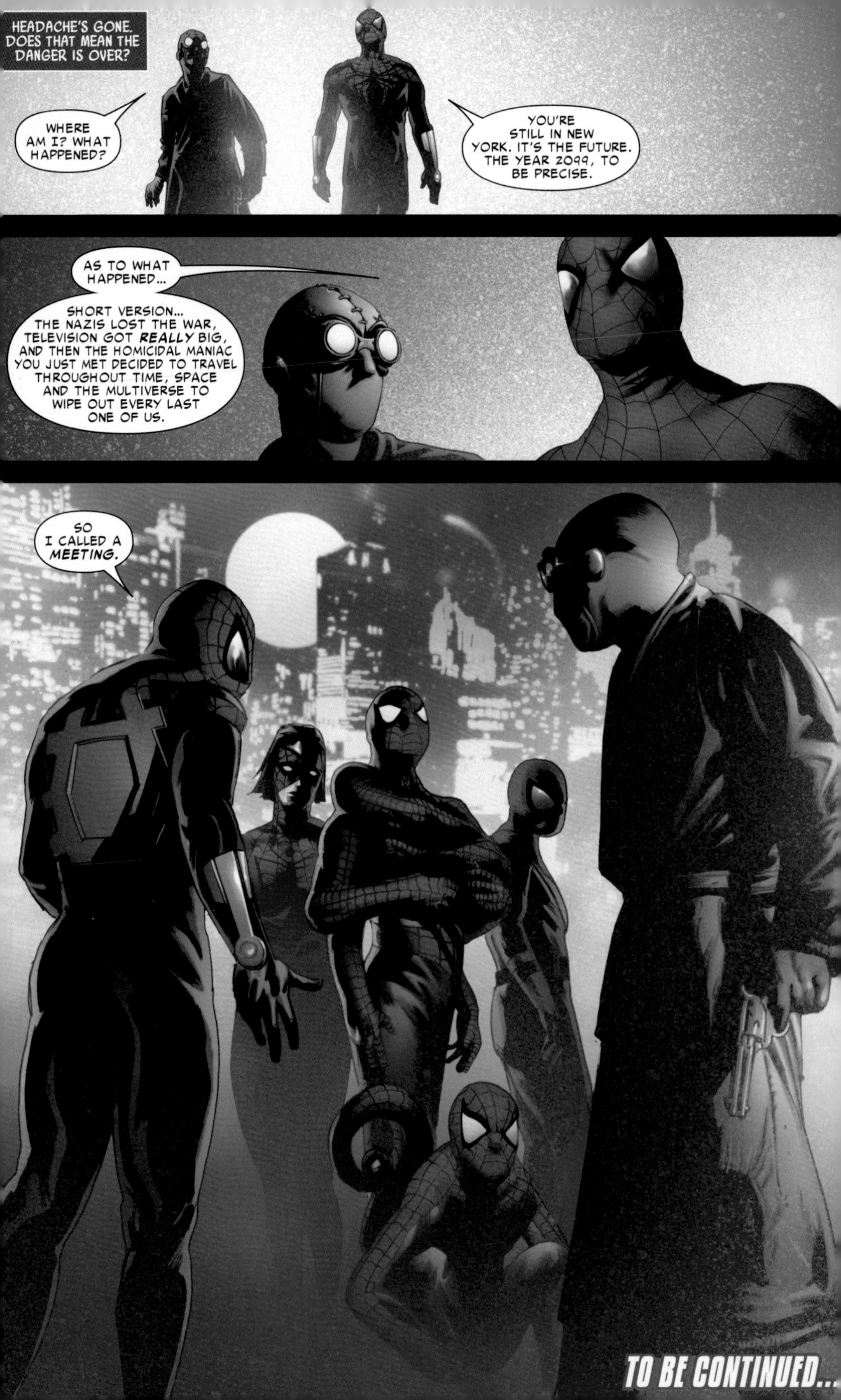
HEADACHE'S GONE. DOES THAT MEAN THE DANGER IS OVER?
WHERE AM I? WHAT HAPPENED?
YOU'RE STILL IN NEW YORK. IT'S THE FUTURE. THE YEAR 2099, TO BE PRECISE.
AS TO WHAT HAPPENED...
SHORT VERSION... THE NAZIS LOST THE WAR, TELEVISION GOT REALLY BIG, AND THEN THE HOMICIDAL MANIAC YOU JUST MET DECIDED TO TRAVEL THROUGHOUT TIME, SPACE AND THE MULTIVERSE TO WIPE OUT EVERY LAST ONE OF US.
SO I CALLED A MEETING.
TO BE CONTINUED...

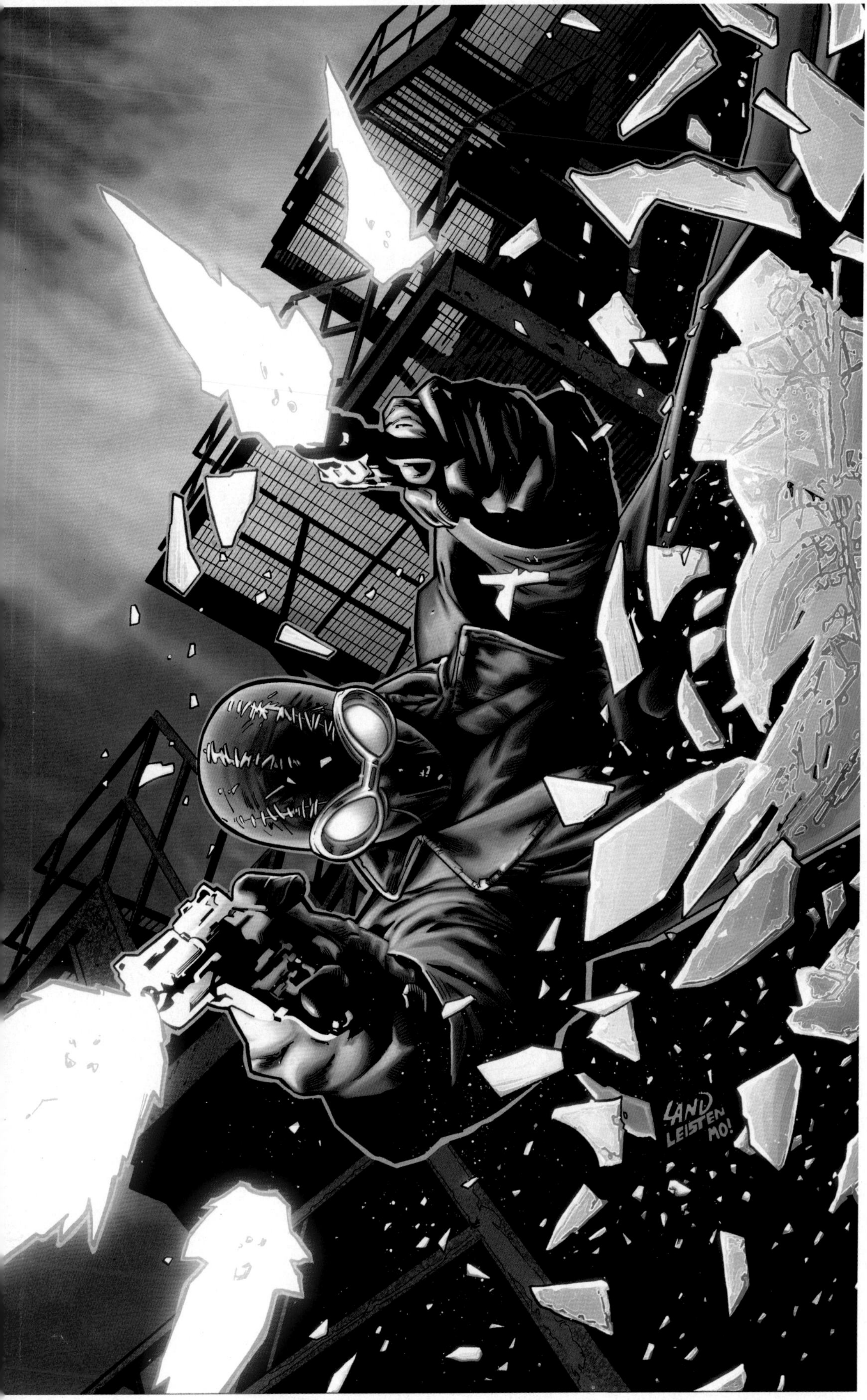
LAND
LEISTEN
MO!
#1 VARIANT BY GREG LAND, JAY LEISTEN & MORRY HOLLOWELL

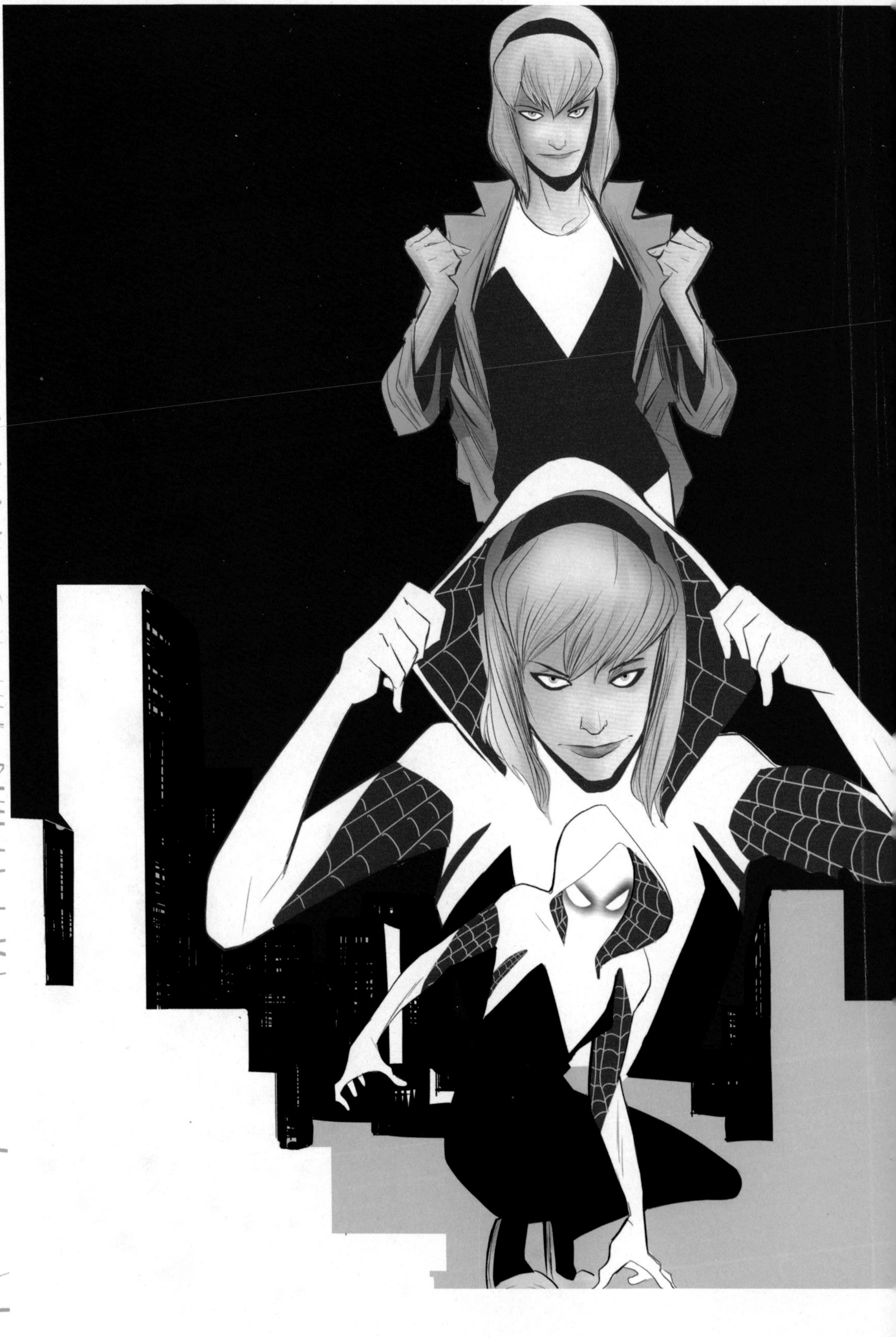

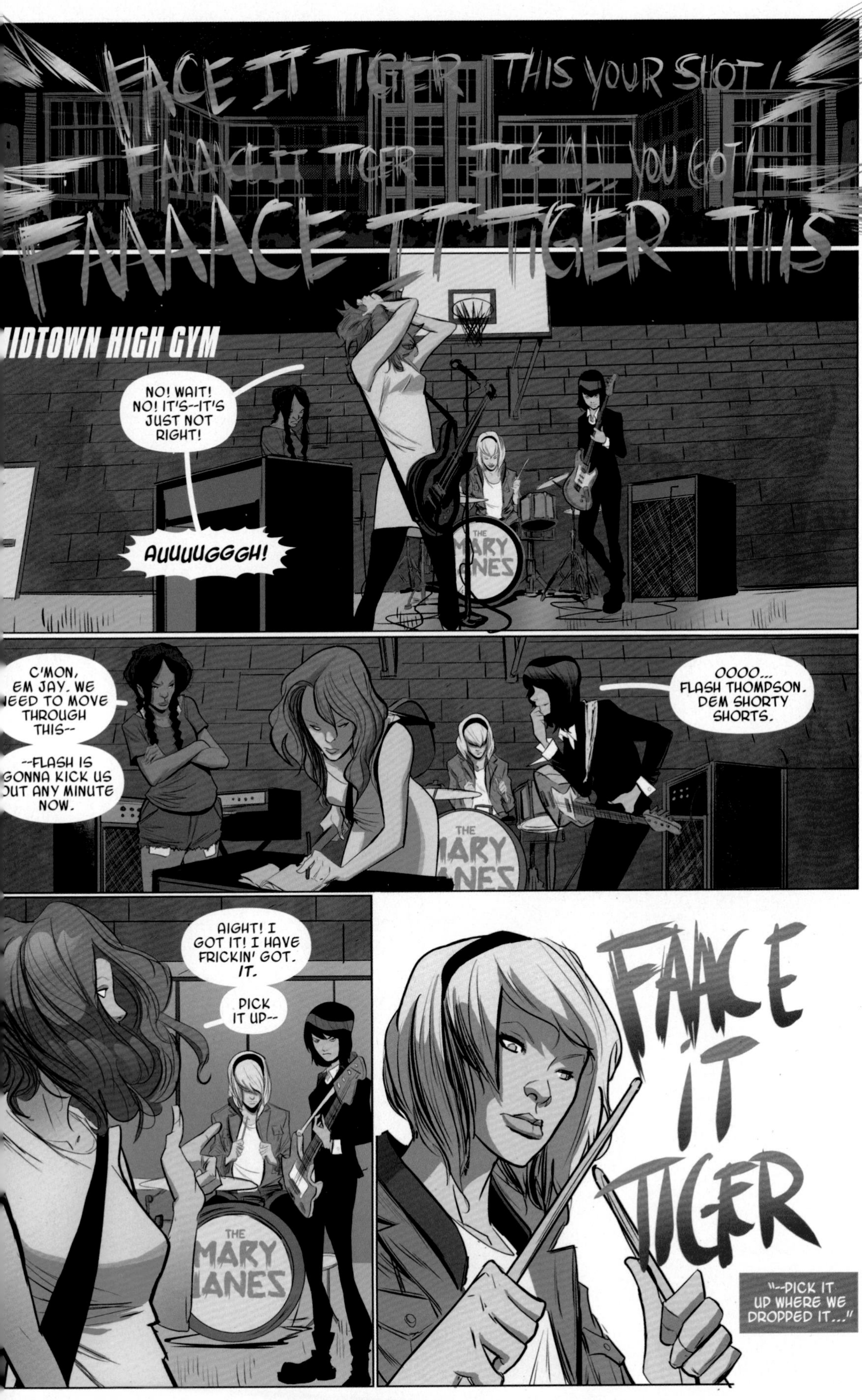

FACE IT TIGER THIS YOUR SHOT!
FAAACE IT TIGER IT'S ALL YOU GOT!
FAAACE IT TIGER THIS
IDTOWN HIGH GYM
NO! WAIT! NO! IT'S--IT'S JUST NOT RIGHT!
AUUUUGGGH!
C'MON, EM JAY. WE NEED TO MOVE THROUGH THIS--
--FLASH IS GONNA KICK US OUT ANY MINUTE NOW.
OOOO... FLASH THOMPSON. DEM SHORTY SHORTS.
AIGHT! I GOT IT! I HAVE FRICKIN' GOT. IT.
PICK IT UP--
FAACE IT TIGER
"--PICK IT UP WHERE WE DROPPED IT..."

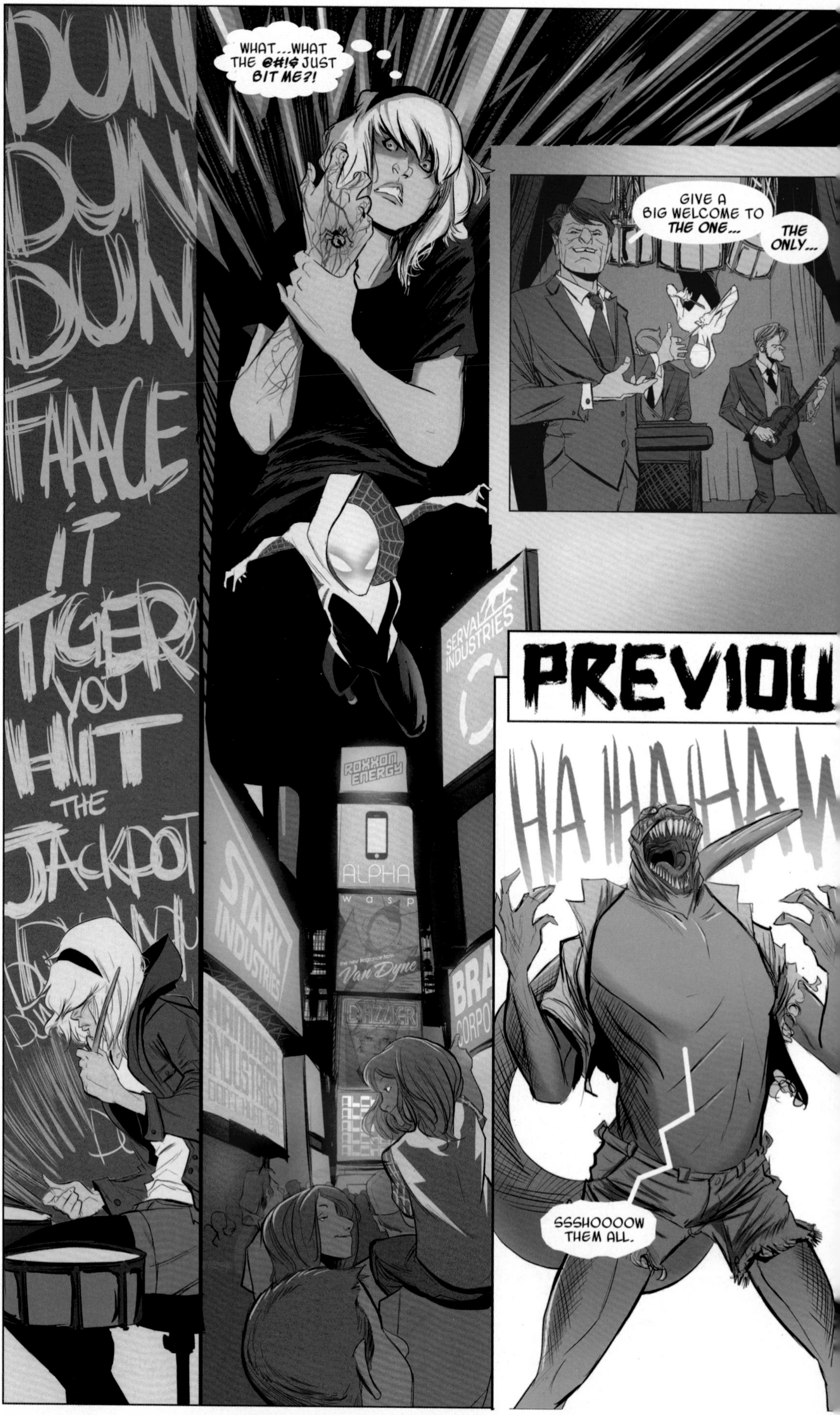

DUN
DUN
DUN
FAAACE
IT
TIGER
YOU
HIT
THE
JACKPOT
WHAT...WHAT
THE @#!$ JUST
BIT ME?!
SERVAL INDUSTRIES
ROXXON ENERGY
ALPHA
wasp
Van Dyne
STARK INDUSTRIES
HAMMER INDUSTRIES
DAZZLER
GIVE A
BIG WELCOME TO
THE ONE...
THE
ONLY...
PREVIOU
HA HAHAHA
SSSHOOOOW
THEM ALL.

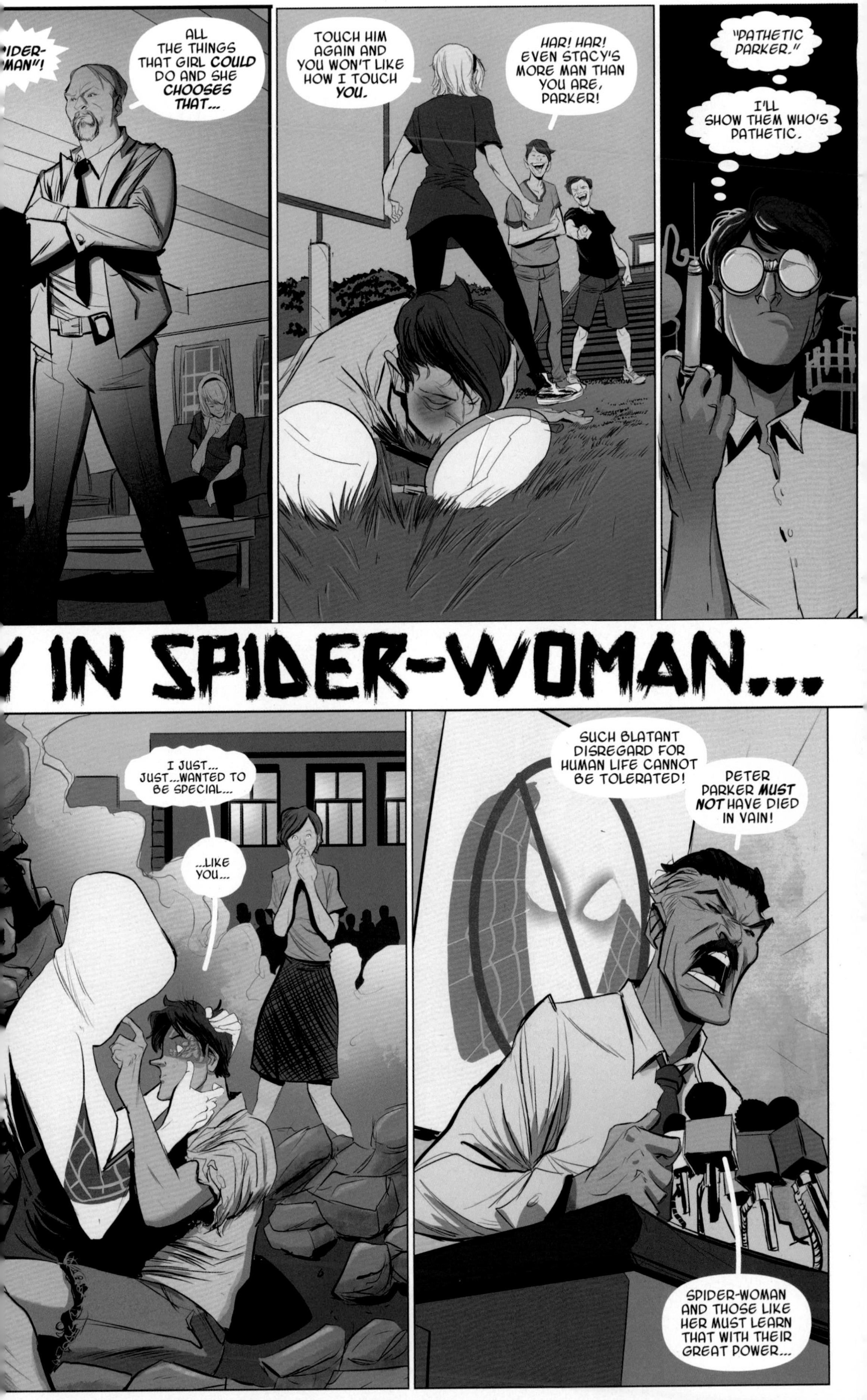

"SPIDER-WOMAN"!
ALL THE THINGS THAT GIRL **COULD** DO AND SHE **CHOOSES** THAT...
TOUCH HIM AGAIN AND YOU WON'T LIKE HOW I TOUCH **YOU.**
HAR! HAR! EVEN STACY'S MORE MAN THAN YOU ARE, PARKER!
"PATHETIC PARKER."
I'LL SHOW THEM WHO'S PATHETIC.
IN SPIDER-WOMAN...
I JUST... JUST...WANTED TO BE SPECIAL...
...LIKE YOU...
SUCH BLATANT DISREGARD FOR HUMAN LIFE CANNOT BE TOLERATED!
PETER PARKER **MUST NOT** HAVE DIED IN VAIN!
SPIDER-WOMAN AND THOSE LIKE HER MUST LEARN THAT WITH THEIR GREAT POWER...

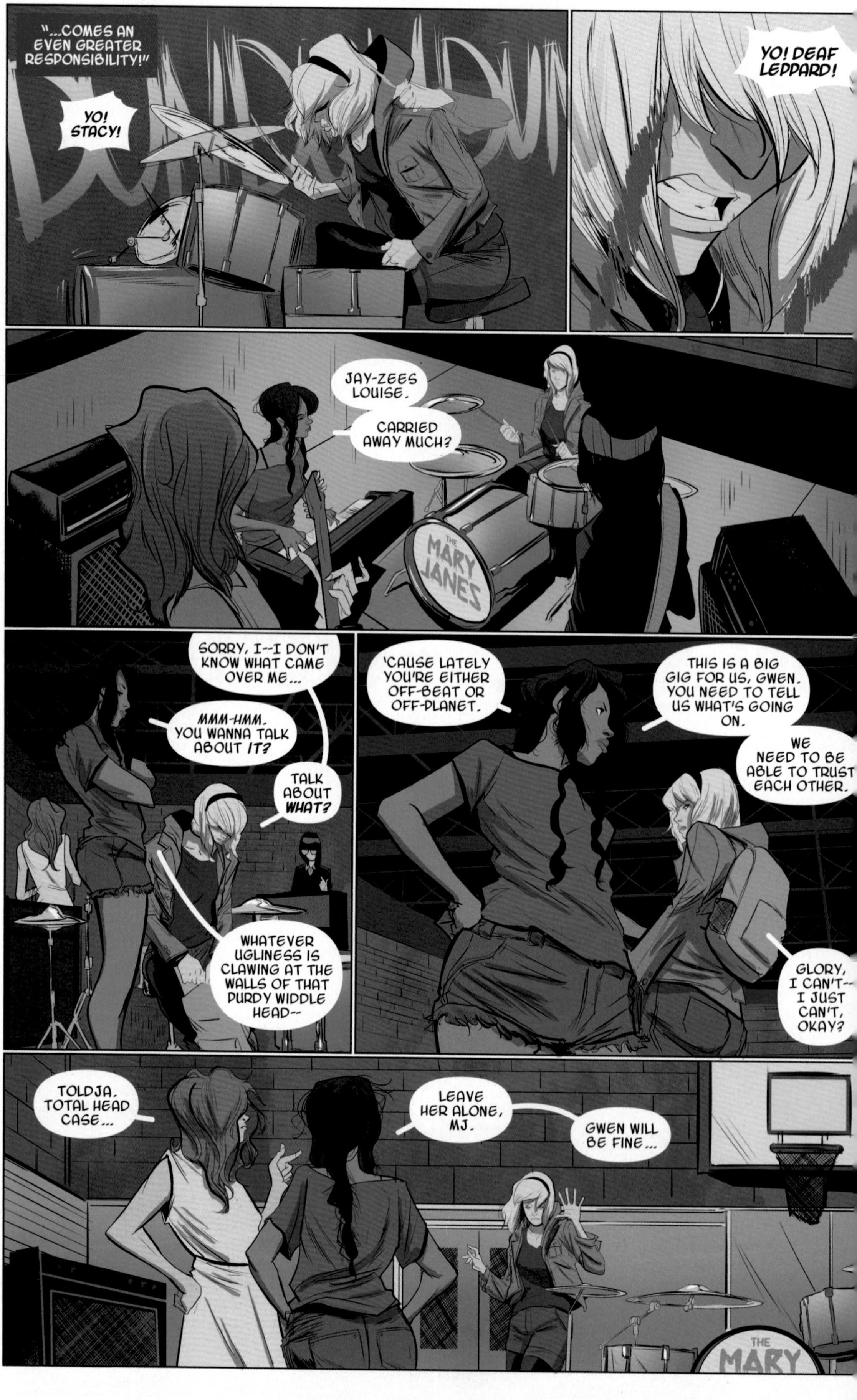
"...COMES AN EVEN GREATER RESPONSIBILITY!"
YO! STACY!
YO! DEAF LEPPARD!
JAY-ZEES LOUISE.
CARRIED AWAY MUCH?
THE MARY JANES
SORRY, I--I DON'T KNOW WHAT CAME OVER ME...
MMM-HMM. YOU WANNA TALK ABOUT IT?
TALK ABOUT WHAT?
WHATEVER UGLINESS IS CLAWING AT THE WALLS OF THAT PURDY WIDDLE HEAD--
'CAUSE LATELY YOU'RE EITHER OFF-BEAT OR OFF-PLANET.
THIS IS A BIG GIG FOR US, GWEN. YOU NEED TO TELL US WHAT'S GOING ON.
WE NEED TO BE ABLE TO TRUST EACH OTHER.
GLORY, I CAN'T-- I JUST CAN'T, OKAY?
TOLDJA. TOTAL HEAD CASE...
LEAVE HER ALONE, MJ.
GWEN WILL BE FINE...
THE MARY

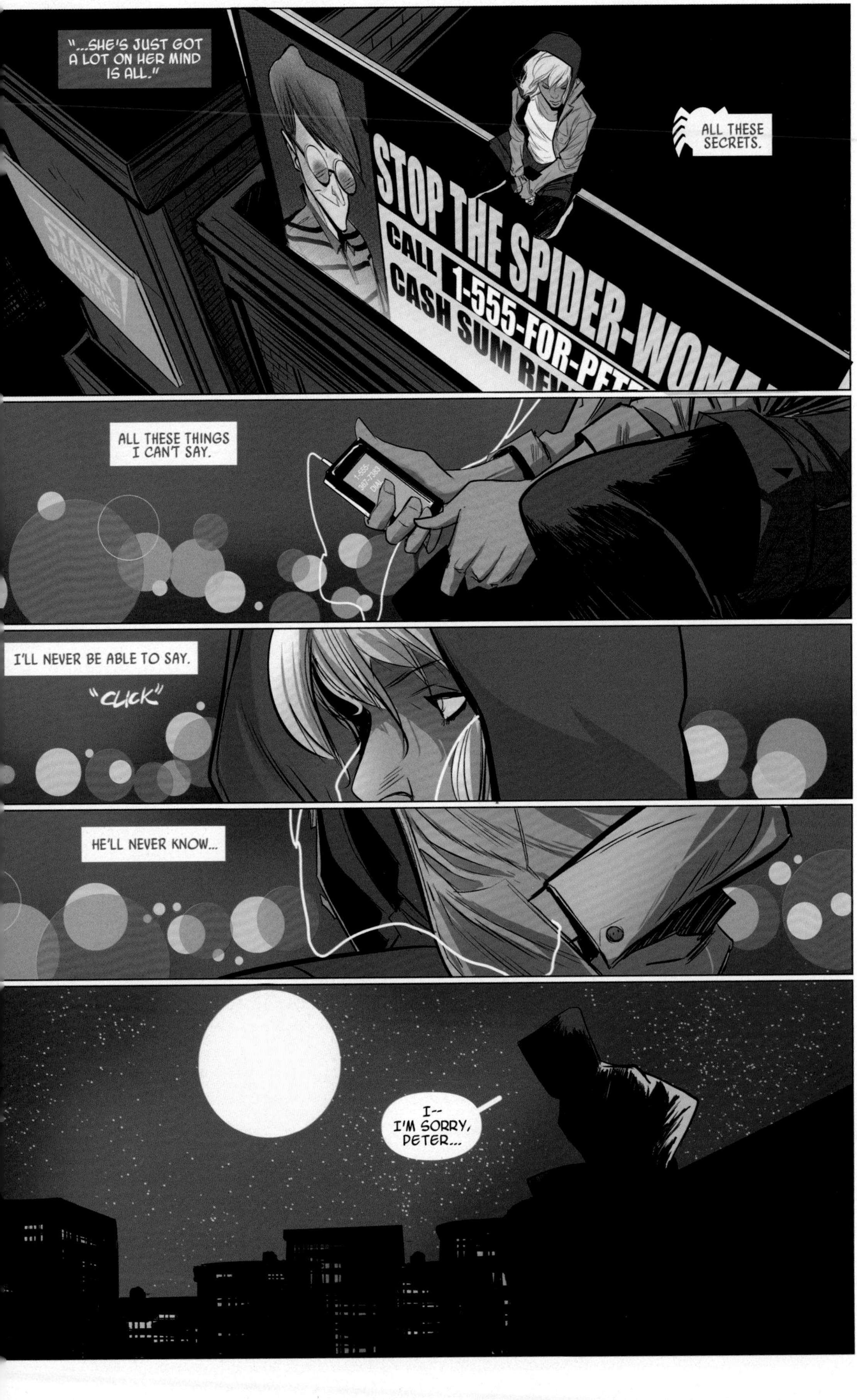
"...SHE'S JUST GOT A LOT ON HER MIND IS ALL."
STOP THE SPIDER-WOMA
CALL 1-555-FOR-PET
CASH SUM RE
STARK INDUSTRIES
ALL THESE SECRETS.
ALL THESE THINGS I CAN'T SAY.
1-555-367-7363 DIAL
I'LL NEVER BE ABLE TO SAY.
"CLICK"
HE'LL NEVER KNOW...
I-- I'M SORRY, PETER...

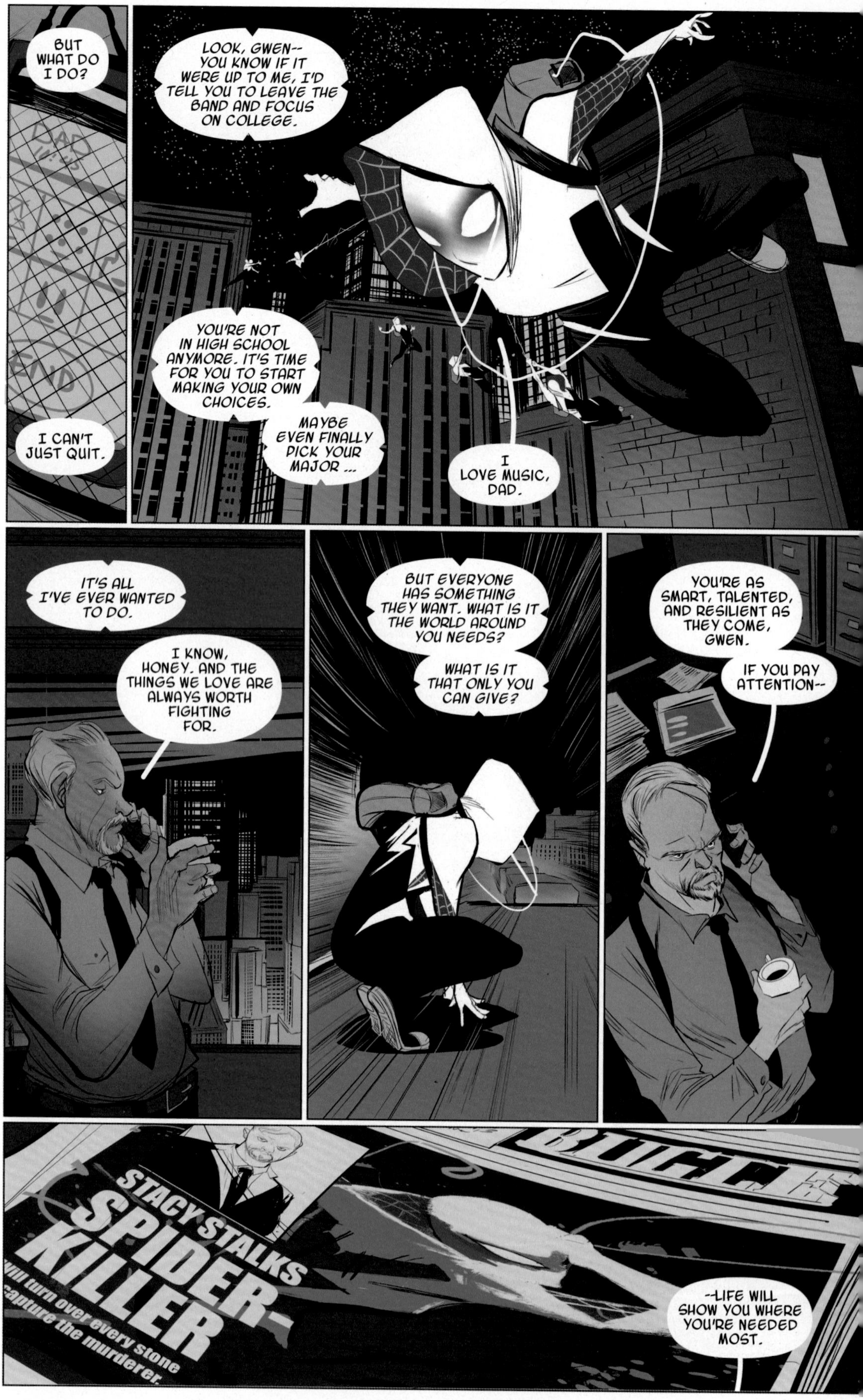
BUT WHAT DO I DO?
LOOK, GWEN-- YOU KNOW IF IT WERE UP TO ME, I'D TELL YOU TO LEAVE THE BAND AND FOCUS ON COLLEGE.
YOU'RE NOT IN HIGH SCHOOL ANYMORE. IT'S TIME FOR YOU TO START MAKING YOUR OWN CHOICES.
MAYBE EVEN FINALLY PICK YOUR MAJOR ...
I CAN'T JUST QUIT.
I LOVE MUSIC, DAD.
IT'S ALL I'VE EVER WANTED TO DO.
I KNOW, HONEY. AND THE THINGS WE LOVE ARE ALWAYS WORTH FIGHTING FOR.
BUT EVERYONE HAS SOMETHING THEY WANT. WHAT IS IT THE WORLD AROUND YOU NEEDS?
WHAT IS IT THAT ONLY YOU CAN GIVE?
YOU'RE AS SMART, TALENTED, AND RESILIENT AS THEY COME, GWEN.
IF YOU PAY ATTENTION--
STACY STALKS SPIDER-KILLER
will turn over every stone
capture the murderer.
--LIFE WILL SHOW YOU WHERE YOU'RE NEEDED MOST.

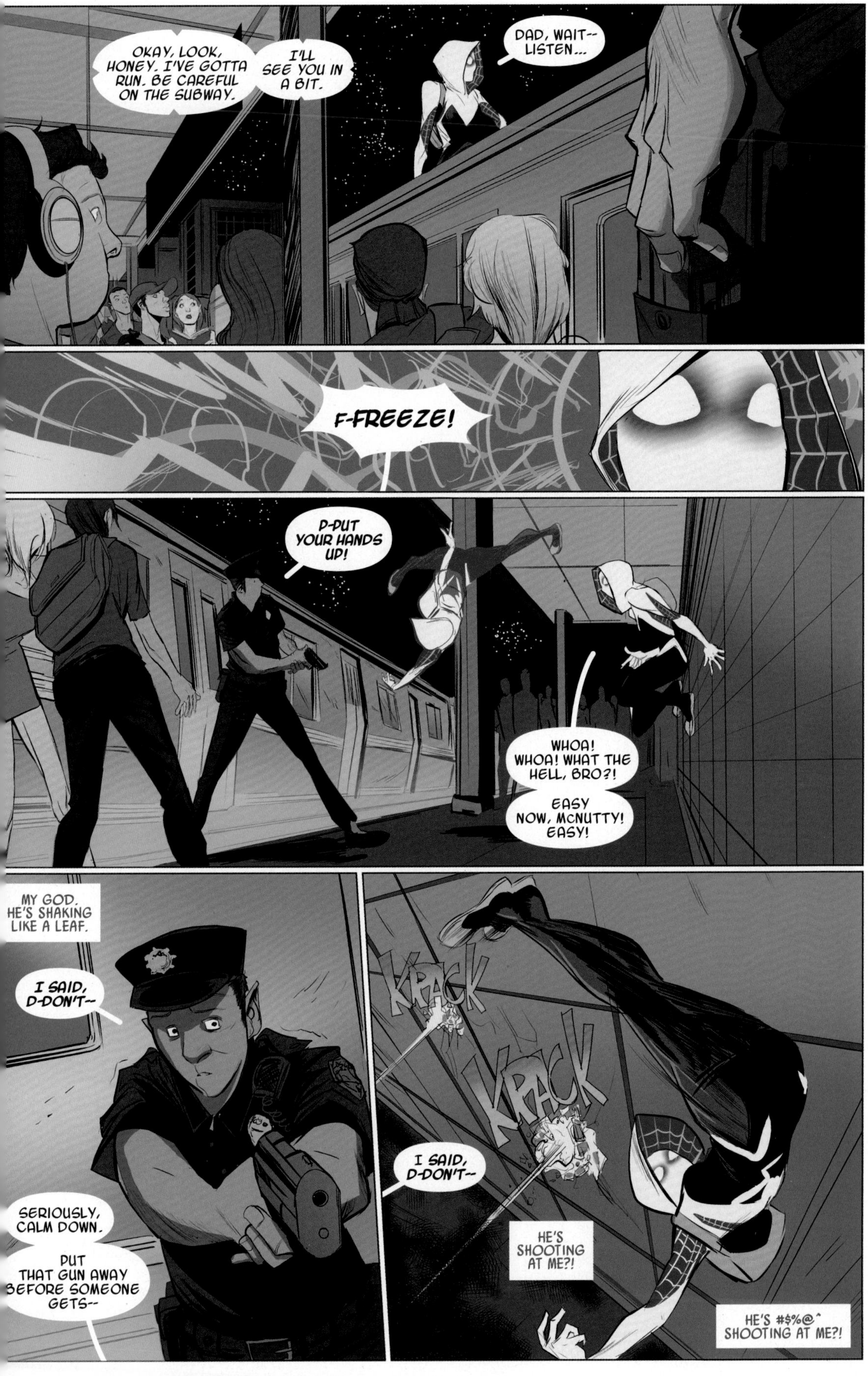
OKAY, LOOK, HONEY. I'VE GOTTA RUN. BE CAREFUL ON THE SUBWAY.
I'LL SEE YOU IN A BIT.
DAD, WAIT-- LISTEN...
F-FREEZE!
D-PUT YOUR HANDS UP!
WHOA! WHOA! WHAT THE HELL, BRO?!
EASY NOW, MCNUTTY! EASY!
MY GOD. HE'S SHAKING LIKE A LEAF.
I SAID, D-DON'T--
SERIOUSLY, CALM DOWN.
PUT THAT GUN AWAY BEFORE SOMEONE GETS--
KRACK
KRACK
I SAID, D-DON'T--
HE'S SHOOTING AT ME?!
HE'S #$%@^ SHOOTING AT ME?!

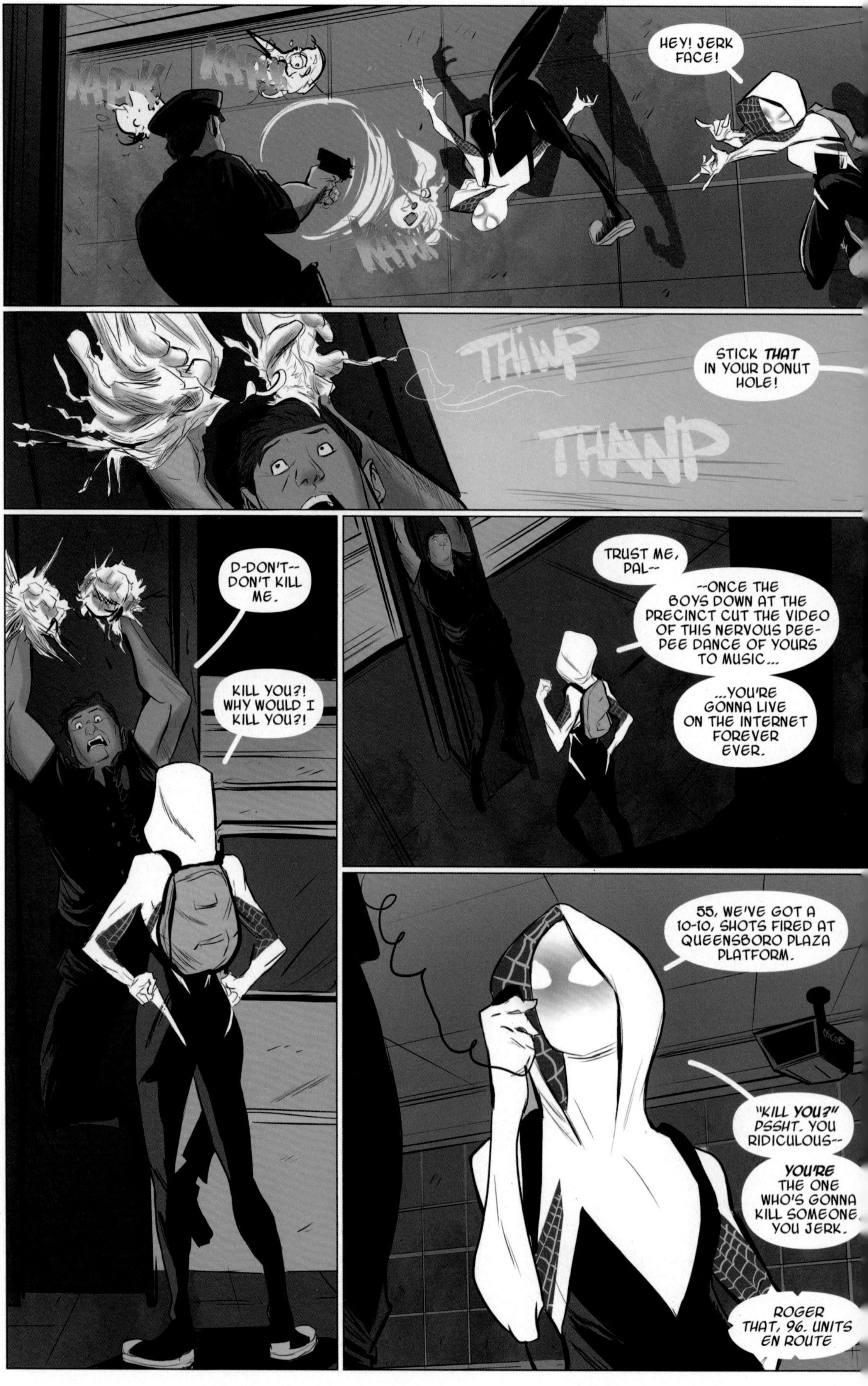
HEY! JERK FACE!
STICK THAT IN YOUR DONUT HOLE!
THAWP
D-DON'T-- DON'T KILL ME.
KILL YOU?! WHY WOULD I KILL YOU?!
TRUST ME, PAL--
--ONCE THE BOYS DOWN AT THE PRECINCT CUT THE VIDEO OF THIS NERVOUS PEE-PEE DANCE OF YOURS TO MUSIC...
...YOU'RE GONNA LIVE ON THE INTERNET FOREVER EVER.
55, WE'VE GOT A 10-10, SHOTS FIRED AT QUEENSBORO PLAZA PLATFORM.
"KILL YOU?" PSSHT. YOU RIDICULOUS--
YOU'RE THE ONE WHO'S GONNA KILL SOMEONE, YOU JERK.
ROGER THAT, 96. UNITS EN ROUTE

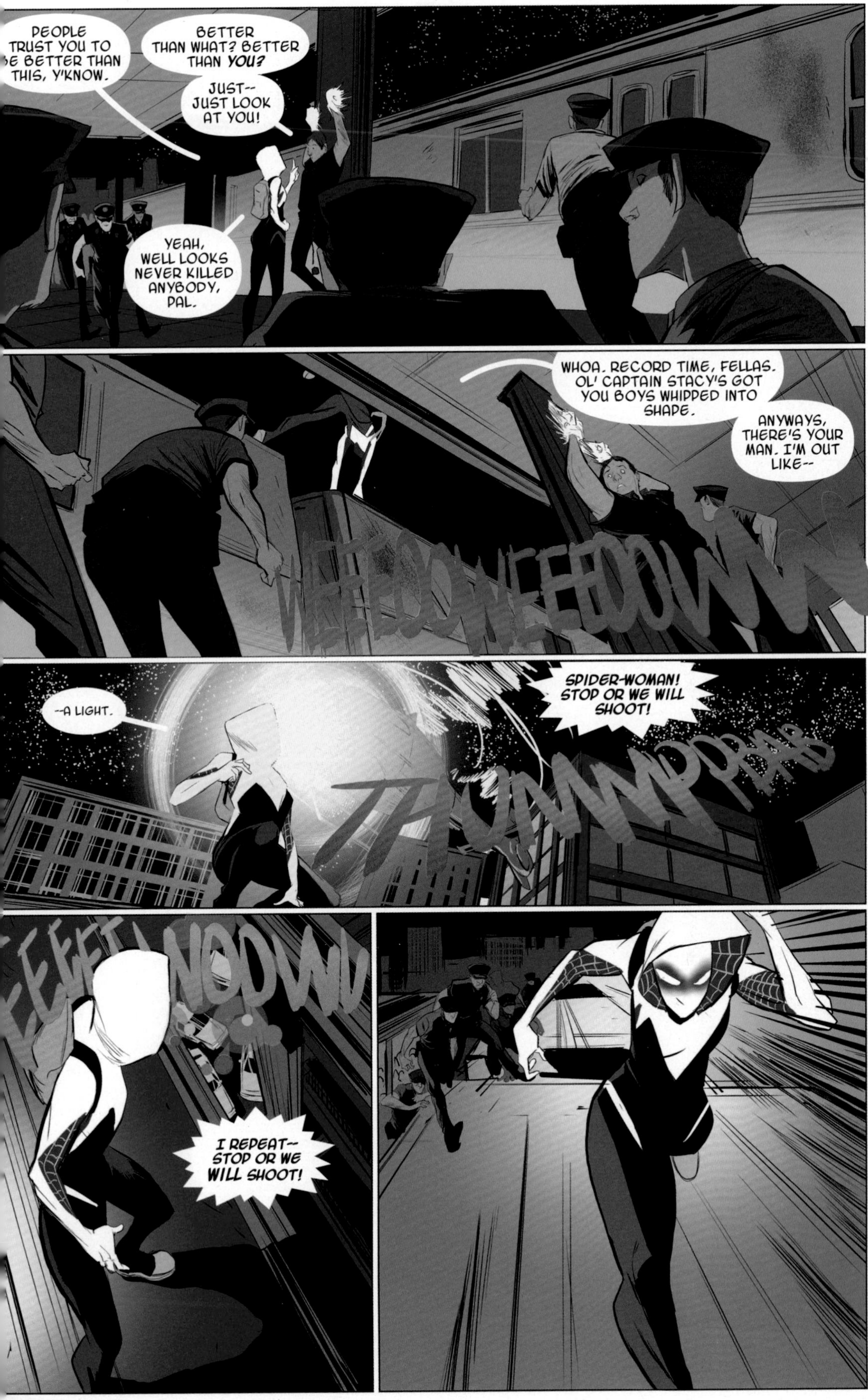
PEOPLE TRUST YOU TO BE BETTER THAN THIS, Y'KNOW.
BETTER THAN WHAT? BETTER THAN YOU?
JUST-- JUST LOOK AT YOU!
YEAH, WELL LOOKS NEVER KILLED ANYBODY, PAL.
WHOA. RECORD TIME, FELLAS. OL' CAPTAIN STACY'S GOT YOU BOYS WHIPPED INTO SHAPE.
ANYWAYS, THERE'S YOUR MAN. I'M OUT LIKE--
--A LIGHT.
SPIDER-WOMAN! STOP OR WE WILL SHOOT!
I REPEAT-- STOP OR WE WILL SHOOT!

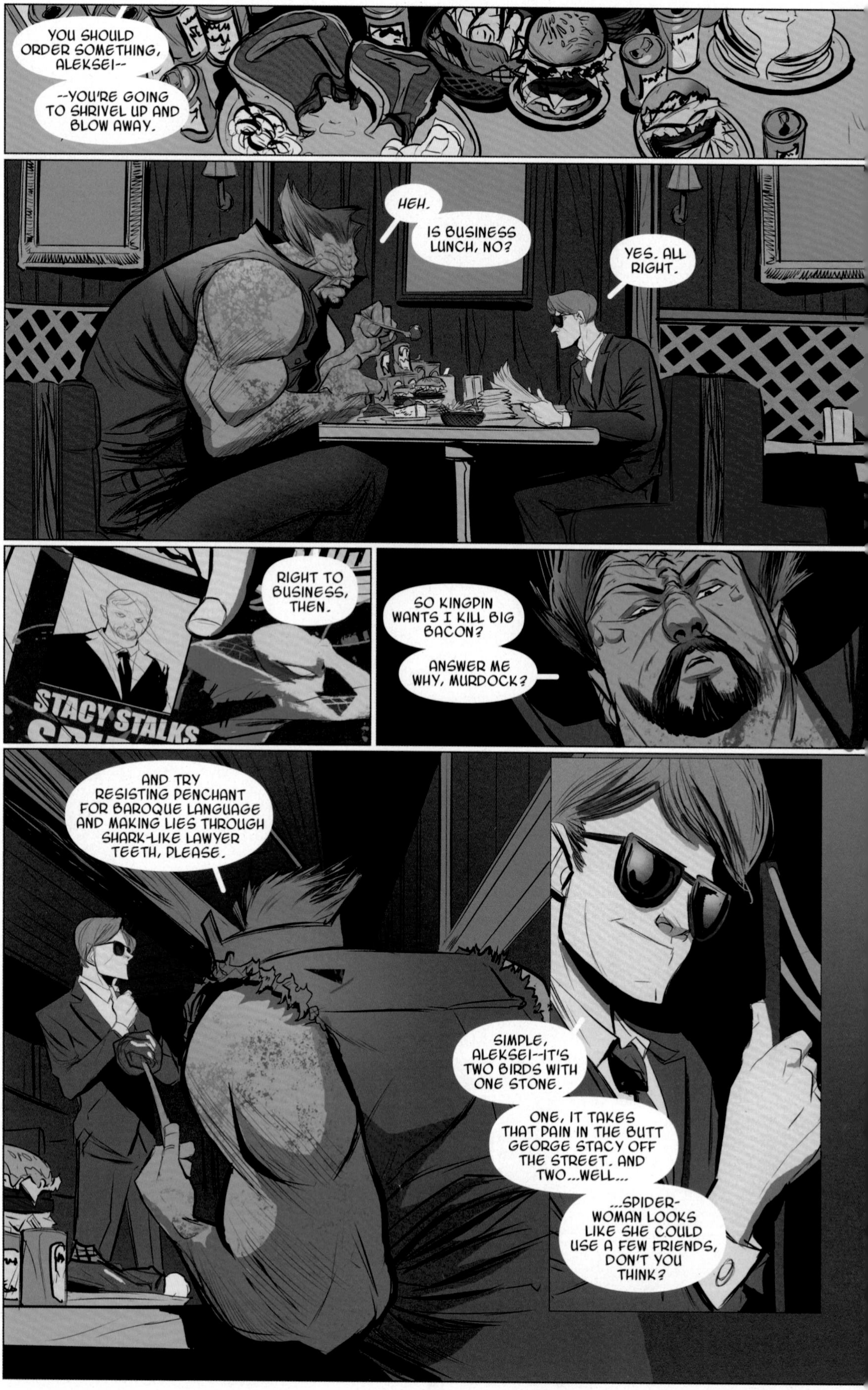
YOU SHOULD ORDER SOMETHING, ALEKSEI--
--YOU'RE GOING TO SHRIVEL UP AND BLOW AWAY.
HEH.
IS BUSINESS LUNCH, NO?
YES. ALL RIGHT.
RIGHT TO BUSINESS, THEN.
STACY STALKS
SO KINGPIN WANTS I KILL BIG BACON?
ANSWER ME WHY, MURDOCK?
AND TRY RESISTING PENCHANT FOR BAROQUE LANGUAGE AND MAKING LIES THROUGH SHARK-LIKE LAWYER TEETH, PLEASE.
SIMPLE, ALEKSEI--IT'S TWO BIRDS WITH ONE STONE.
ONE, IT TAKES THAT PAIN IN THE BUTT GEORGE STACY OFF THE STREET. AND TWO...WELL...
...SPIDER-WOMAN LOOKS LIKE SHE COULD USE A FEW FRIENDS, DON'T YOU THINK?

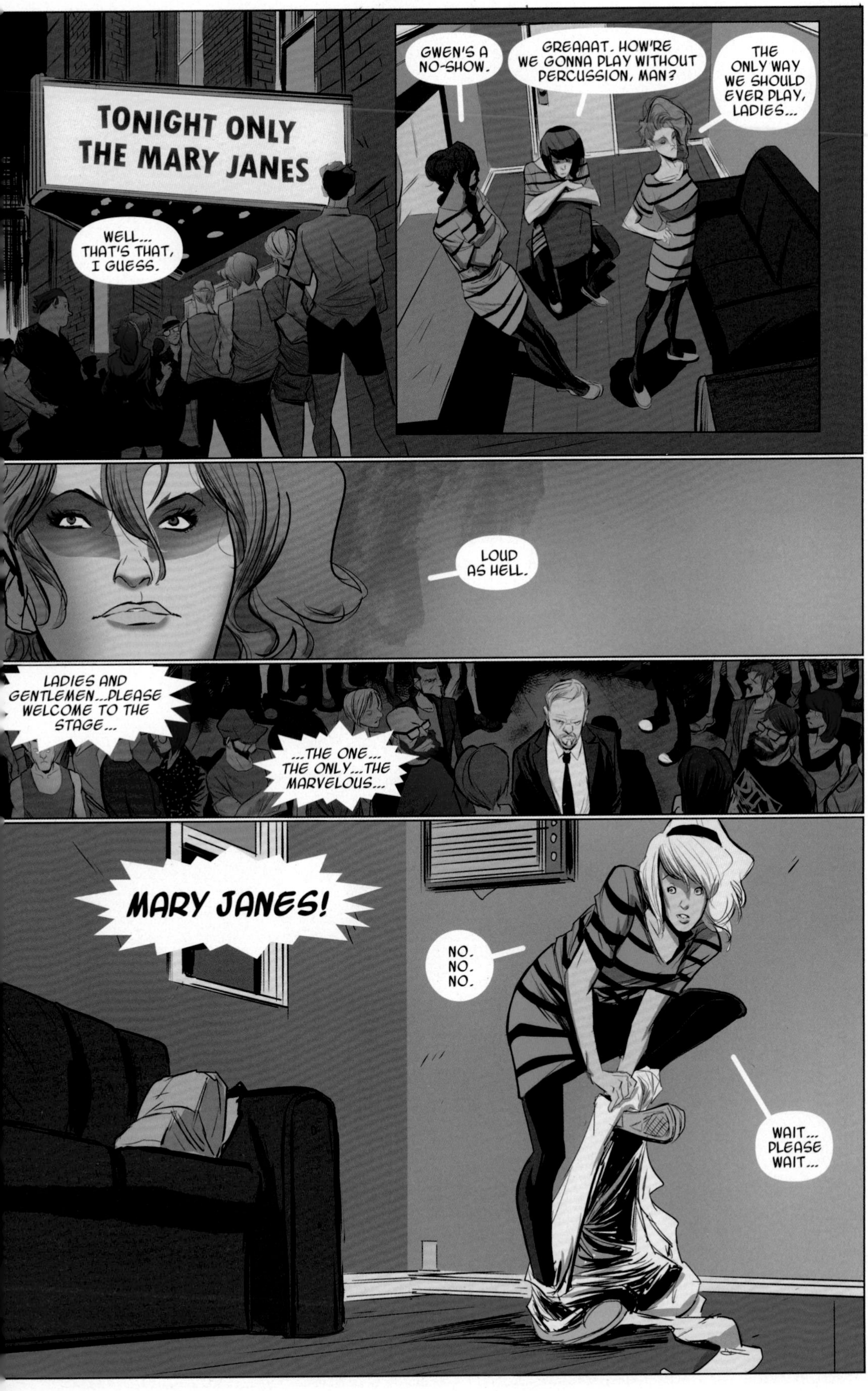
TONIGHT ONLY
THE MARY JANES
WELL... THAT'S THAT, I GUESS.
GWEN'S A NO-SHOW.
GREAAAT. HOW'RE WE GONNA PLAY WITHOUT PERCUSSION, MAN?
THE ONLY WAY WE SHOULD EVER PLAY, LADIES...
LOUD AS HELL.
LADIES AND GENTLEMEN...PLEASE WELCOME TO THE STAGE...
...THE ONE... THE ONLY...THE MARVELOUS...
MARY JANES!
NO. NO. NO.
WAIT... PLEASE WAIT...

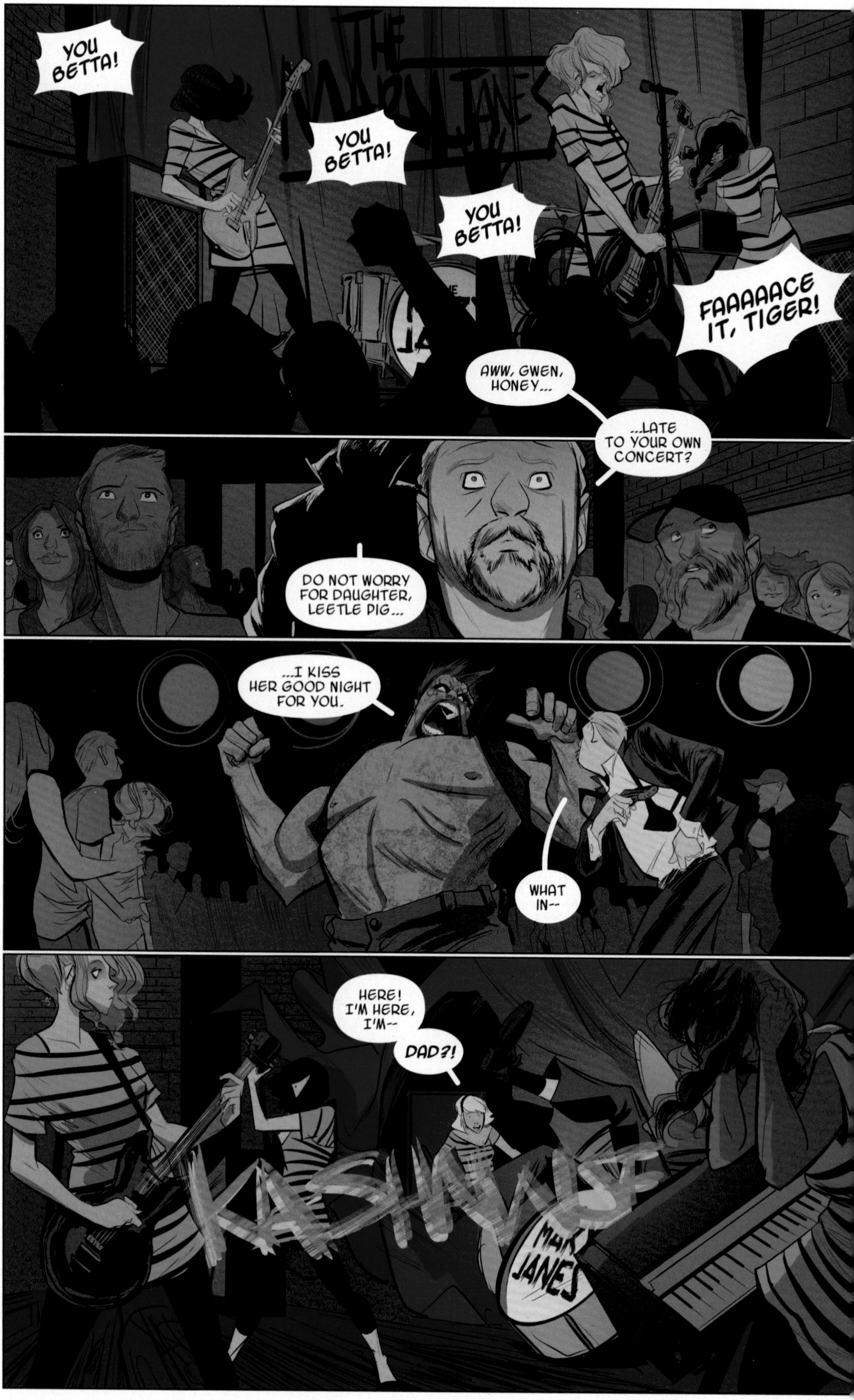
YOU BETTA!
YOU BETTA!
YOU BETTA!
FAAAAACE IT, TIGER!
AWW, GWEN, HONEY...
...LATE TO YOUR OWN CONCERT?
DO NOT WORRY FOR DAUGHTER, LEETLE PIG...
...I KISS HER GOOD NIGHT FOR YOU.
WHAT IN--
HERE! I'M HERE, I'M--
DAD?!
KASHWISE

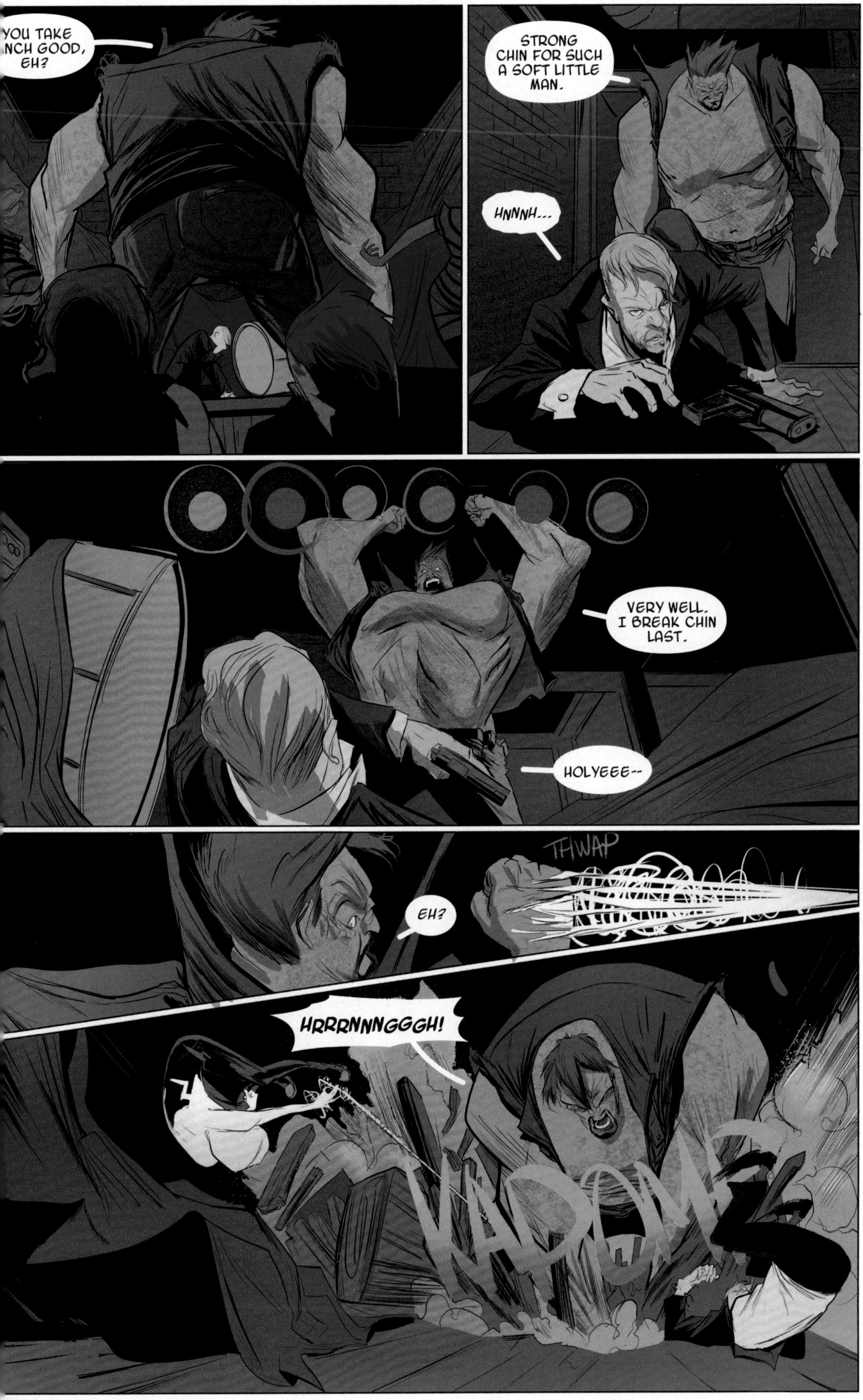
YOU TAKE
NCH GOOD,
EH?
STRONG CHIN FOR SUCH A SOFT LITTLE MAN.
HNNNH...
VERY WELL. I BREAK CHIN LAST.
HOLYEEE--
THWAP
EH?
HRRRNNNGGGH!
VAPOOM

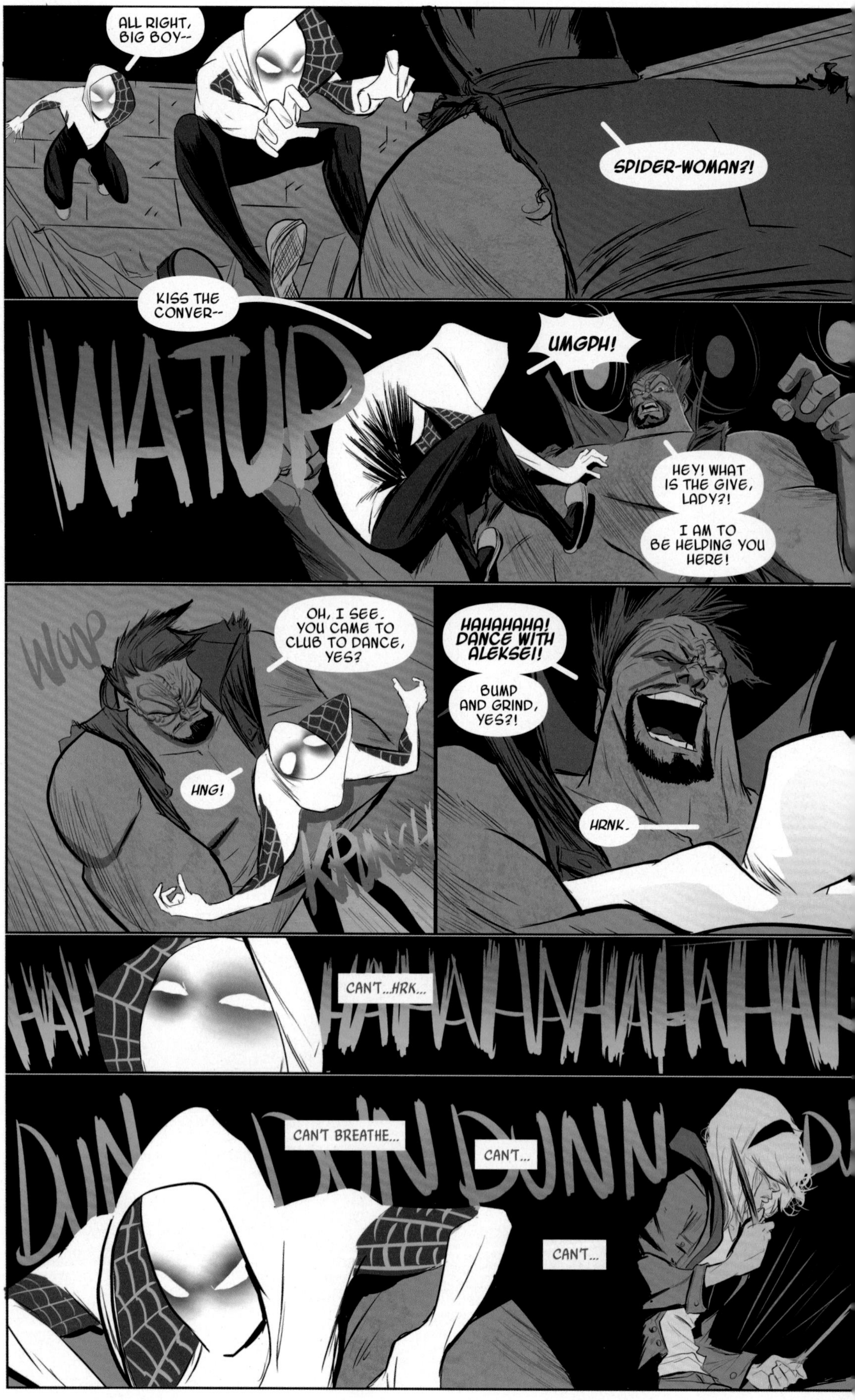

ALL RIGHT, BIG BOY--
SPIDER-WOMAN?!
KISS THE CONVER--
WATUP
UMGPH!
HEY! WHAT IS THE GIVE, LADY?!
I AM TO BE HELPING YOU HERE!
WOOP
OH, I SEE. YOU CAME TO CLUB TO DANCE, YES?
HNG!
HAHAHAHA! DANCE WITH ALEKSEI!
BUMP AND GRIND, YES?!
HRNK.
CAN'T...HRK...
CAN'T BREATHE...
CAN'T...
CAN'T...

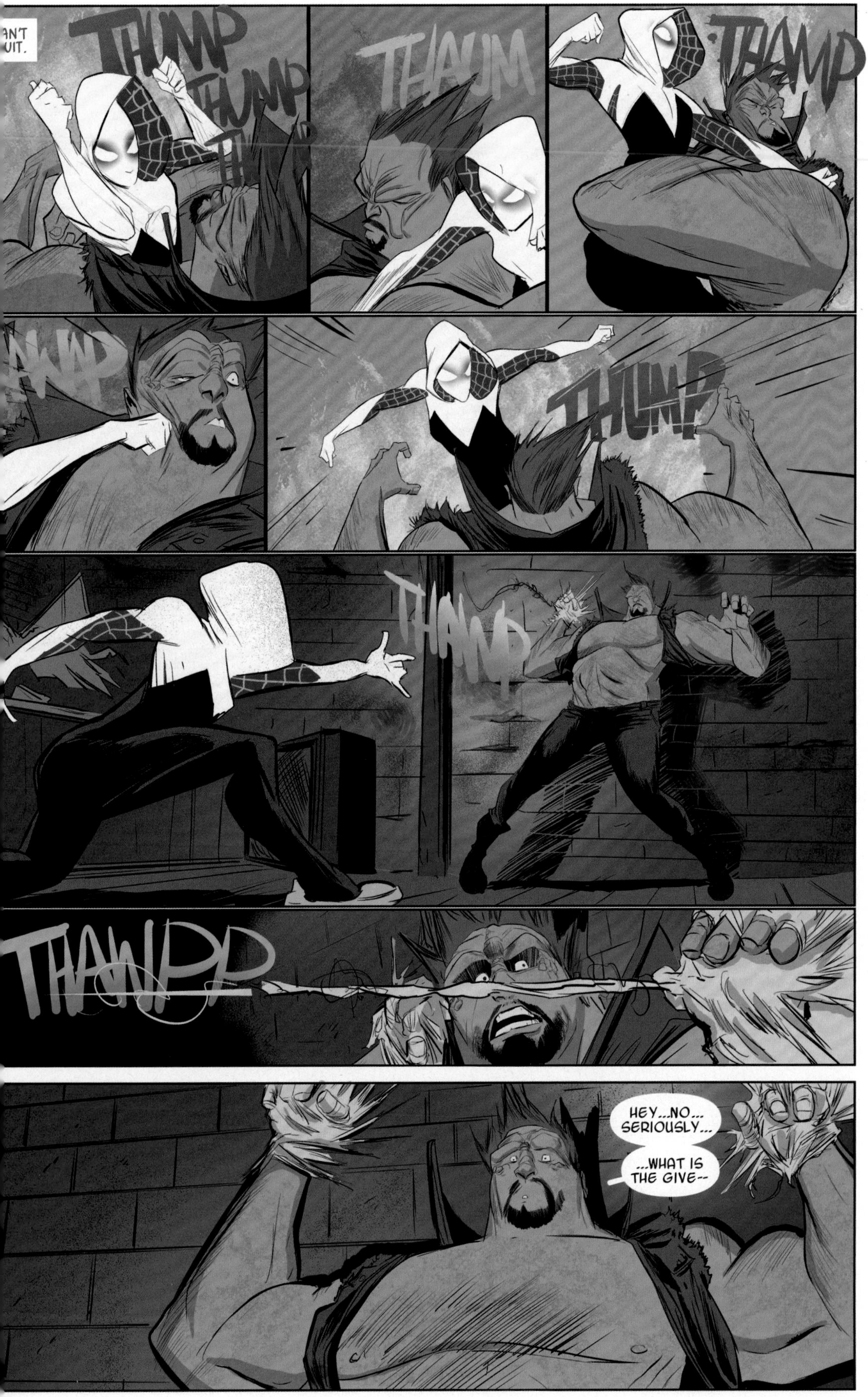
AN'T
UIT.
THUMP
THUMP
THAUM
THAMP
THUMP
THAWP
THAWPP
HEY...NO...
SERIOUSLY...
...WHAT IS
THE GIVE--

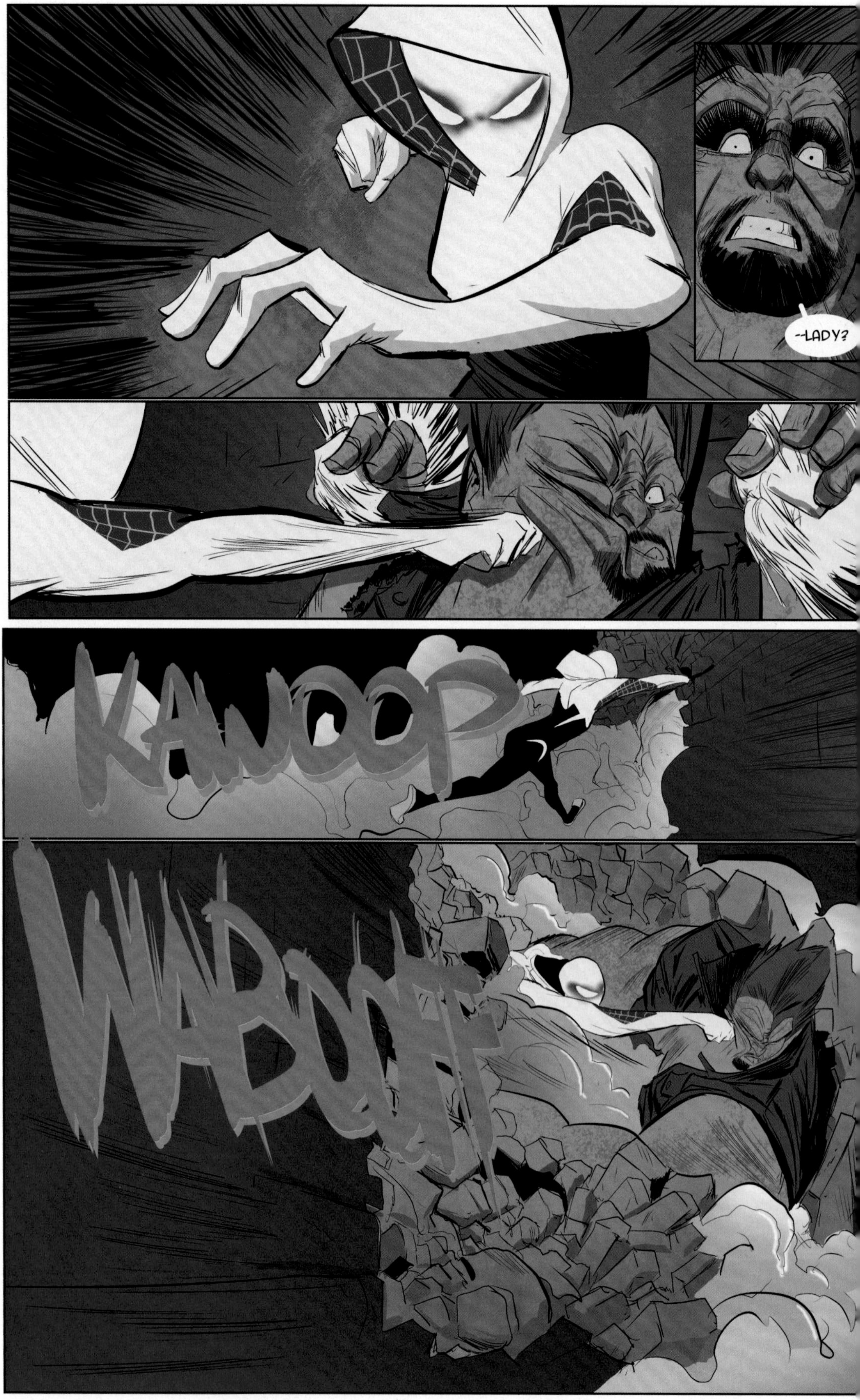
--LADY?
KAWOOP
WABOOFF

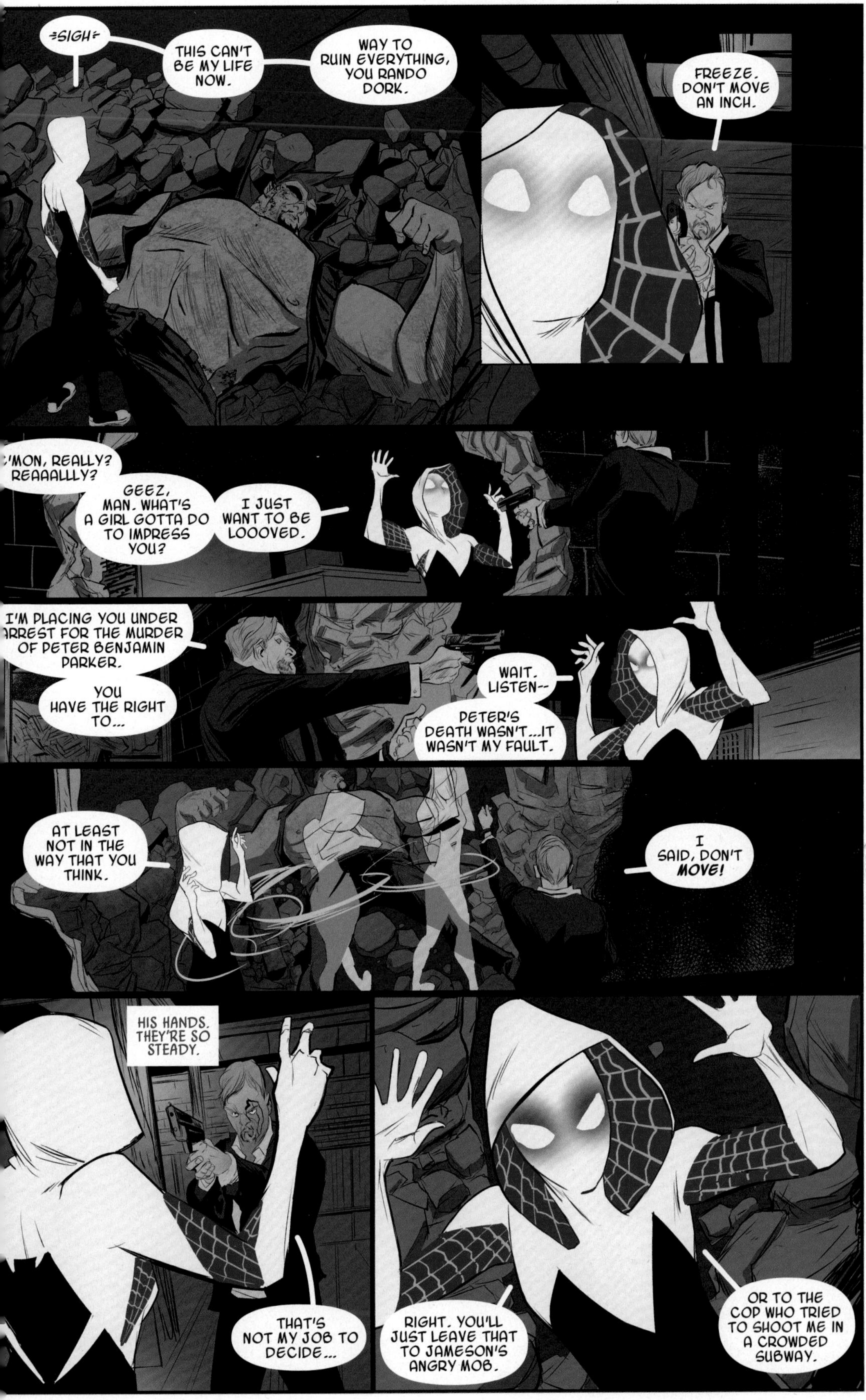

≡SIGH≡
THIS CAN'T BE MY LIFE NOW.
WAY TO RUIN EVERYTHING, YOU RANDO DORK.
FREEZE. DON'T MOVE AN INCH.
C'MON, REALLY? REAAALLLY?
GEEZ, MAN. WHAT'S A GIRL GOTTA DO TO IMPRESS YOU?
I JUST WANT TO BE LOOOVED.
I'M PLACING YOU UNDER ARREST FOR THE MURDER OF PETER BENJAMIN PARKER.
YOU HAVE THE RIGHT TO...
WAIT. LISTEN--
PETER'S DEATH WASN'T...IT WASN'T MY FAULT.
AT LEAST NOT IN THE WAY THAT YOU THINK.
I SAID, DON'T MOVE!
HIS HANDS. THEY'RE SO STEADY.
THAT'S NOT MY JOB TO DECIDE...
RIGHT. YOU'LL JUST LEAVE THAT TO JAMESON'S ANGRY MOB.
OR TO THE COP WHO TRIED TO SHOOT ME IN A CROWDED SUBWAY.

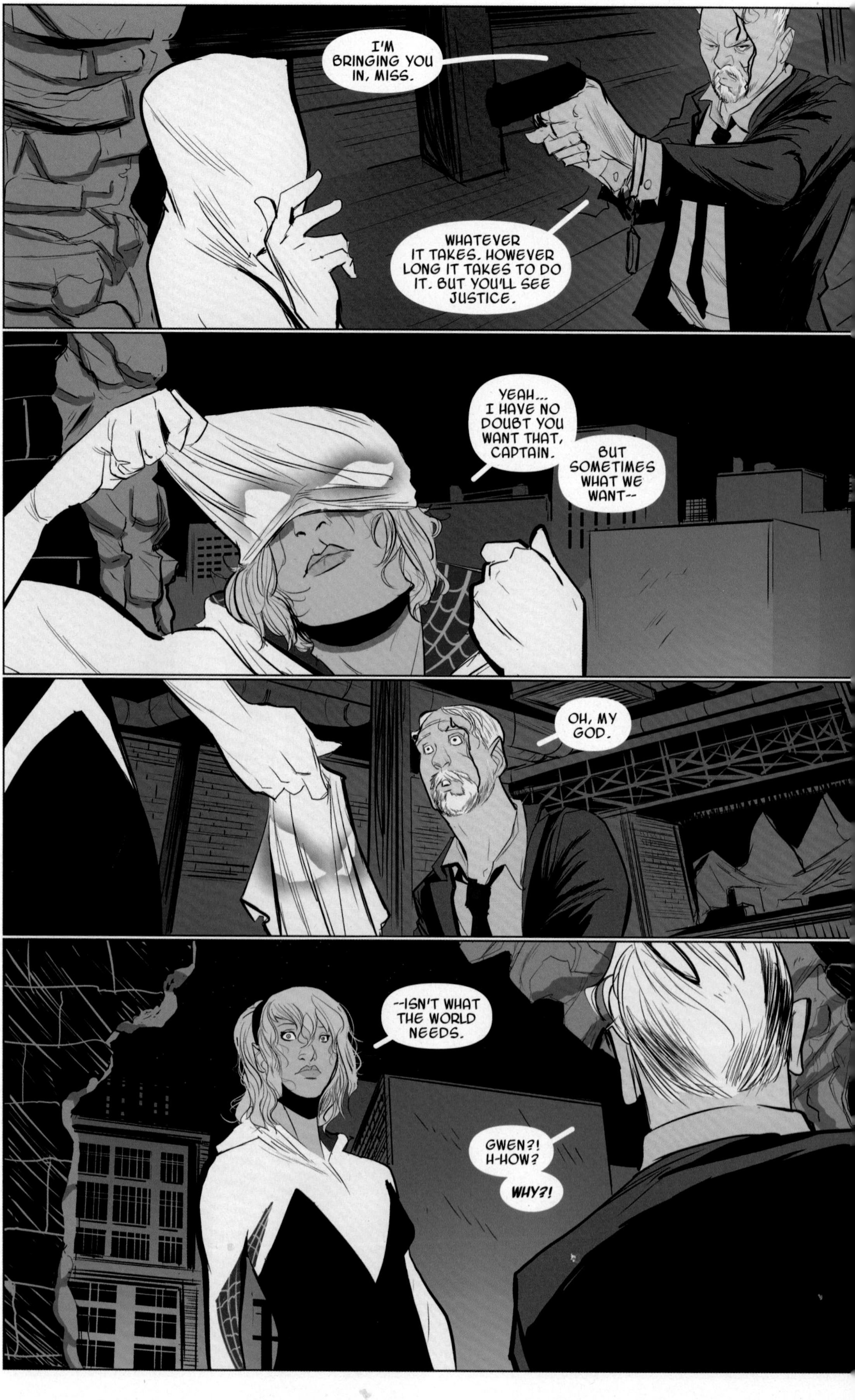
I'M BRINGING YOU IN, MISS.
WHATEVER IT TAKES. HOWEVER LONG IT TAKES TO DO IT. BUT YOU'LL SEE JUSTICE.
YEAH... I HAVE NO DOUBT YOU WANT THAT, CAPTAIN.
BUT SOMETIMES WHAT WE WANT--
OH, MY GOD.
--ISN'T WHAT THE WORLD NEEDS.
GWEN?! H-HOW?
WHY?!

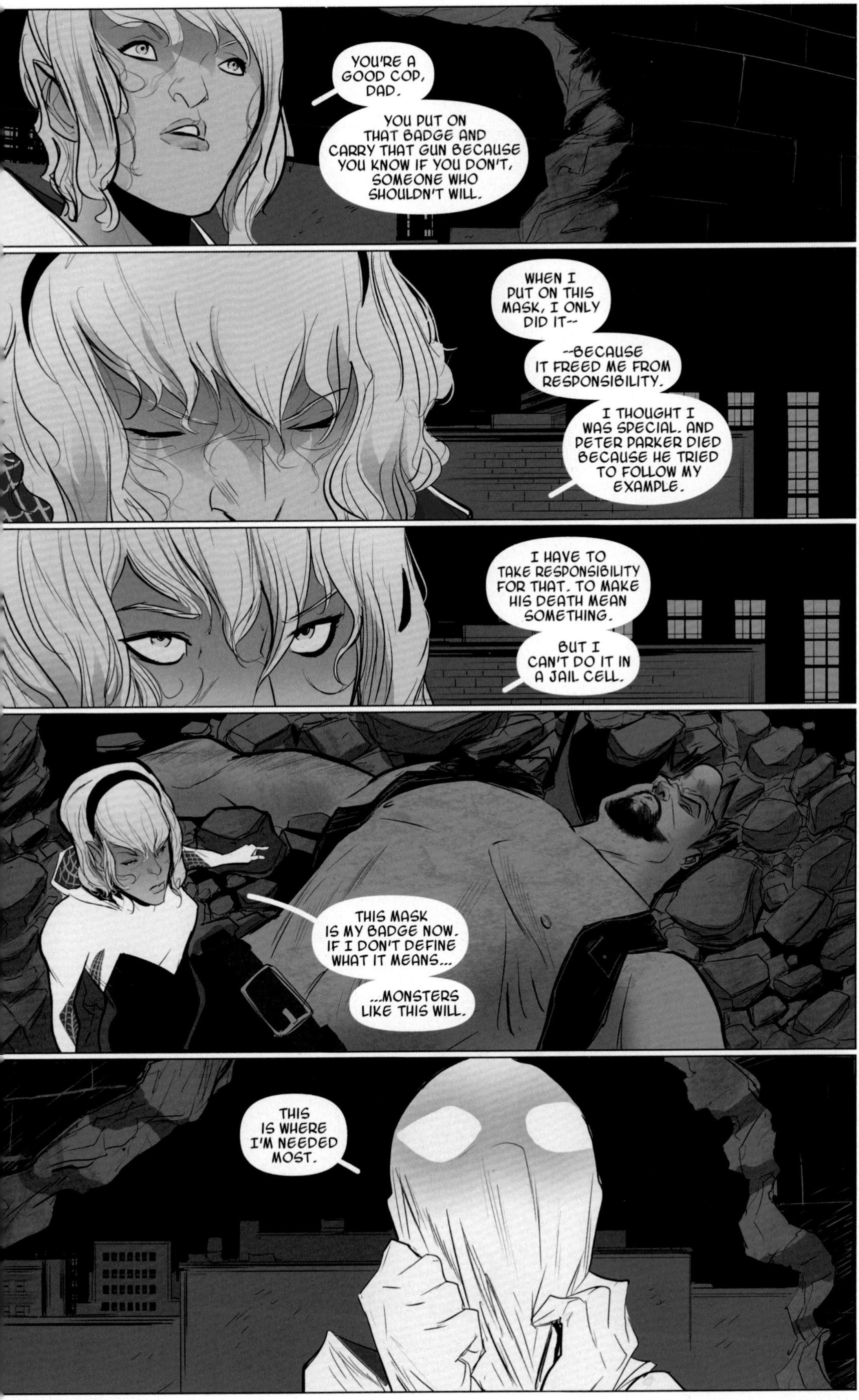
YOU'RE A GOOD COP, DAD.
YOU PUT ON THAT BADGE AND CARRY THAT GUN BECAUSE YOU KNOW IF YOU DON'T, SOMEONE WHO SHOULDN'T WILL.
WHEN I PUT ON THIS MASK, I ONLY DID IT--
--BECAUSE IT FREED ME FROM RESPONSIBILITY.
I THOUGHT I WAS SPECIAL. AND PETER PARKER DIED BECAUSE HE TRIED TO FOLLOW MY EXAMPLE.
I HAVE TO TAKE RESPONSIBILITY FOR THAT. TO MAKE HIS DEATH MEAN SOMETHING.
BUT I CAN'T DO IT IN A JAIL CELL.
THIS MASK IS MY BADGE NOW. IF I DON'T DEFINE WHAT IT MEANS...
...MONSTERS LIKE THIS WILL.
THIS IS WHERE I'M NEEDED MOST.

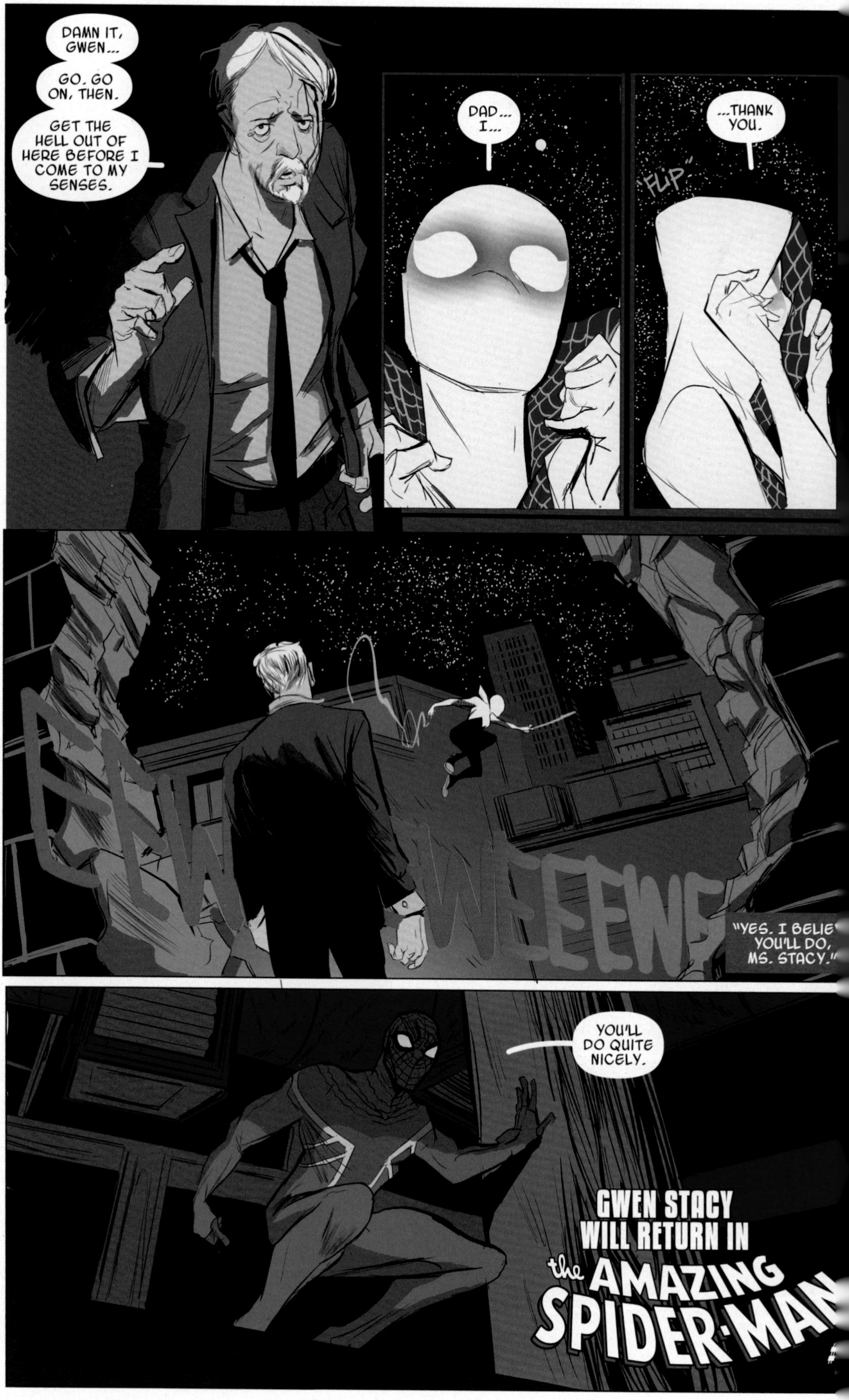
DAMN IT, GWEN...
GO. GO ON, THEN.
GET THE HELL OUT OF HERE BEFORE I COME TO MY SENSES.
DAD... I...
...THANK YOU.
FLIP
"YES. I BELIE
YOU'LL DO,
MS. STACY."
YOU'LL DO QUITE NICELY.
GWEN STACY WILL RETURN IN
the AMAZING SPIDER-MAN

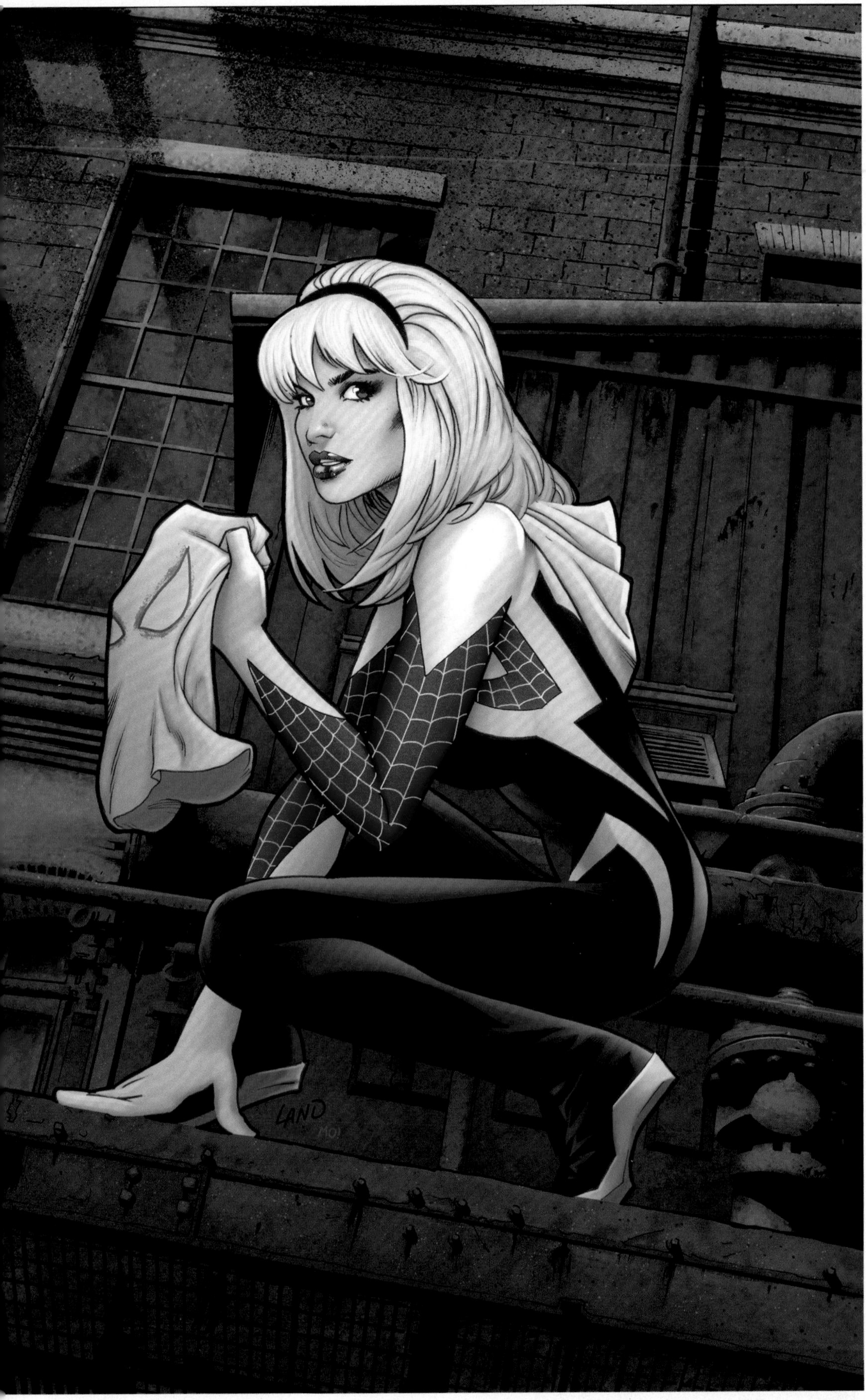
LAND
MO!

#2 VARIANT BY GREG LAND & MORRY HOLLOWELL

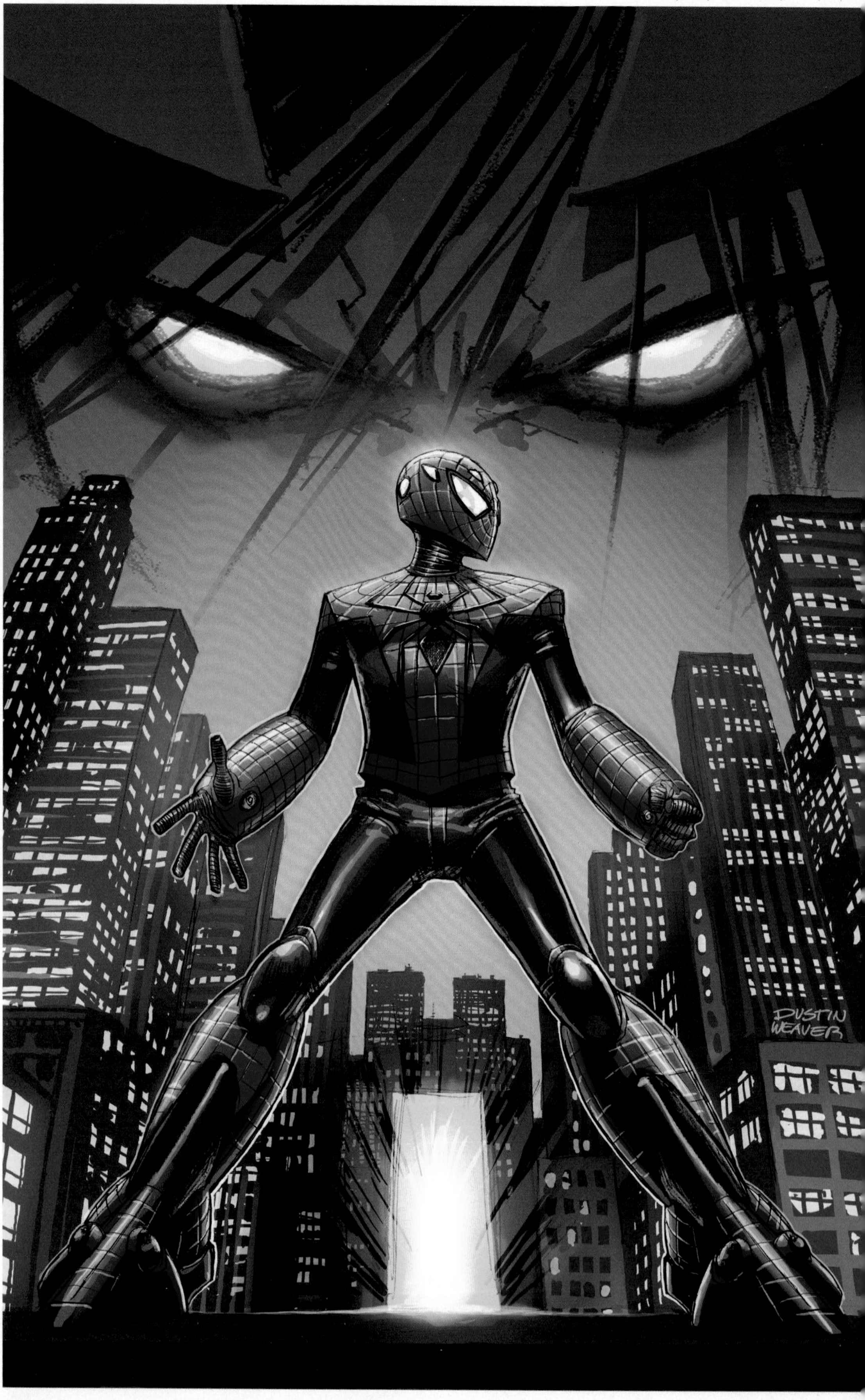
DUSTIN
WEAVER

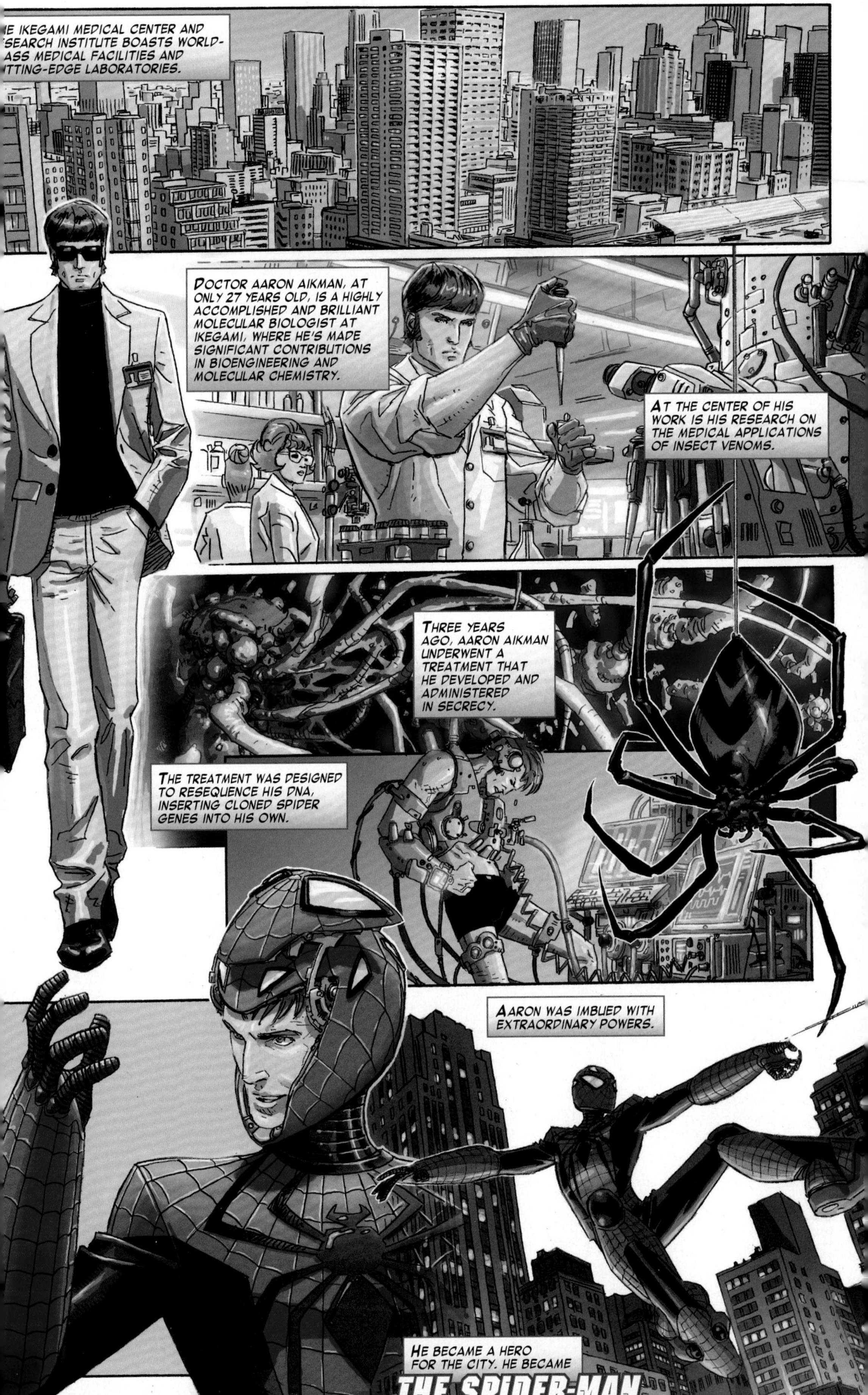
E IKEGAMI MEDICAL CENTER AND
ESEARCH INSTITUTE BOASTS WORLD-
ASS MEDICAL FACILITIES AND
TTING-EDGE LABORATORIES.
DOCTOR AARON AIKMAN, AT ONLY 27 YEARS OLD, IS A HIGHLY ACCOMPLISHED AND BRILLIANT MOLECULAR BIOLOGIST AT IKEGAMI, WHERE HE'S MADE SIGNIFICANT CONTRIBUTIONS IN BIOENGINEERING AND MOLECULAR CHEMISTRY.
AT THE CENTER OF HIS WORK IS HIS RESEARCH ON THE MEDICAL APPLICATIONS OF INSECT VENOMS.
THREE YEARS AGO, AARON AIKMAN UNDERWENT A TREATMENT THAT HE DEVELOPED AND ADMINISTERED IN SECRECY.
THE TREATMENT WAS DESIGNED TO RESEQUENCE HIS DNA, INSERTING CLONED SPIDER GENES INTO HIS OWN.
AARON WAS IMBUED WITH EXTRAORDINARY POWERS.
HE BECAME A HERO FOR THE CITY. HE BECAME
THE SPIDER-MAN.

As the Spider-Man, Aaron has fantastic strength and agility. He is able to crawl on walls and, using his molecular bioengineering genius, has formulated a silk webbing solution.

HELMET WITH AN ARRAY OF SENSORS AND HEADS-UP DISPLAYS

BORN IN THE GREAT RED STORM OF JUPITER, REDEYE WILL DESTROY YOU ALL!

REDEYE WAS THE REASON AARON BECAME THE SPIDER-MAN. HE WAS HIS FIRST FOE.

REDEYE

SILK-SPINNER, SILK SOLUTION CARTRIDGE (CONCEALED IN THE ARM CASING)

NEURO-PULSE STINGER (LOCATED ON A RETRACTABLE CABLE ON HIS BELT)

REDEYE™

Real Name: Rick Landress
Group Affiliation: The Apoc
Height: 6'6   **Weight:** 370 l
Battles Fought: 9
Wins: 7   **Losses:** 1   Tie
Win Percentage: 77%
Arch-enemies: The Spider-M
Devil Recuse, Bullwhip
First Appearance: (as Rick
Landress) THE SPIDER-MAN #1 (as Red-Eye) THE SPIDER-MAN #3

Commander Rick Landress was an astronaut on the manned mission to the moons of Jupiter. When one the crew was mysteriously found dead, the rest turne each other. Rick soon discovered that their mission v not what they were lead to believe and that the ship in danger. He tried leaving in an escape pod, but it v too late. The ship was bombarded with cosmic radia and Rick's pod hurtled out of control into Jupiter. W Rick returned to Earth as Redeye he had the power t create huge gusts of wind and storms.

Did You Know: Redeye is currently believed dead, c ed by The Spider-Man under a barrage of falling build

AFTER THE "JOVIAN DESTROYER," MORE VILLAINS ROSE TO TAKE HIS PLACE, AND WITH EACH, DR. AIKMAN ROSE TO STOP THEM AS THE SPIDER-MAN.

up Chroni

OVER 100 VICTIM NAAMURAH KIDNAPPIN A CITY GRIPPED IN FEA

their doors and close and bolt their windows at night. Naamurah's attacks have been focused in the South East quadrant. Residents of these neighborhoods should take every precaution."

Can The Spide Stop Her?

For months Police have been on the hunt for the mysteri- Atlas City kidnapper, but a few vague eye wit- om or what

This past W City hero, The Spi- der-Man, gave police our

was unc

Jackson, the at the ave re- ion to.

Naamurah pears to be a cyborg. Though the extent is har

ONE YEAR AGO, A NEW, EXCEEDINGLY ELUSIVE AND MYSTERIOUS VILLAIN, KNOWN AS NAAMURAH, APPEARED IN THE CITY.

CATAPULT PROPULSION BOOTS

IN THEIR ONE CONFRONTATION, SHE NEARLY DEFEATED HIM. HIS STINGER HAD NO EFFECT, AND SHE EASILY BROKE THROUGH HIS SILK.

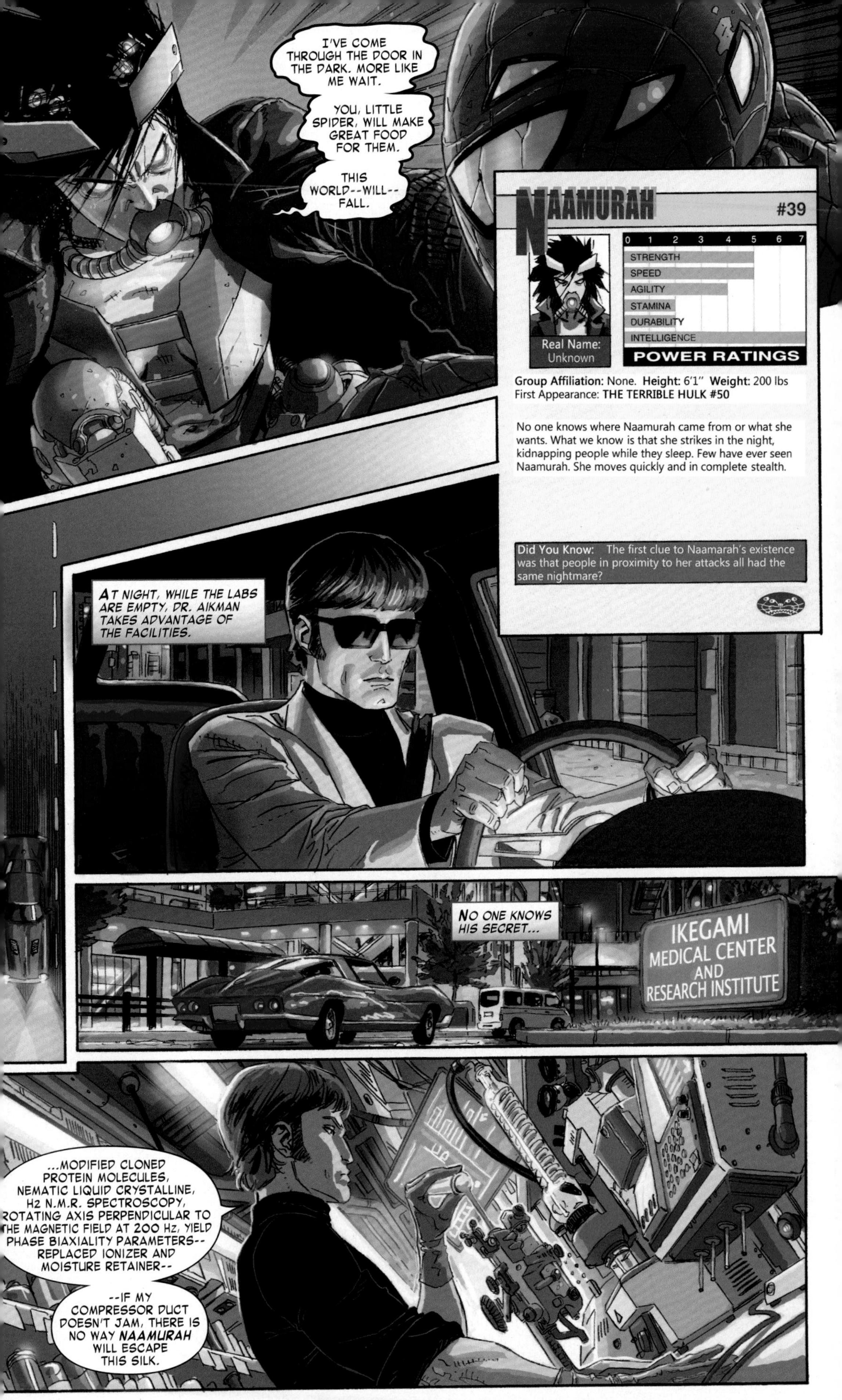

I'VE COME THROUGH THE DOOR IN THE DARK. MORE LIKE ME WAIT.
YOU, LITTLE SPIDER, WILL MAKE GREAT FOOD FOR THEM.
THIS WORLD--WILL--FALL.
NAAMURAH
#39
0 1 2 3 4 5 6 7
STRENGTH
SPEED
AGILITY
STAMINA
DURABILITY
INTELLIGENCE
Real Name: Unknown
POWER RATINGS
Group Affiliation: None. Height: 6'1" Weight: 200 lbs
First Appearance: THE TERRIBLE HULK #50
No one knows where Naamurah came from or what she wants. What we know is that she strikes in the night, kidnapping people while they sleep. Few have ever seen Naamurah. She moves quickly and in complete stealth.
Did You Know: The first clue to Naamarah's existence was that people in proximity to her attacks all had the same nightmare?
AT NIGHT, WHILE THE LABS ARE EMPTY, DR. AIKMAN TAKES ADVANTAGE OF THE FACILITIES.
NO ONE KNOWS HIS SECRET...
IKEGAMI MEDICAL CENTER AND RESEARCH INSTITUTE
...MODIFIED CLONED PROTEIN MOLECULES, NEMATIC LIQUID CRYSTALLINE, H2 N.M.R. SPECTROSCOPY, ROTATING AXIS PERPENDICULAR TO THE MAGNETIC FIELD AT 200 Hz, YIELD PHASE BIAXIALITY PARAMETERS-- REPLACED IONIZER AND MOISTURE RETAINER--
--IF MY COMPRESSOR DUCT DOESN'T JAM, THERE IS NO WAY NAAMURAH WILL ESCAPE THIS SILK.

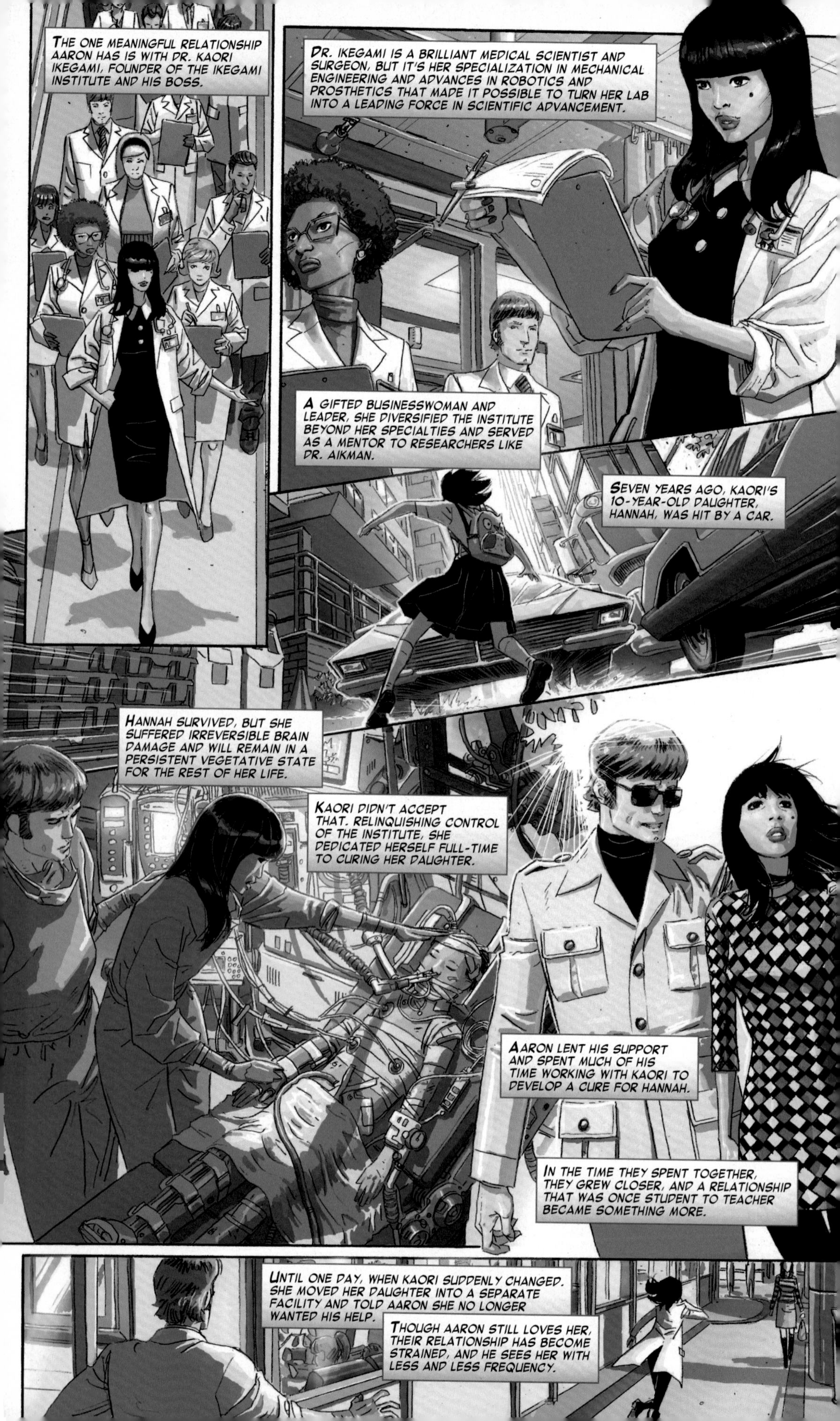

THE ONE MEANINGFUL RELATIONSHIP AARON HAS IS WITH DR. KAORI IKEGAMI, FOUNDER OF THE IKEGAMI INSTITUTE AND HIS BOSS.
DR. IKEGAMI IS A BRILLIANT MEDICAL SCIENTIST AND SURGEON, BUT IT'S HER SPECIALIZATION IN MECHANICAL ENGINEERING AND ADVANCES IN ROBOTICS AND PROSTHETICS THAT MADE IT POSSIBLE TO TURN HER LAB INTO A LEADING FORCE IN SCIENTIFIC ADVANCEMENT.
A GIFTED BUSINESSWOMAN AND LEADER, SHE DIVERSIFIED THE INSTITUTE BEYOND HER SPECIALTIES AND SERVED AS A MENTOR TO RESEARCHERS LIKE DR. AIKMAN.
SEVEN YEARS AGO, KAORI'S 10-YEAR-OLD DAUGHTER, HANNAH, WAS HIT BY A CAR.
HANNAH SURVIVED, BUT SHE SUFFERED IRREVERSIBLE BRAIN DAMAGE AND WILL REMAIN IN A PERSISTENT VEGETATIVE STATE FOR THE REST OF HER LIFE.
KAORI DIDN'T ACCEPT THAT. RELINQUISHING CONTROL OF THE INSTITUTE, SHE DEDICATED HERSELF FULL-TIME TO CURING HER DAUGHTER.
AARON LENT HIS SUPPORT AND SPENT MUCH OF HIS TIME WORKING WITH KAORI TO DEVELOP A CURE FOR HANNAH.
IN THE TIME THEY SPENT TOGETHER, THEY GREW CLOSER, AND A RELATIONSHIP THAT WAS ONCE STUDENT TO TEACHER BECAME SOMETHING MORE.
UNTIL ONE DAY, WHEN KAORI SUDDENLY CHANGED. SHE MOVED HER DAUGHTER INTO A SEPARATE FACILITY AND TOLD AARON SHE NO LONGER WANTED HIS HELP.
THOUGH AARON STILL LOVES HER, THEIR RELATIONSHIP HAS BECOME STRAINED, AND HE SEES HER WITH LESS AND LESS FREQUENCY.

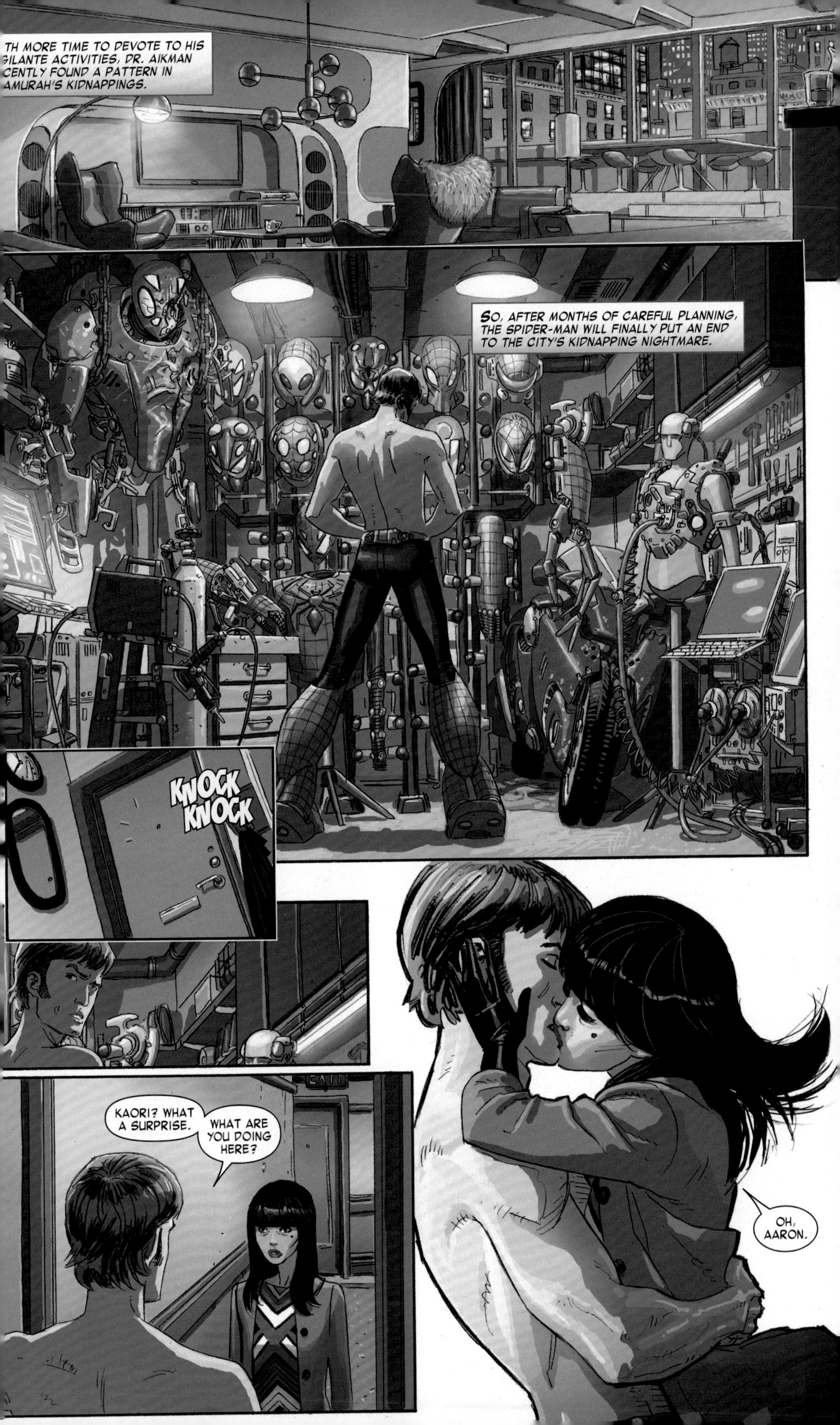
TH MORE TIME TO DEVOTE TO HIS GILANTE ACTIVITIES, DR. AIKMAN CENTLY FOUND A PATTERN IN AMURAH'S KIDNAPPINGS.
SO, AFTER MONTHS OF CAREFUL PLANNING, THE SPIDER-MAN WILL FINALLY PUT AN END TO THE CITY'S KIDNAPPING NIGHTMARE.
KNOCK KNOCK
KAORI? WHAT A SURPRISE.
WHAT ARE YOU DOING HERE?
OH, AARON.

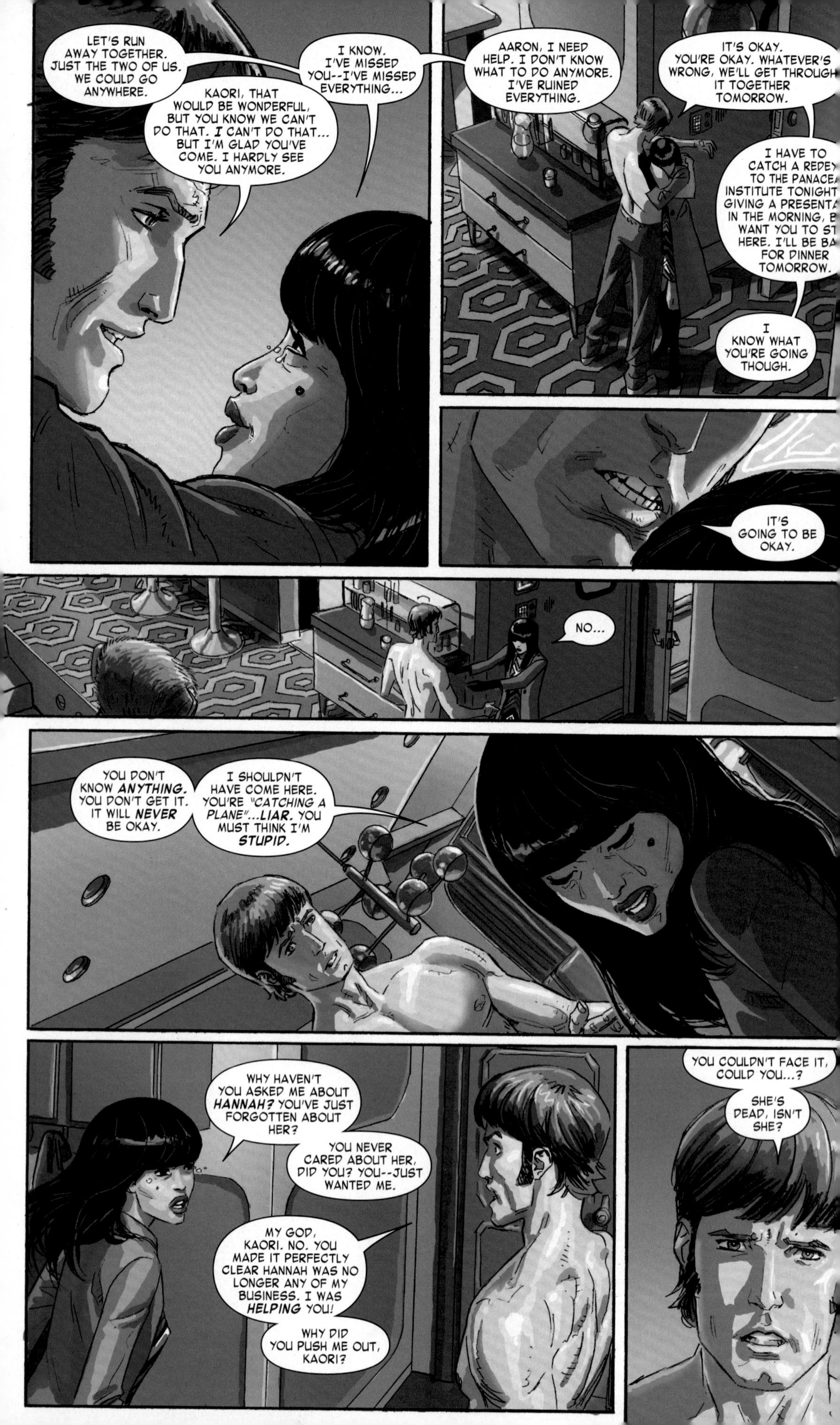
LET'S RUN AWAY TOGETHER. JUST THE TWO OF US. WE COULD GO ANYWHERE.
KAORI, THAT WOULD BE WONDERFUL, BUT YOU KNOW WE CAN'T DO THAT. *I* CAN'T DO THAT... BUT I'M GLAD YOU'VE COME. I HARDLY SEE YOU ANYMORE.
I KNOW. I'VE MISSED YOU--I'VE MISSED EVERYTHING...
AARON, I NEED HELP. I DON'T KNOW WHAT TO DO ANYMORE. I'VE RUINED EVERYTHING.
IT'S OKAY. YOU'RE OKAY. WHATEVER'S WRONG, WE'LL GET THROUGH IT TOGETHER TOMORROW.
I HAVE TO CATCH A REDE TO THE PANACE INSTITUTE TONIGH GIVING A PRESENTA IN THE MORNING, B WANT YOU TO ST HERE. I'LL BE BA FOR DINNER TOMORROW.
I KNOW WHAT YOU'RE GOING THOUGH.
IT'S GOING TO BE OKAY.
NO...
YOU DON'T KNOW ***ANYTHING.*** YOU DON'T GET IT. IT WILL ***NEVER*** BE OKAY.
I SHOULDN'T HAVE COME HERE. YOU'RE *"CATCHING A PLANE"*...***LIAR.*** YOU MUST THINK I'M ***STUPID.***
WHY HAVEN'T YOU ASKED ME ABOUT ***HANNAH?*** YOU'VE JUST FORGOTTEN ABOUT HER?
YOU NEVER CARED ABOUT HER, DID YOU? YOU--JUST WANTED ME.
MY GOD, KAORI. NO. YOU MADE IT PERFECTLY CLEAR HANNAH WAS NO LONGER ANY OF MY BUSINESS. I WAS ***HELPING*** YOU!
WHY DID YOU PUSH ME OUT, KAORI?
YOU COULDN'T FACE IT, COULD YOU...?
SHE'S DEAD, ISN'T SHE?

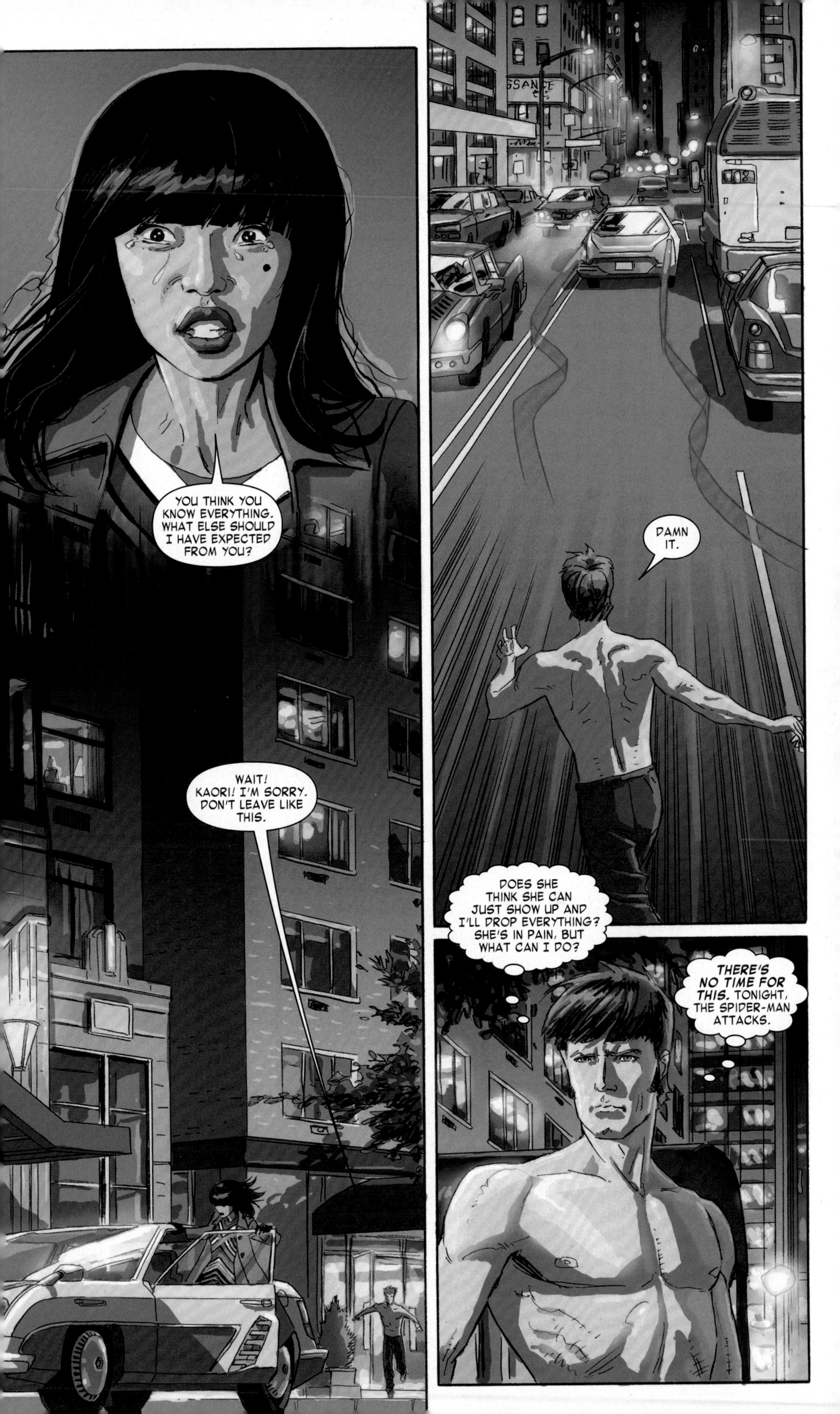

YOU THINK YOU KNOW EVERYTHING. WHAT ELSE SHOULD I HAVE EXPECTED FROM YOU?
WAIT! KAORI! I'M SORRY. DON'T LEAVE LIKE THIS.
DAMN IT.
DOES SHE THINK SHE CAN JUST SHOW UP AND I'LL DROP EVERYTHING? SHE'S IN PAIN, BUT WHAT CAN I DO?
THERE'S NO TIME FOR THIS. TONIGHT, THE SPIDER-MAN ATTACKS.

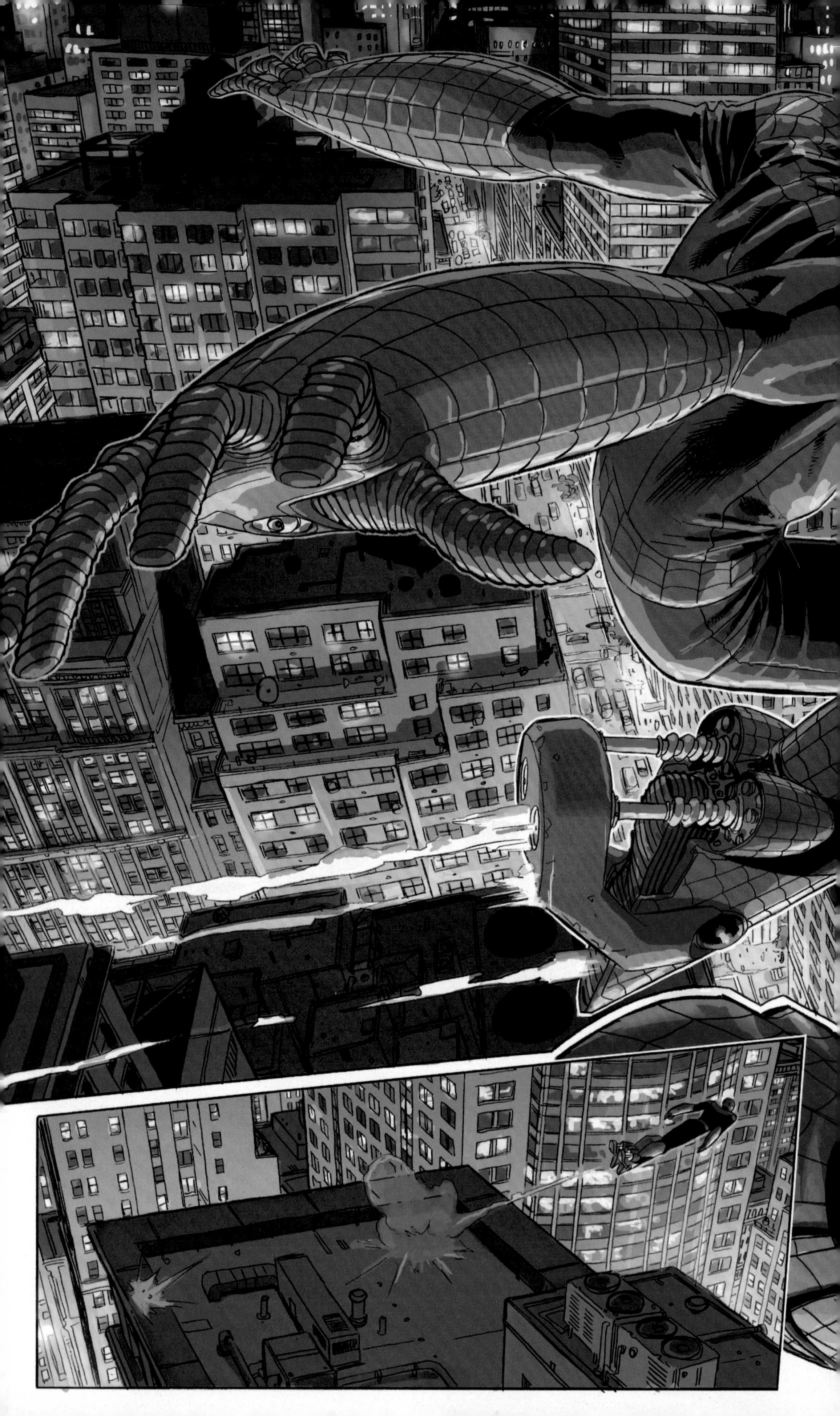

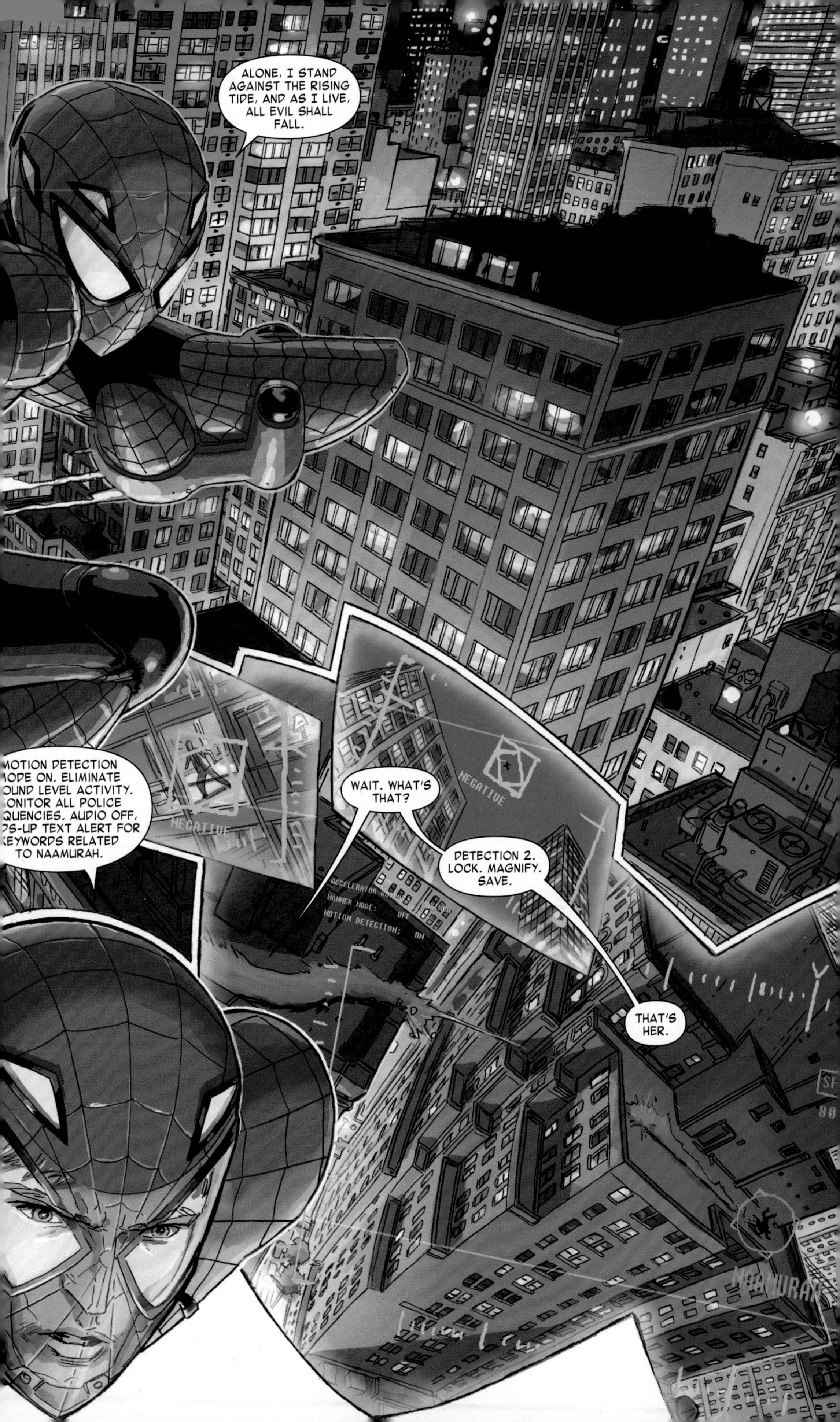

ALONE, I STAND AGAINST THE RISING TIDE, AND AS I LIVE, ALL EVIL SHALL FALL.
MOTION DETECTION MODE ON. ELIMINATE GROUND LEVEL ACTIVITY. MONITOR ALL POLICE FREQUENCIES. AUDIO OFF, HEADS-UP TEXT ALERT FOR KEYWORDS RELATED TO NAAMURAH.
NEGATIVE
NEGATIVE
WAIT. WHAT'S THAT?
MOTION DETECTION: ON
DETECTION 2. LOCK. MAGNIFY. SAVE.
THAT'S HER.

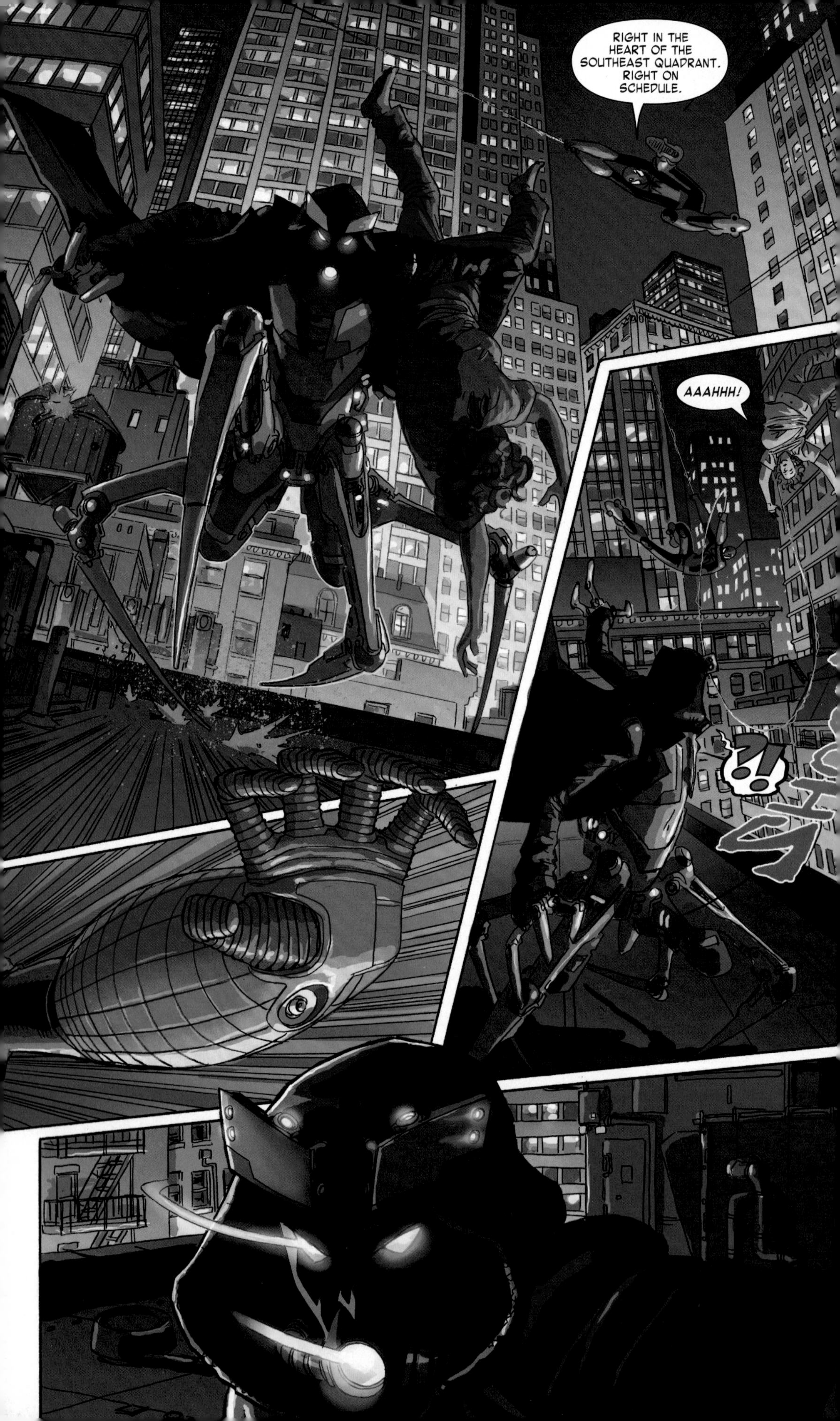
RIGHT IN THE HEART OF THE SOUTHEAST QUADRANT. RIGHT ON SCHEDULE.
AAAHHH!
?!

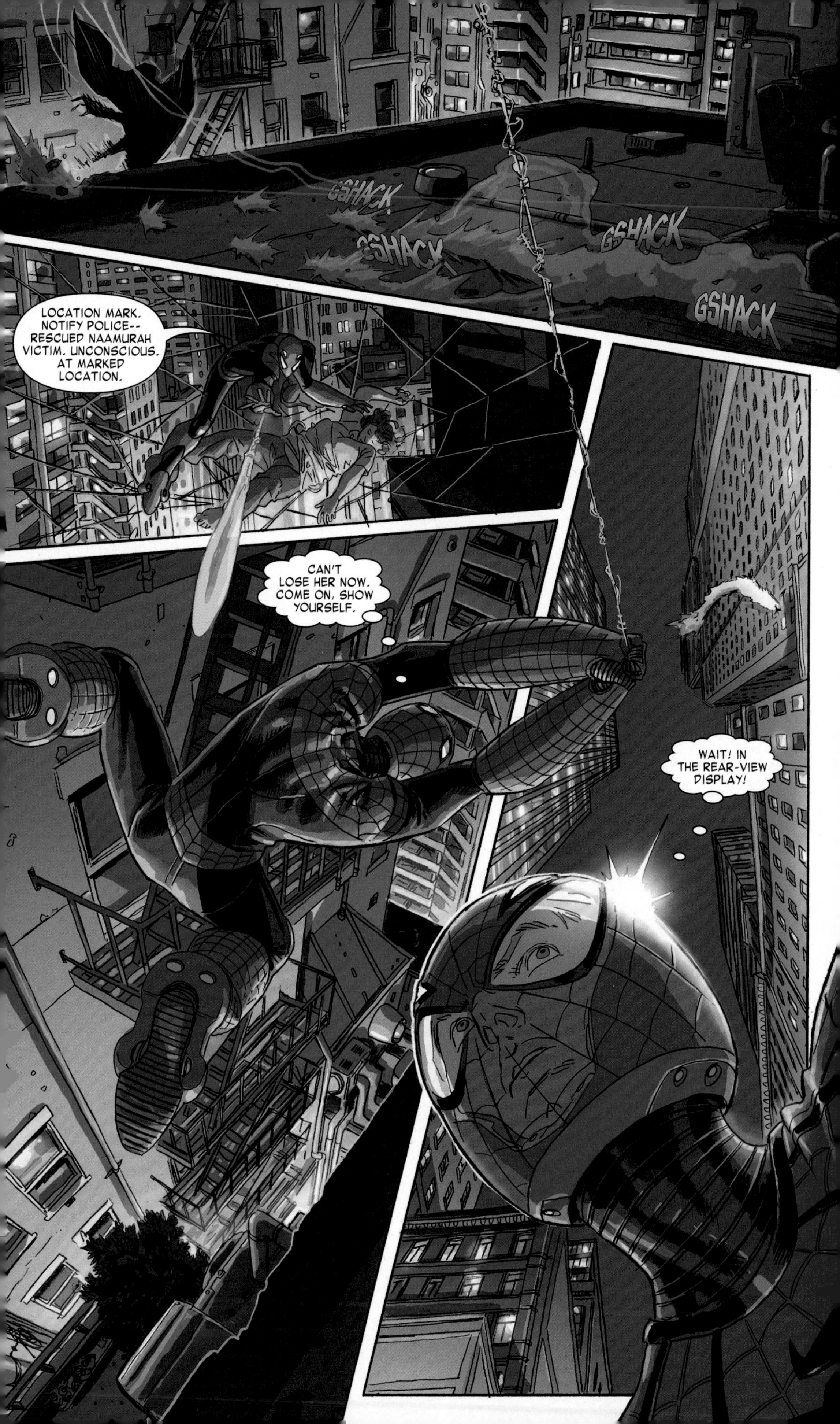
GSHACK
GSHACK
GSHACK
GSHACK
LOCATION MARK. NOTIFY POLICE-- RESCUED NAAMURAH VICTIM. UNCONSCIOUS. AT MARKED LOCATION.
CAN'T LOSE HER NOW. COME ON, SHOW YOURSELF.
WAIT! IN THE REAR-VIEW DISPLAY!

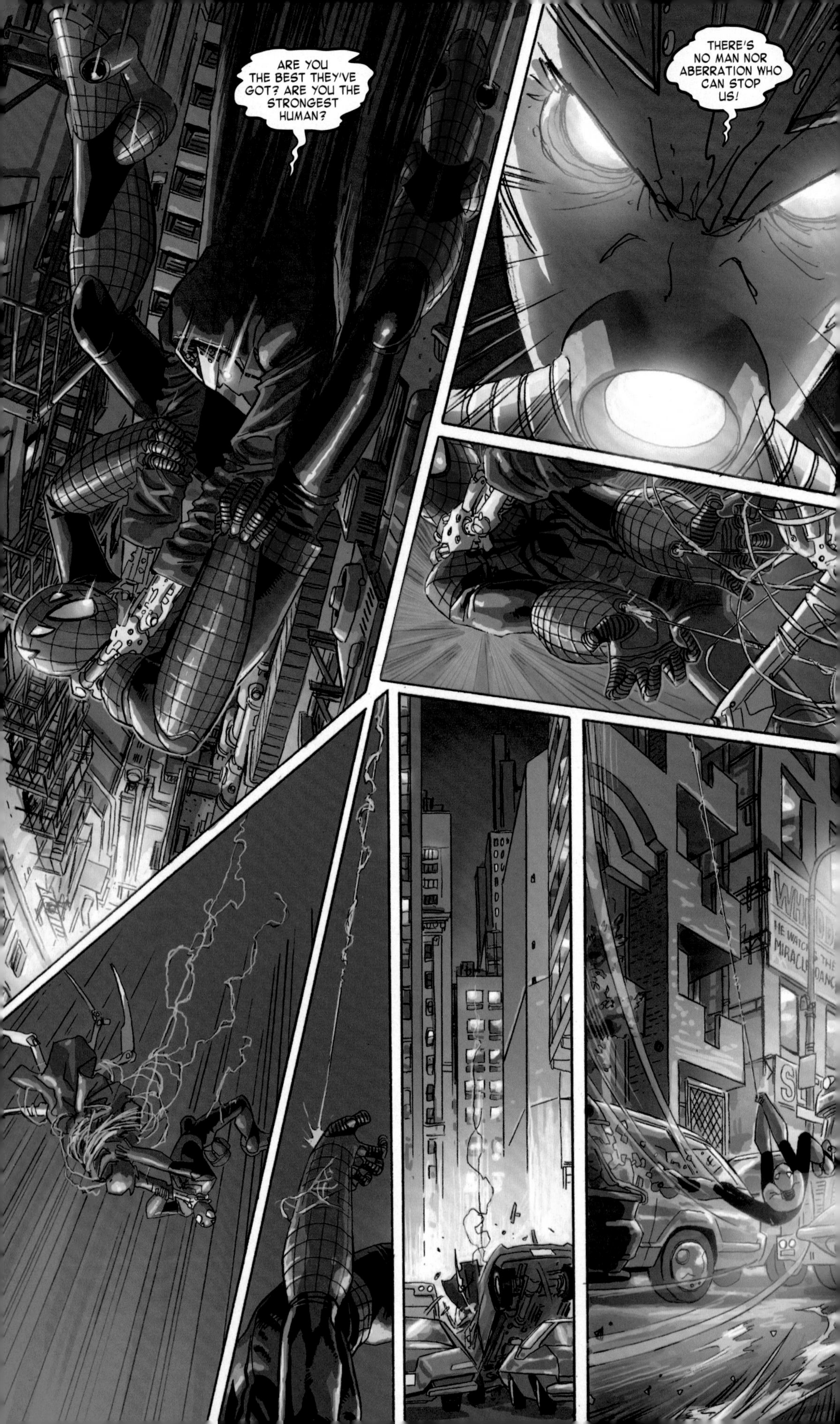
ARE YOU THE BEST THEY'VE GOT? ARE YOU THE STRONGEST HUMAN?
THERE'S NO MAN NOR ABERRATION WHO CAN STOP US!

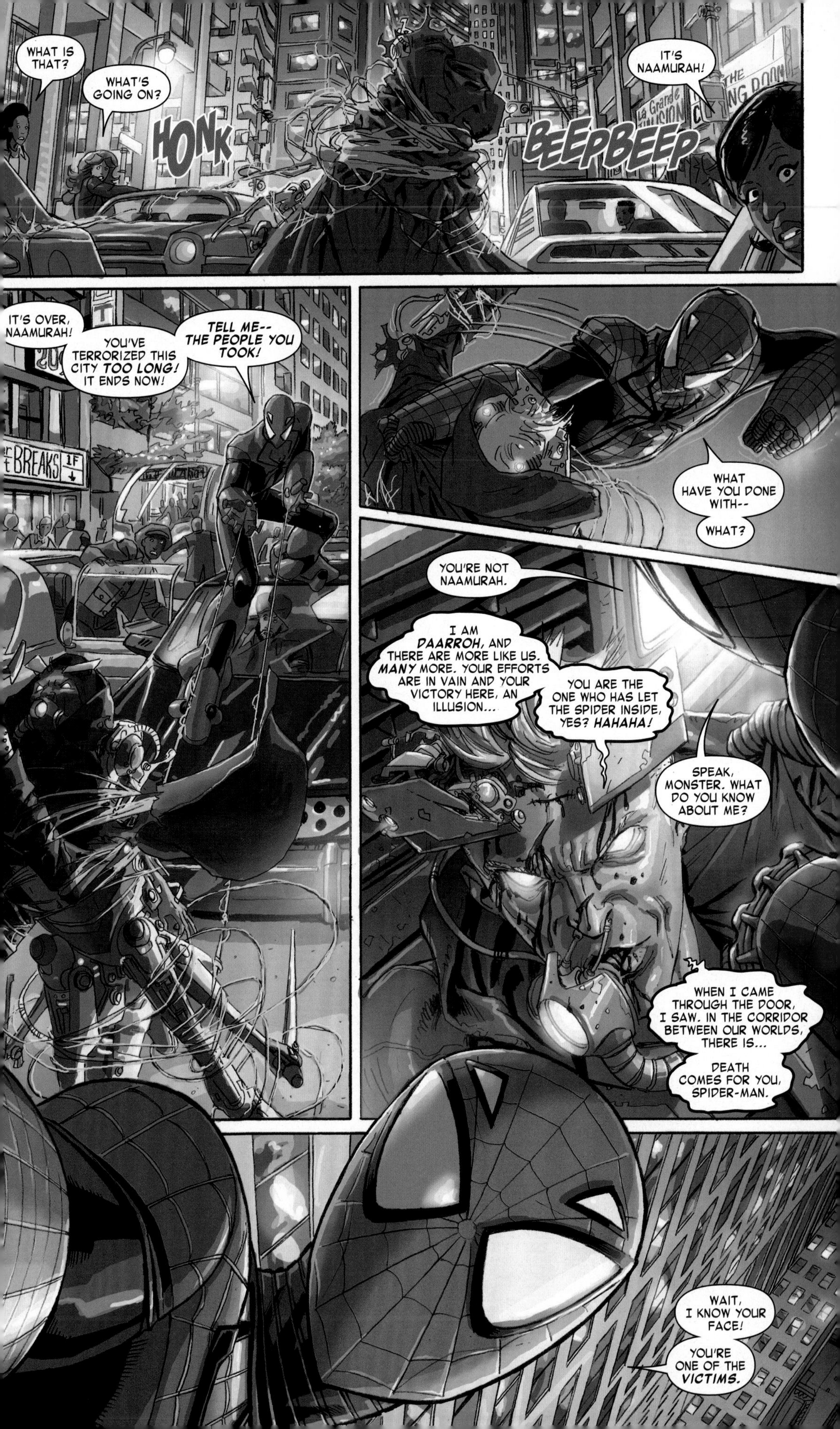
WHAT IS THAT?
WHAT'S GOING ON?
HONK
IT'S NAAMURAH!
BEEPBEEP
IT'S OVER, NAAMURAH!
YOU'VE TERRORIZED THIS CITY TOO LONG! IT ENDS NOW!
TELL ME-- THE PEOPLE YOU TOOK!
WHAT HAVE YOU DONE WITH--
WHAT?
YOU'RE NOT NAAMURAH.
I AM DAARROH, AND THERE ARE MORE LIKE US. MANY MORE. YOUR EFFORTS ARE IN VAIN AND YOUR VICTORY HERE, AN ILLUSION...
YOU ARE THE ONE WHO HAS LET THE SPIDER INSIDE, YES? HAHAHA!
SPEAK, MONSTER. WHAT DO YOU KNOW ABOUT ME?
WHEN I CAME THROUGH THE DOOR, I SAW. IN THE CORRIDOR BETWEEN OUR WORLDS, THERE IS...
DEATH COMES FOR YOU, SPIDER-MAN.
WAIT, I KNOW YOUR FACE!
YOU'RE ONE OF THE VICTIMS.

YOU CAN'T BE THEIR HERO, LITTLE SPIDER-MAN. MANKIND IS DOOMED.

WHERE ARE THEY, DAARROH? THE OTHER VICTIMS! ANSWER ME!

...

DON'T YOU DIE ON ME!

IKEGAMI MEDICAL CENTER AND RESEARCH INSTITUTE

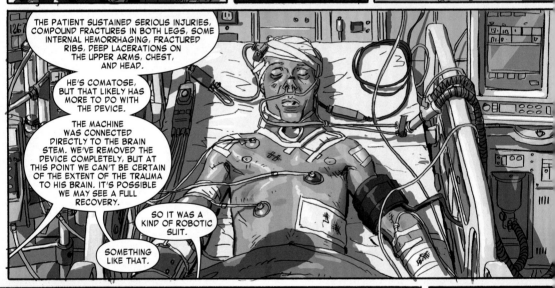

THE PATIENT SUSTAINED SERIOUS INJURIES, COMPOUND FRACTURES IN BOTH LEGS, SOME INTERNAL HEMORRHAGING, FRACTURED RIBS, DEEP LACERATIONS ON THE UPPER ARMS, CHEST, AND HEAD.

HE'S COMATOSE, BUT THAT LIKELY HAS MORE TO DO WITH THE DEVICE.

THE MACHINE WAS CONNECTED DIRECTLY TO THE BRAIN STEM. WE'VE REMOVED THE DEVICE COMPLETELY, BUT AT THIS POINT WE CAN'T BE CERTAIN OF THE EXTENT OF THE TRAUMA TO HIS BRAIN. IT'S POSSIBLE WE MAY SEE A FULL RECOVERY.

SO IT WAS A KIND OF ROBOTIC SUIT.

SOMETHING LIKE THAT.

ACTUALLY, THIS PATIENT MIGHT NOT HAVE MADE IT IF IT WEREN'T FOR SPIDER-MAN'S AID AT THE SCENE. I WOULDN'T BE SURPRISED IF HIS SECRET IDENTITY IS AN E.M.T.

THE ROBOTIC SUIT. DO YOU STILL HAVE IT?

THAT'S WHY I ASKED YOU HERE, DR. AIKMAN.

POLICE ARE TAKING IT AS EVIDENCE, BUT ARE LEAVING IT WITH US OVERNIGHT. THEY WANT OUR EXPERT ANALYSIS, AND WITH DR. IKEGAMI...UNREACHABLE, I HOPED YOU WOULD BE ABLE TO HELP.

I'M NOT A ROBOTICIST.

WHAT? HAVE YOU BEC— SUDDENLY MOD AIKMAN? THA— NOT LIKE YO—

BUT YOU'RE RIGHT NOT ABOUT MACHINE

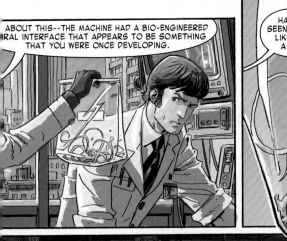
ABOUT THIS--THE MACHINE HAD A BIO-ENGINEERED NEURAL INTERFACE THAT APPEARS TO BE SOMETHING THAT YOU WERE ONCE DEVELOPING.

HAVE YOU SEEN ANYTHING LIKE IT, DR. AIKMAN?

OH, MY GOD!

IT'S YOU...

DR. IKEGAMI, WHERE IS HANNAH?

NOT HERE. SHE'S--SHE'S GONE.

DON'T HURT HER, AARON. PLEASE-- DON'T HURT ME FOR WHAT I'VE DONE.

KAORI, STOP.

WHAT IS THE MEANING OF THIS? WHO IS NAAMURAH? WHERE IS YOUR DAUGHTER? WHERE IS HANNAH?!

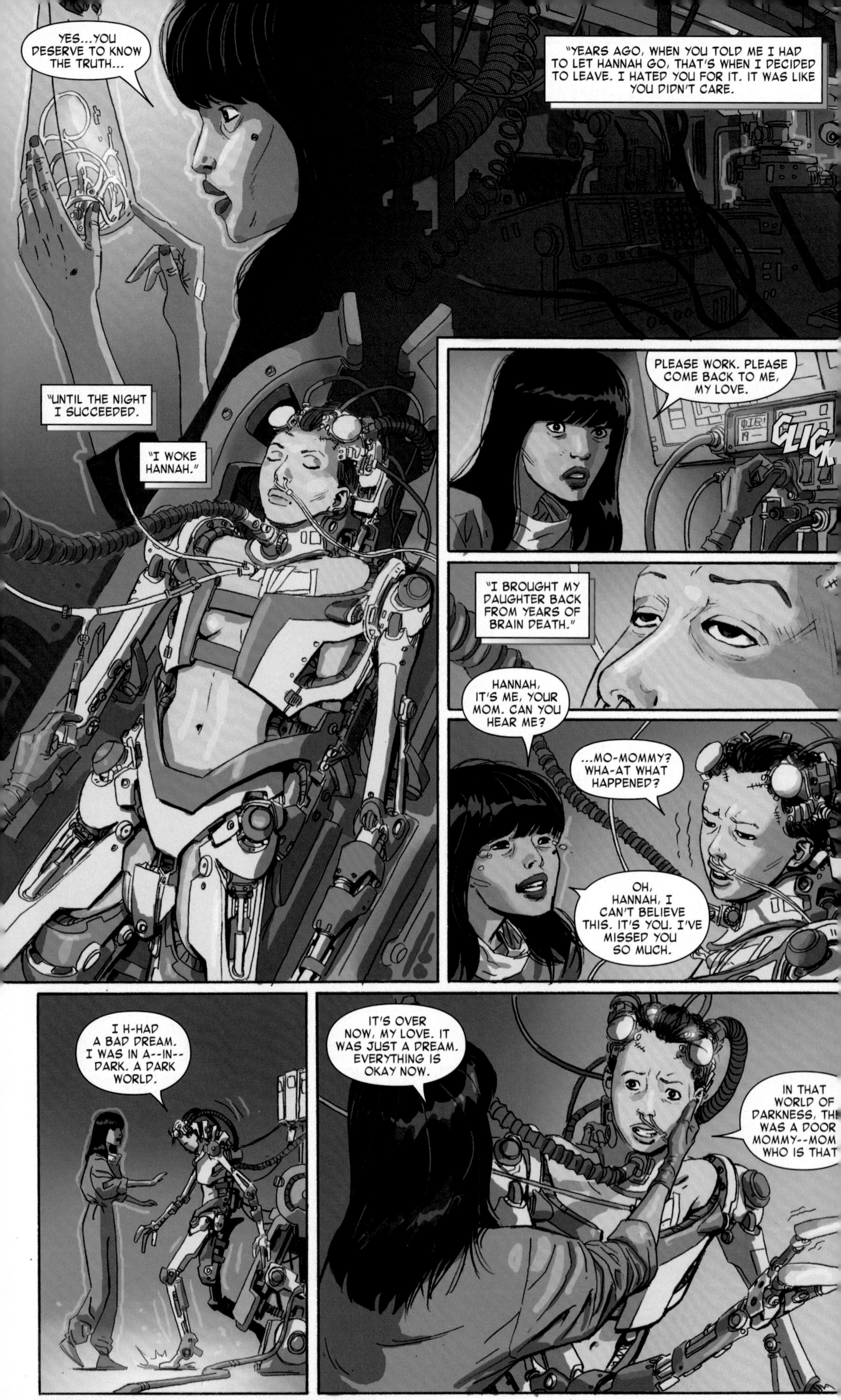
YES...YOU DESERVE TO KNOW THE TRUTH...
"YEARS AGO, WHEN YOU TOLD ME I HAD TO LET HANNAH GO, THAT'S WHEN I DECIDED TO LEAVE. I HATED YOU FOR IT. IT WAS LIKE YOU DIDN'T CARE.
"UNTIL THE NIGHT I SUCCEEDED.
"I WOKE HANNAH."
PLEASE WORK. PLEASE COME BACK TO ME, MY LOVE.
CLICK
"I BROUGHT MY DAUGHTER BACK FROM YEARS OF BRAIN DEATH."
HANNAH, IT'S ME, YOUR MOM. CAN YOU HEAR ME?
...MO-MOMMY? WHA-AT WHAT HAPPENED?
OH, HANNAH, I CAN'T BELIEVE THIS. IT'S YOU. I'VE MISSED YOU SO MUCH.
I H-HAD A BAD DREAM. I WAS IN A--IN--DARK. A DARK WORLD.
IT'S OVER NOW, MY LOVE. IT WAS JUST A DREAM. EVERYTHING IS OKAY NOW.
IN THAT WORLD OF DARKNESS, TH WAS A DOOR MOMMY--MOM WHO IS THAT

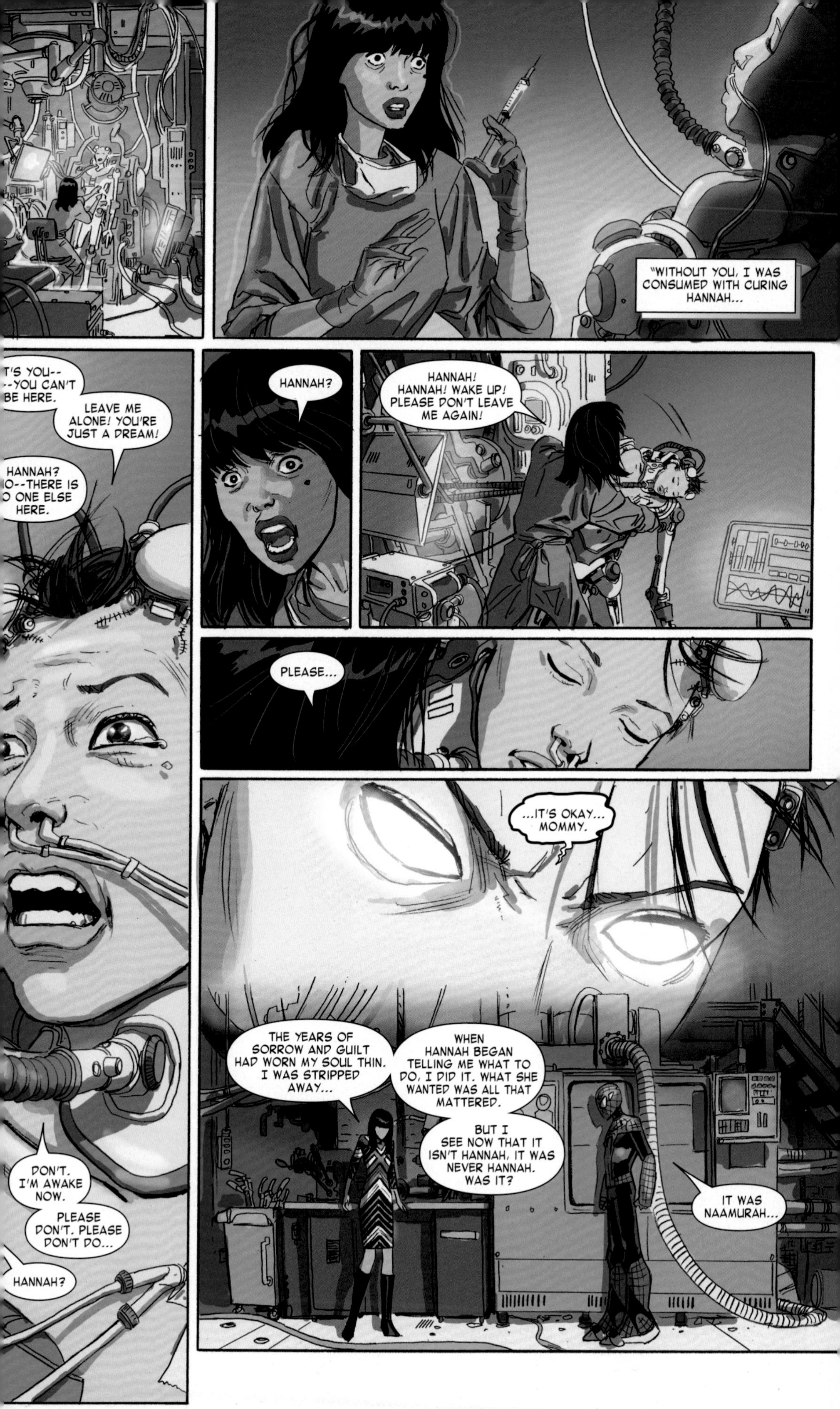
"WITHOUT YOU, I WAS CONSUMED WITH CURING HANNAH...
T'S YOU-- --YOU CAN'T BE HERE.
LEAVE ME ALONE! YOU'RE JUST A DREAM!
HANNAH? O--THERE IS O ONE ELSE HERE.
HANNAH?
HANNAH! HANNAH! WAKE UP! PLEASE DON'T LEAVE ME AGAIN!
PLEASE...
DON'T. I'M AWAKE NOW.
PLEASE DON'T. PLEASE DON'T DO...
HANNAH?
...IT'S OKAY... MOMMY.
THE YEARS OF SORROW AND GUILT HAD WORN MY SOUL THIN. I WAS STRIPPED AWAY...
WHEN HANNAH BEGAN TELLING ME WHAT TO DO, I DID IT. WHAT SHE WANTED WAS ALL THAT MATTERED.
BUT I SEE NOW THAT IT ISN'T HANNAH, IT WAS NEVER HANNAH. WAS IT?
IT WAS NAAMURAH...

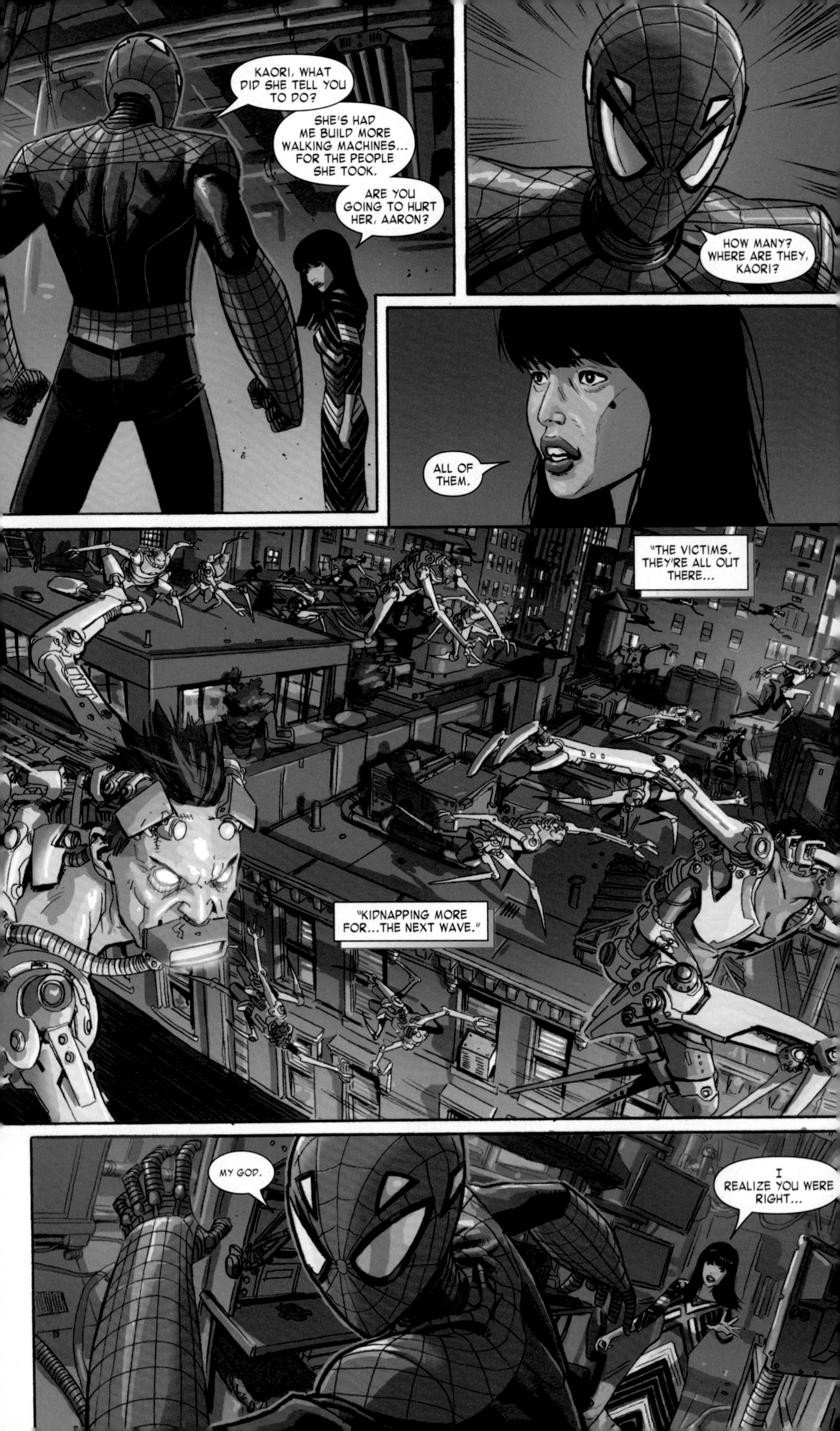
KAORI, WHAT DID SHE TELL YOU TO DO?
SHE'S HAD ME BUILD MORE WALKING MACHINES... FOR THE PEOPLE SHE TOOK.
ARE YOU GOING TO HURT HER, AARON?
HOW MANY? WHERE ARE THEY, KAORI?
ALL OF THEM.
"THE VICTIMS. THEY'RE ALL OUT THERE...
"KIDNAPPING MORE FOR...THE NEXT WAVE."
MY GOD.
I REALIZE YOU WERE RIGHT...

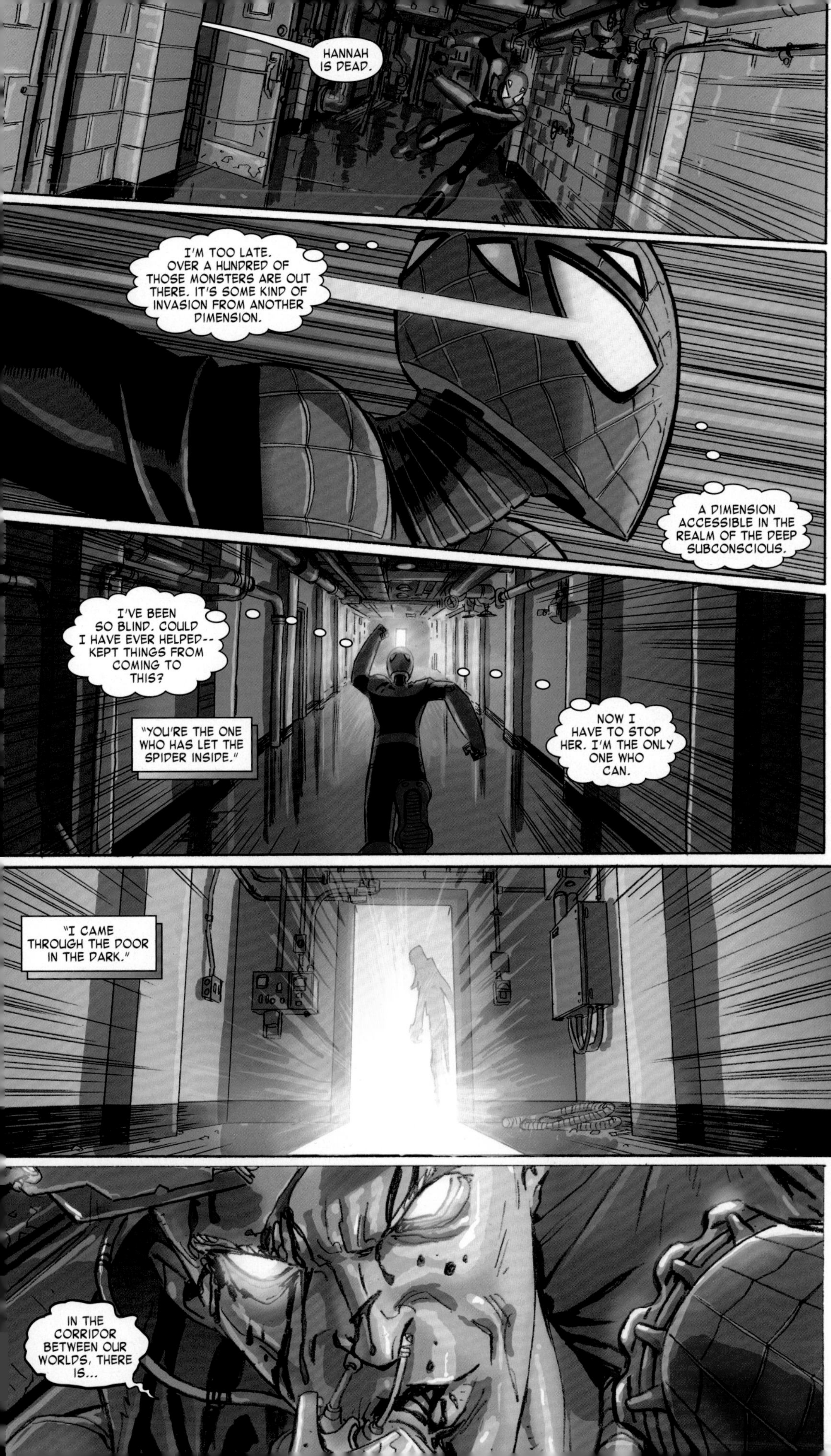
HANNAH IS DEAD.
I'M TOO LATE. OVER A HUNDRED OF THOSE MONSTERS ARE OUT THERE. IT'S SOME KIND OF INVASION FROM ANOTHER DIMENSION.
A DIMENSION ACCESSIBLE IN THE REALM OF THE DEEP SUBCONSCIOUS.
I'VE BEEN SO BLIND. COULD I HAVE EVER HELPED-- KEPT THINGS FROM COMING TO THIS?
"YOU'RE THE ONE WHO HAS LET THE SPIDER INSIDE."
NOW I HAVE TO STOP HER. I'M THE ONLY ONE WHO CAN.
"I CAME THROUGH THE DOOR IN THE DARK."
IN THE CORRIDOR BETWEEN OUR WORLDS, THERE IS...

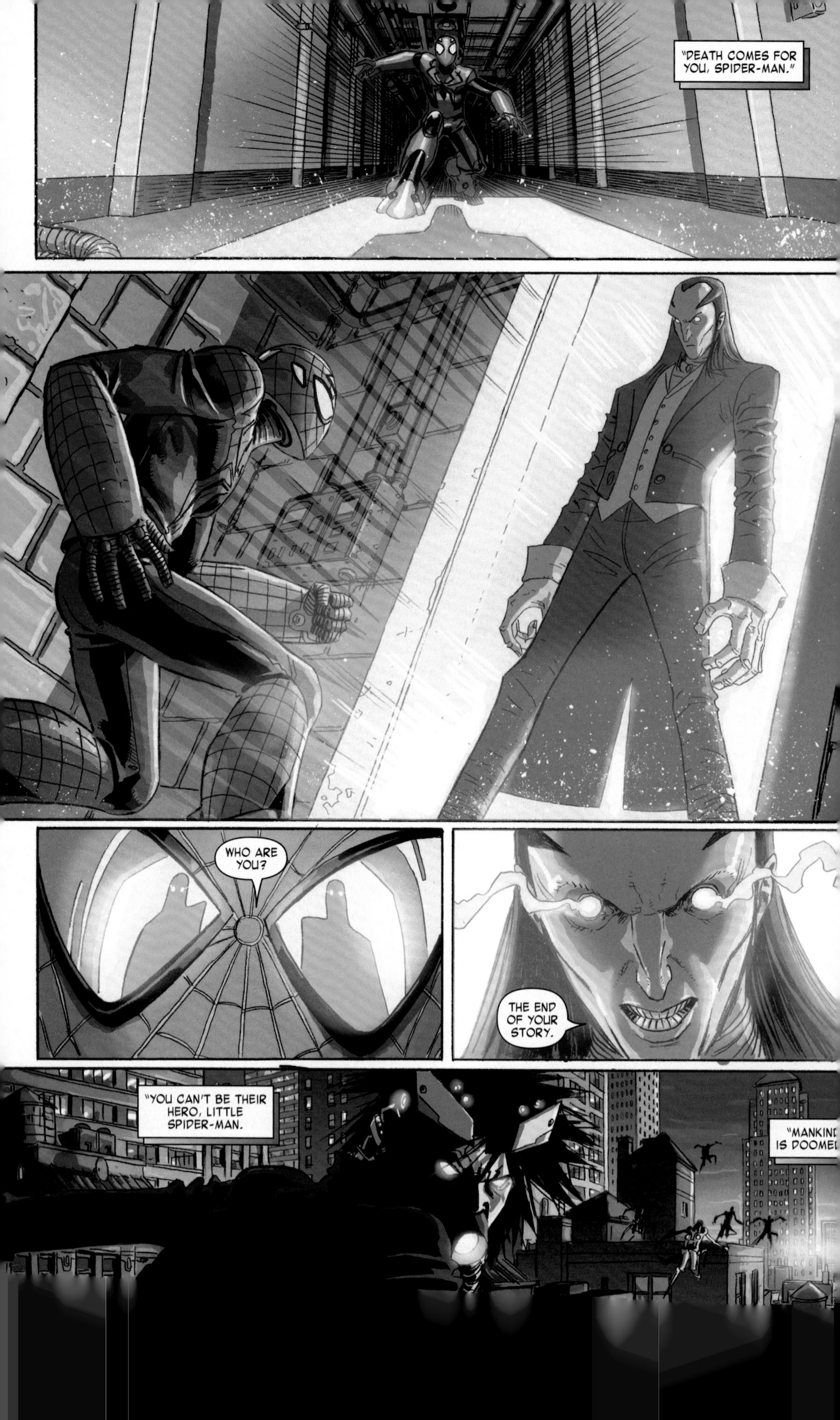
"DEATH COMES FOR YOU, SPIDER-MAN."
WHO ARE YOU?
THE END OF YOUR STORY.
"YOU CAN'T BE THEIR HERO, LITTLE SPIDER-MAN.
"MANKIND IS DOOMED

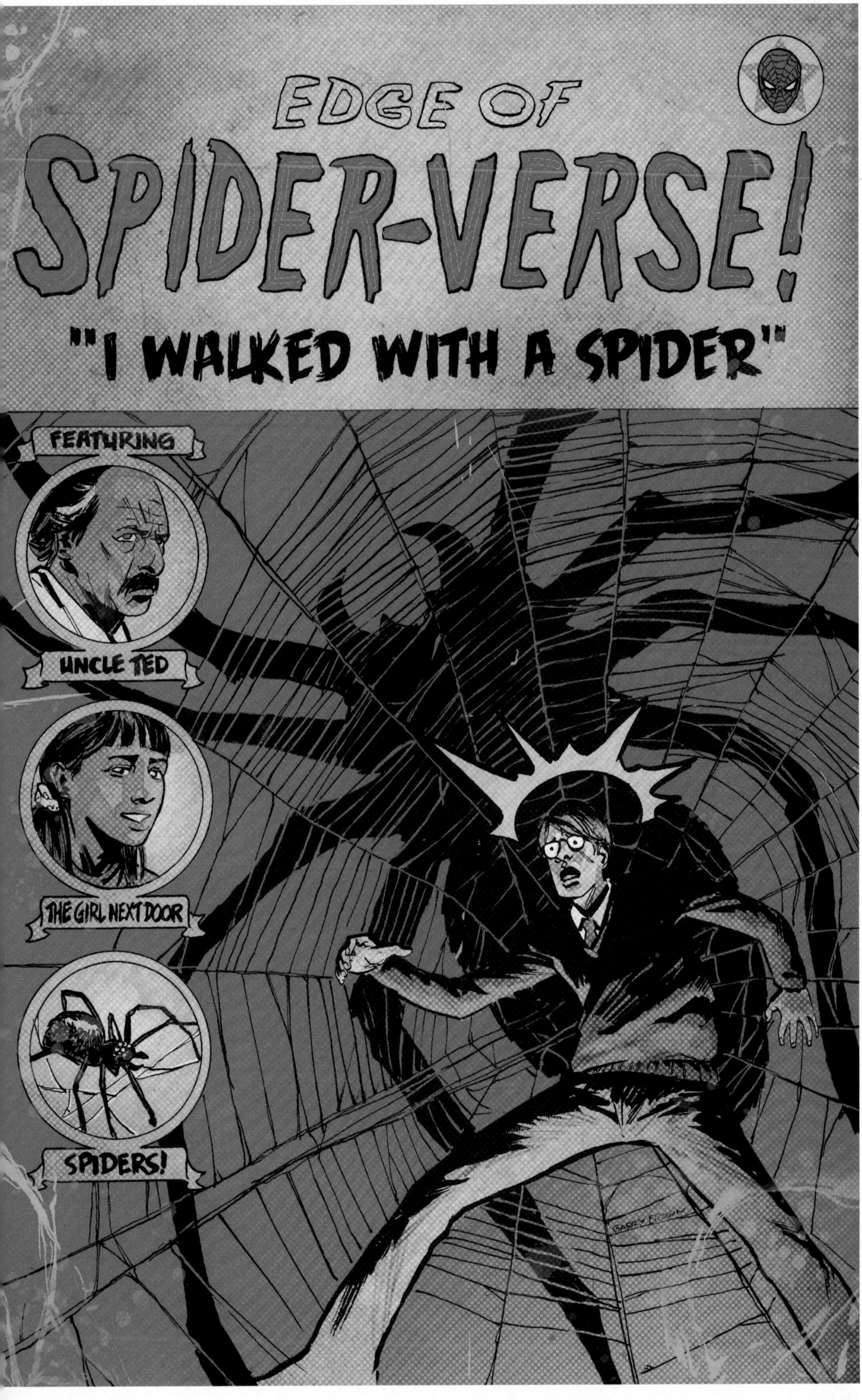
EDGE OF
SPIDER-VERSE!
"I WALKED WITH A SPIDER"
FEATURING
UNCLE TED
THE GIRL NEXT DOOR
SPIDERS!

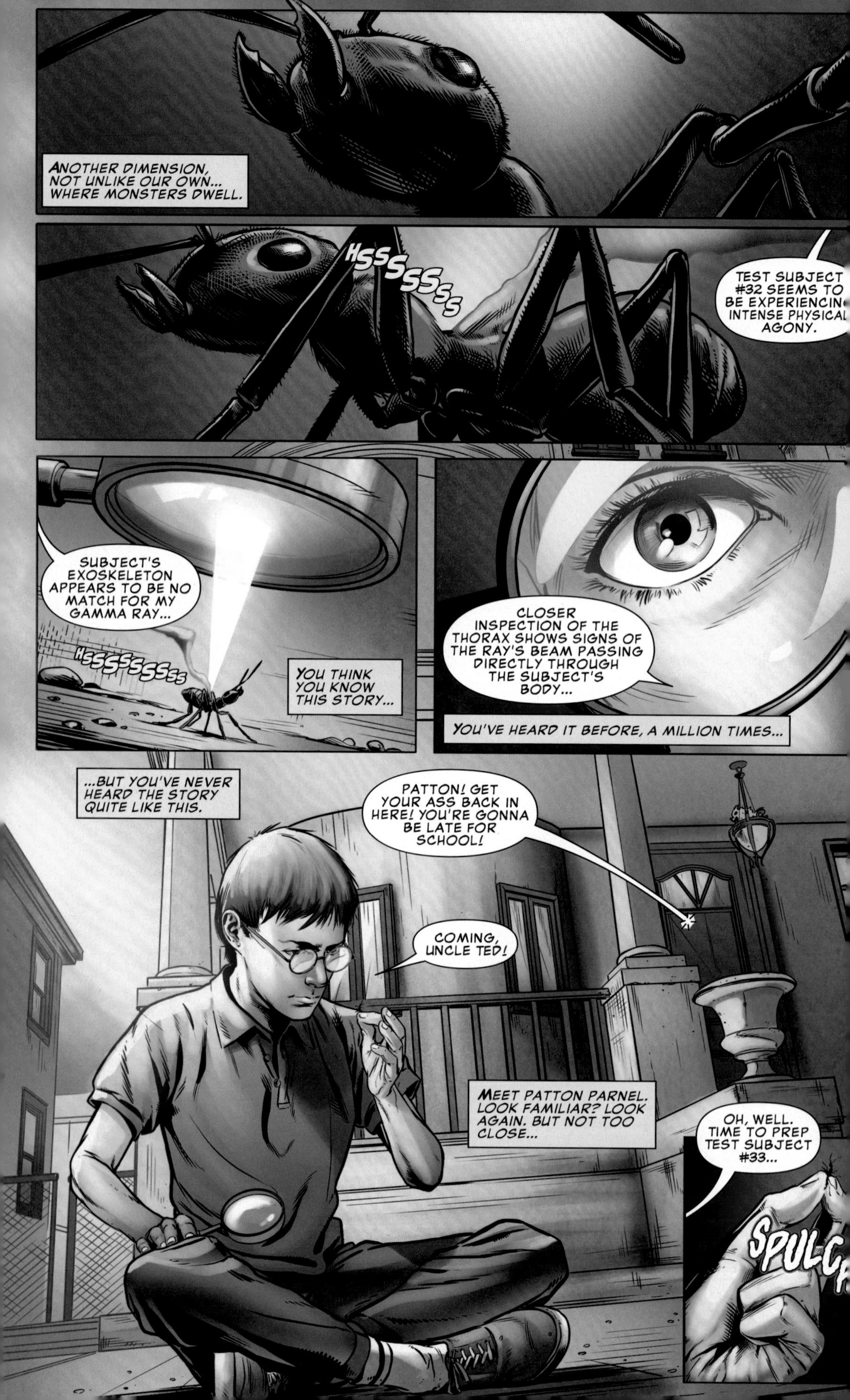
ANOTHER DIMENSION, NOT UNLIKE OUR OWN... WHERE MONSTERS DWELL.
HSSSSSSS
TEST SUBJECT #32 SEEMS TO BE EXPERIENCIN INTENSE PHYSICAL AGONY.
SUBJECT'S EXOSKELETON APPEARS TO BE NO MATCH FOR MY GAMMA RAY...
HSSSSSSSSS
YOU THINK YOU KNOW THIS STORY...
CLOSER INSPECTION OF THE THORAX SHOWS SIGNS OF THE RAY'S BEAM PASSING DIRECTLY THROUGH THE SUBJECT'S BODY...
YOU'VE HEARD IT BEFORE, A MILLION TIMES...
...BUT YOU'VE NEVER HEARD THE STORY QUITE LIKE THIS.
PATTON! GET YOUR ASS BACK IN HERE! YOU'RE GONNA BE LATE FOR SCHOOL!
COMING, UNCLE TED!
MEET PATTON PARNEL. LOOK FAMILIAR? LOOK AGAIN. BUT NOT TOO CLOSE...
OH, WELL. TIME TO PREP TEST SUBJECT #33...
SPULC

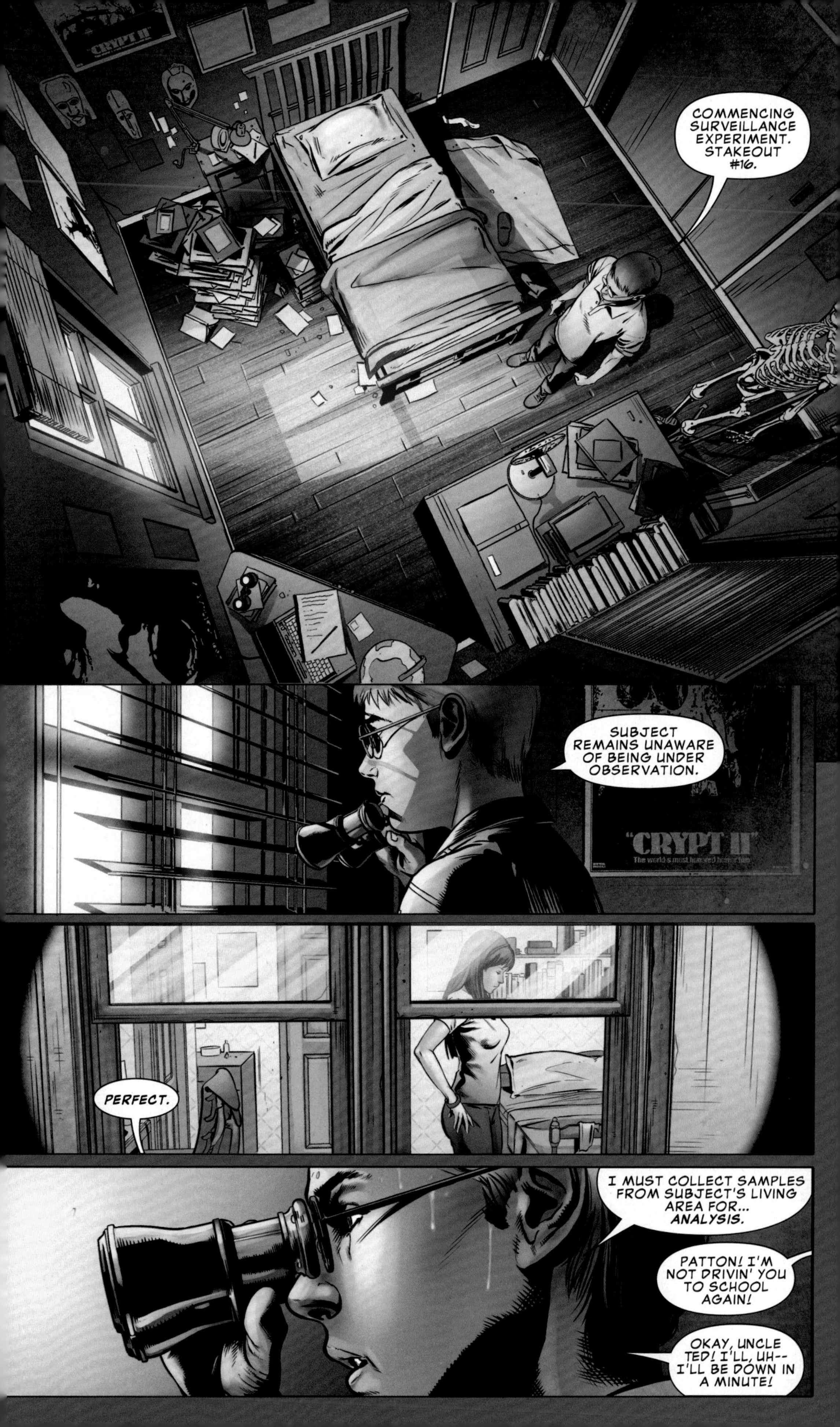
COMMENCING SURVEILLANCE EXPERIMENT. STAKEOUT #16.
SUBJECT REMAINS UNAWARE OF BEING UNDER OBSERVATION.
"CRYPT II"
The world's most honored horror film
PERFECT.
I MUST COLLECT SAMPLES FROM SUBJECT'S LIVING AREA FOR... ANALYSIS.
PATTON! I'M NOT DRIVIN' YOU TO SCHOOL AGAIN!
OKAY, UNCLE TED! I'LL, UH-- I'LL BE DOWN IN A MINUTE!

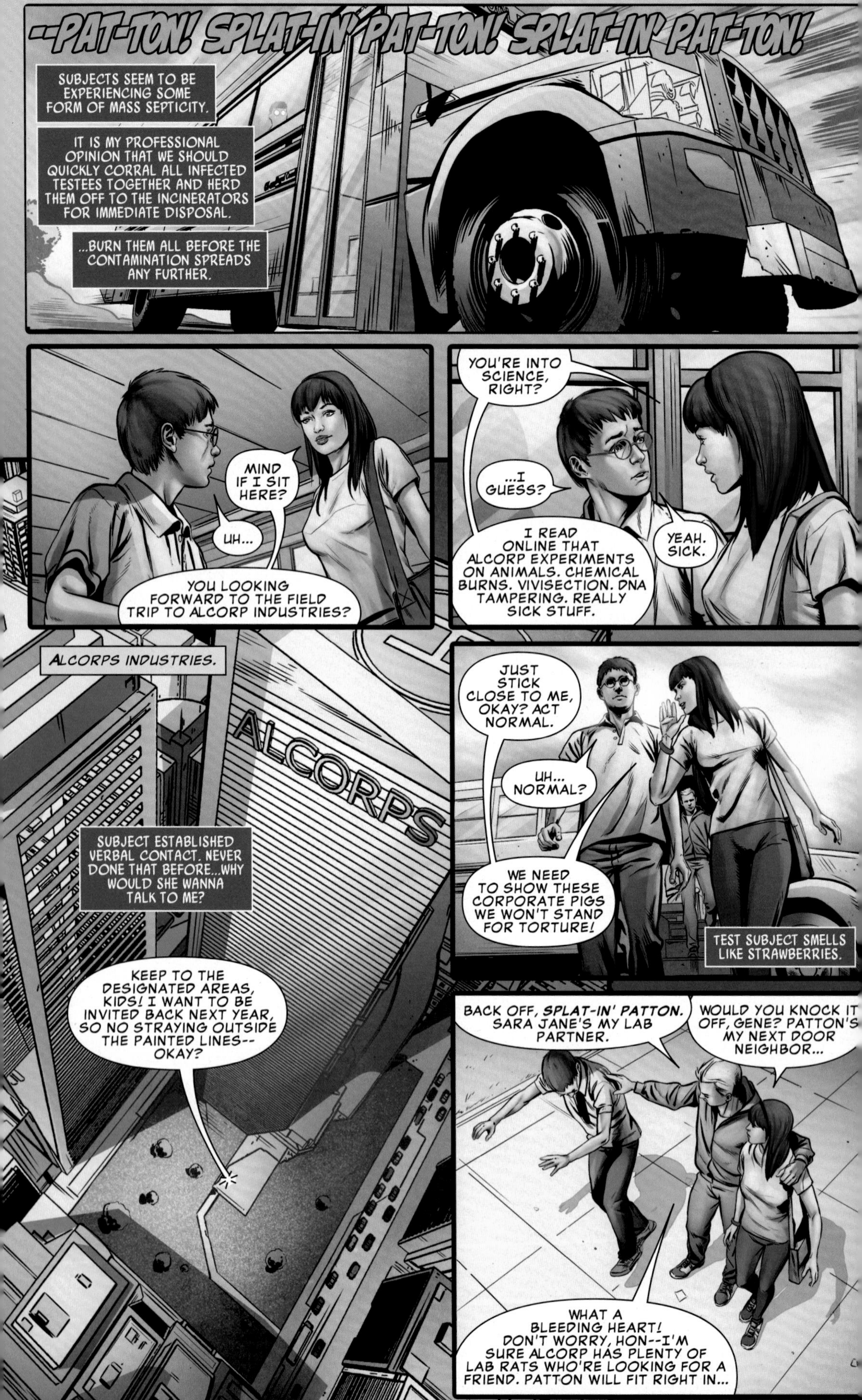
--PAT-TON! SPLAT-IN' PAT-TON! SPLAT-IN' PAT-TON!
SUBJECTS SEEM TO BE EXPERIENCING SOME FORM OF MASS SEPTICITY.
IT IS MY PROFESSIONAL OPINION THAT WE SHOULD QUICKLY CORRAL ALL INFECTED TESTEES TOGETHER AND HERD THEM OFF TO THE INCINERATORS FOR IMMEDIATE DISPOSAL.
...BURN THEM ALL BEFORE THE CONTAMINATION SPREADS ANY FURTHER.
MIND IF I SIT HERE?
UH...
YOU LOOKING FORWARD TO THE FIELD TRIP TO ALCORP INDUSTRIES?
YOU'RE INTO SCIENCE, RIGHT?
...I GUESS?
I READ ONLINE THAT ALCORP EXPERIMENTS ON ANIMALS. CHEMICAL BURNS. VIVISECTION. DNA TAMPERING. REALLY SICK STUFF.
YEAH. SICK.
ALCORPS INDUSTRIES.
ALCORPS
SUBJECT ESTABLISHED VERBAL CONTACT. NEVER DONE THAT BEFORE...WHY WOULD SHE WANNA TALK TO ME?
KEEP TO THE DESIGNATED AREAS, KIDS! I WANT TO BE INVITED BACK NEXT YEAR, SO NO STRAYING OUTSIDE THE PAINTED LINES--OKAY?
JUST STICK CLOSE TO ME, OKAY? ACT NORMAL.
UH... NORMAL?
WE NEED TO SHOW THESE CORPORATE PIGS WE WON'T STAND FOR TORTURE!
TEST SUBJECT SMELLS LIKE STRAWBERRIES.
BACK OFF, *SPLAT-IN' PATTON.* SARA JANE'S MY LAB PARTNER.
WOULD YOU KNOCK IT OFF, GENE? PATTON'S MY NEXT DOOR NEIGHBOR...
WHAT A BLEEDING HEART! DON'T WORRY, HON--I'M SURE ALCORP HAS PLENTY OF LAB RATS WHO'RE LOOKING FOR A FRIEND. PATTON WILL FIT RIGHT IN...

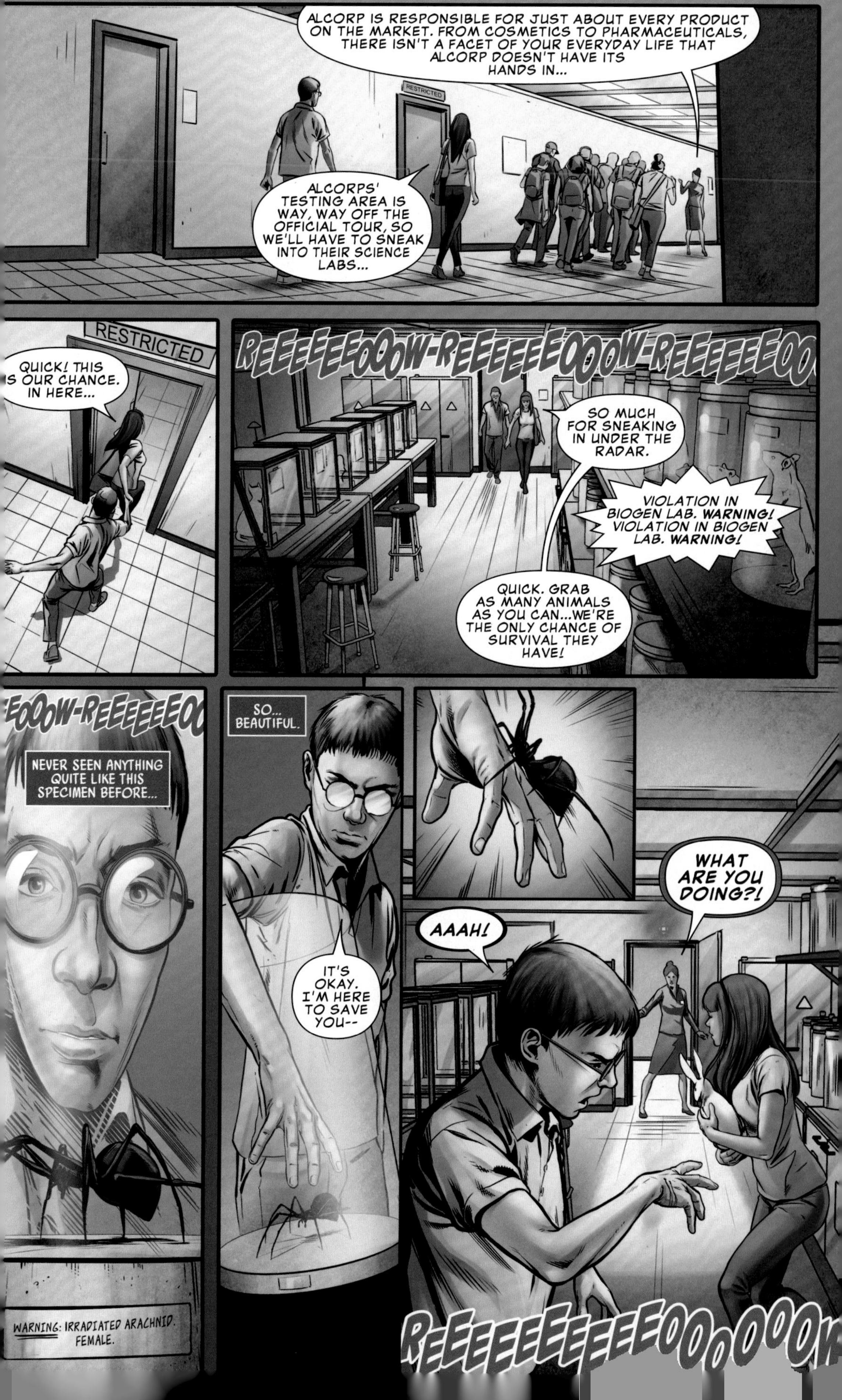
ALCORP IS RESPONSIBLE FOR JUST ABOUT EVERY PRODUCT ON THE MARKET. FROM COSMETICS TO PHARMACEUTICALS, THERE ISN'T A FACET OF YOUR EVERYDAY LIFE THAT ALCORP DOESN'T HAVE ITS HANDS IN...
RESTRICTED
ALCORPS' TESTING AREA IS WAY, WAY OFF THE OFFICIAL TOUR, SO WE'LL HAVE TO SNEAK INTO THEIR SCIENCE LABS...
RESTRICTED
QUICK! THIS IS OUR CHANCE. IN HERE...
REEEEEEOOOW-REEEEEEOOOW-REEEEEEOO
SO MUCH FOR SNEAKING IN UNDER THE RADAR.
VIOLATION IN BIOGEN LAB. WARNING! VIOLATION IN BIOGEN LAB. WARNING!
QUICK. GRAB AS MANY ANIMALS AS YOU CAN...WE'RE THE ONLY CHANCE OF SURVIVAL THEY HAVE!
EOOOW-REEEEEEOO
NEVER SEEN ANYTHING QUITE LIKE THIS SPECIMEN BEFORE...
WARNING: IRRADIATED ARACHNID. FEMALE.
SO... BEAUTIFUL.
IT'S OKAY. I'M HERE TO SAVE YOU--
AAAH!
WHAT ARE YOU DOING?!
REEEEEEEEEEOOOOOOW

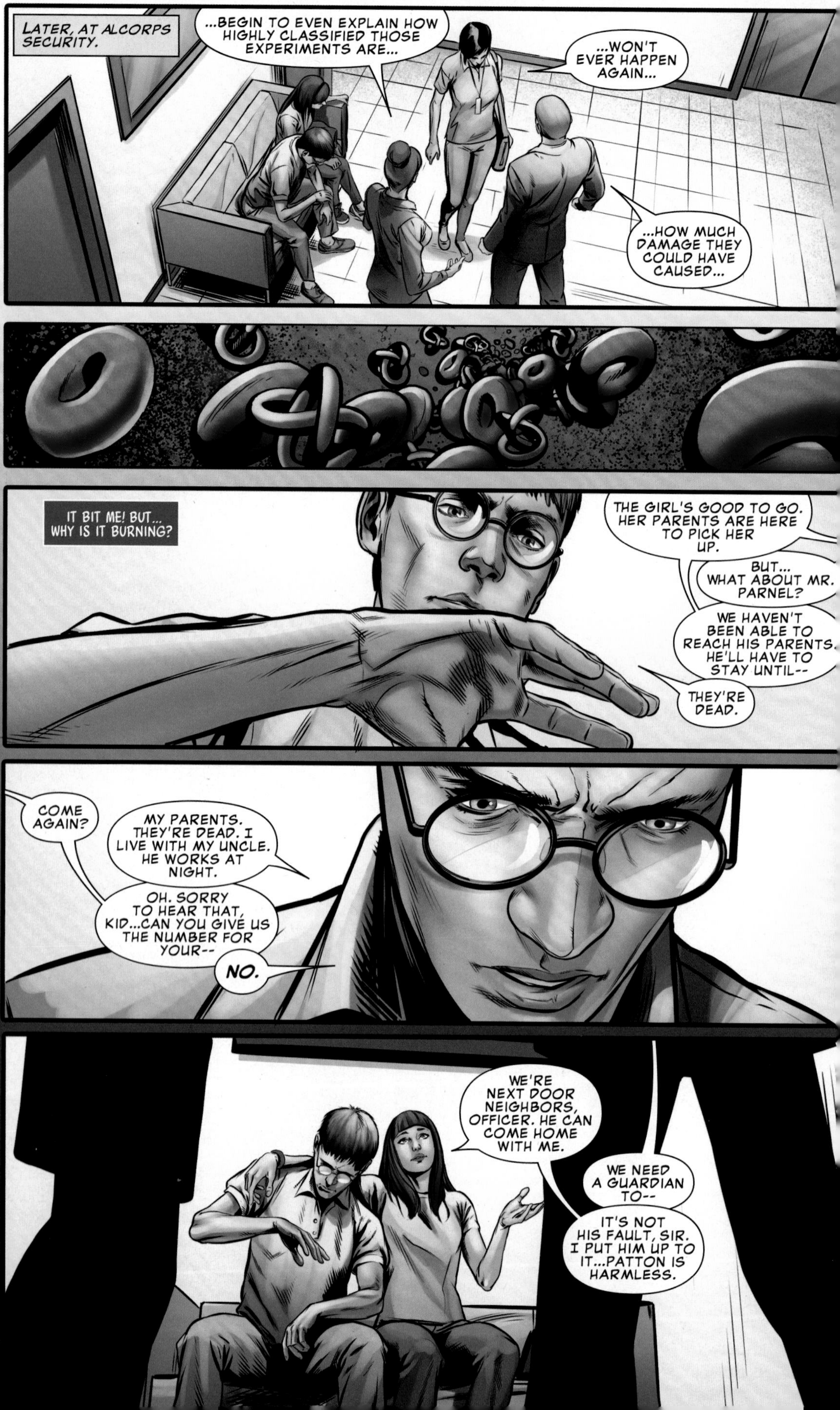

LATER, AT ALCORPS SECURITY.
...BEGIN TO EVEN EXPLAIN HOW HIGHLY CLASSIFIED THOSE EXPERIMENTS ARE...
...WON'T EVER HAPPEN AGAIN...
...HOW MUCH DAMAGE THEY COULD HAVE CAUSED...
IT BIT ME! BUT... WHY IS IT BURNING?
THE GIRL'S GOOD TO GO. HER PARENTS ARE HERE TO PICK HER UP.
BUT... WHAT ABOUT MR. PARNEL?
WE HAVEN'T BEEN ABLE TO REACH HIS PARENTS. HE'LL HAVE TO STAY UNTIL--
THEY'RE DEAD.
COME AGAIN?
MY PARENTS. THEY'RE DEAD. I LIVE WITH MY UNCLE. HE WORKS AT NIGHT.
OH. SORRY TO HEAR THAT, KID...CAN YOU GIVE US THE NUMBER FOR YOUR--
NO.
WE'RE NEXT DOOR NEIGHBORS, OFFICER. HE CAN COME HOME WITH ME.
WE NEED A GUARDIAN TO--
IT'S NOT HIS FAULT, SIR. I PUT HIM UP TO IT...PATTON IS HARMLESS.

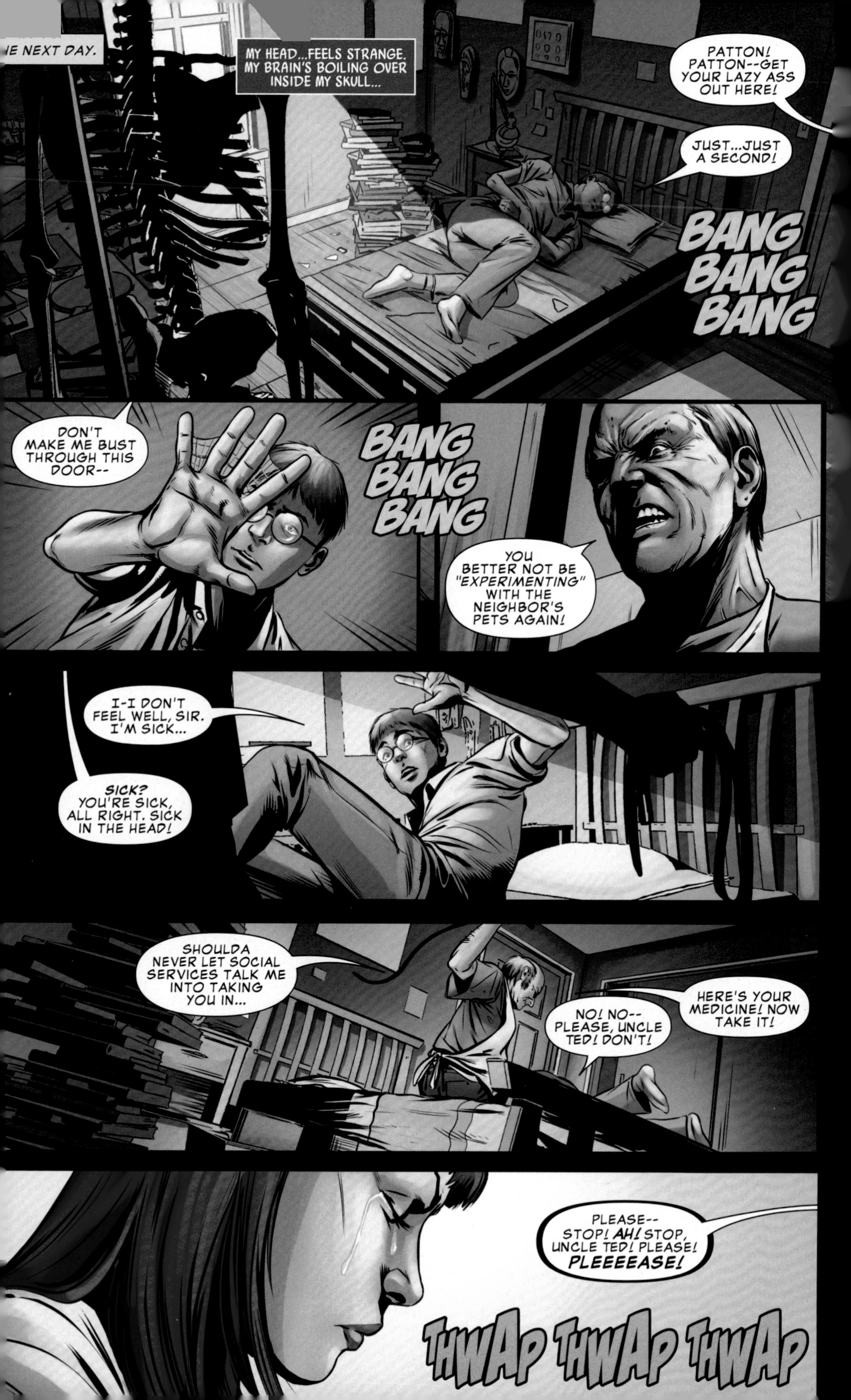

...E NEXT DAY.
MY HEAD...FEELS STRANGE. MY BRAIN'S BOILING OVER INSIDE MY SKULL...
PATTON! PATTON--GET YOUR LAZY ASS OUT HERE!
JUST...JUST A SECOND!
BANG BANG BANG
DON'T MAKE ME BUST THROUGH THIS DOOR--
BANG BANG BANG
YOU BETTER NOT BE "EXPERIMENTING" WITH THE NEIGHBOR'S PETS AGAIN!
I-I DON'T FEEL WELL, SIR. I'M SICK...
SICK? YOU'RE SICK, ALL RIGHT. SICK IN THE HEAD!
SHOULDA NEVER LET SOCIAL SERVICES TALK ME INTO TAKING YOU IN...
HERE'S YOUR MEDICINE! NOW TAKE IT!
NO! NO--PLEASE, UNCLE TED! DON'T!
PLEASE--STOP! AH! STOP, UNCLE TED! PLEASE! PLEEEEASE!
THWAP THWAP THWAP

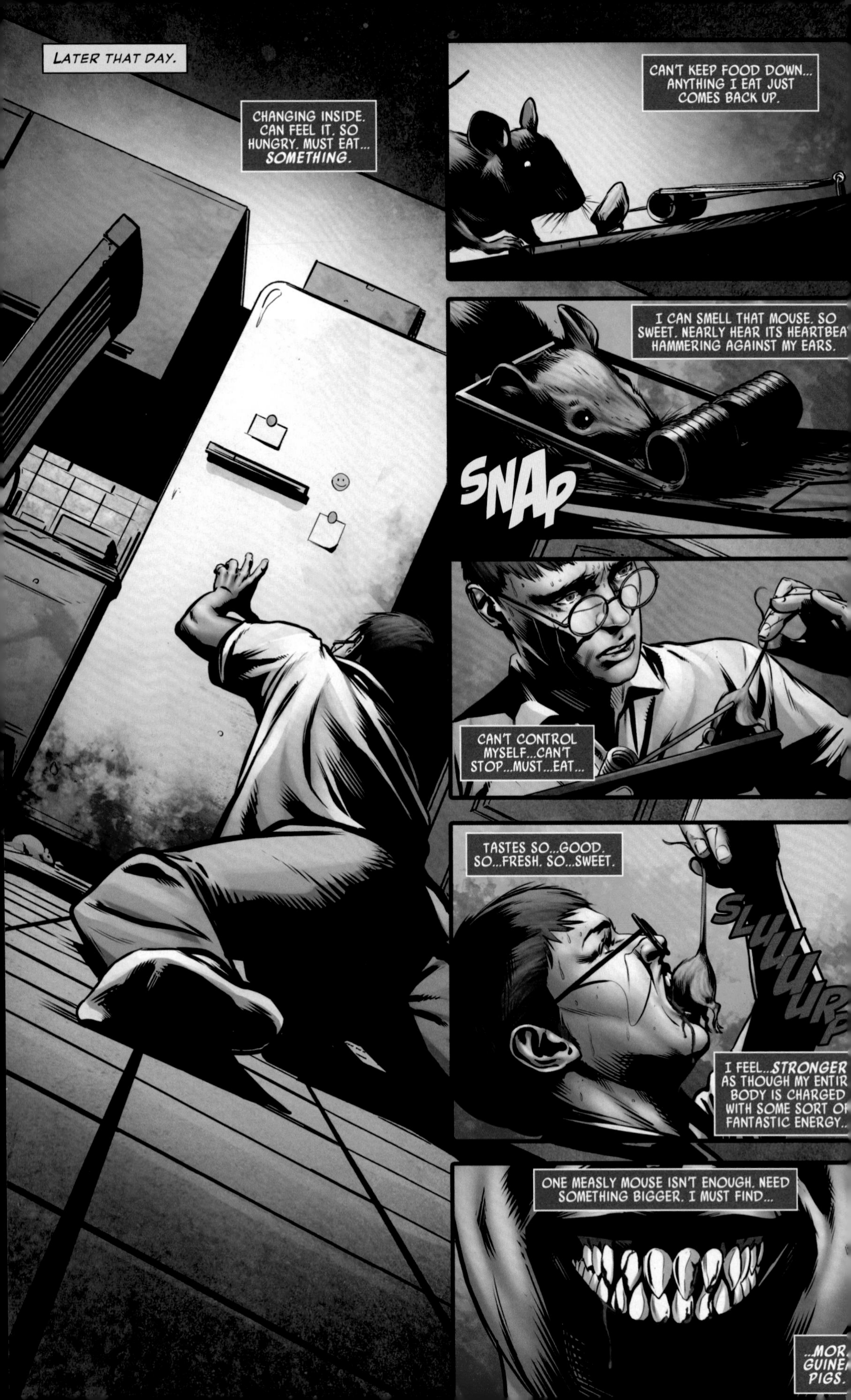
LATER THAT DAY.
CHANGING INSIDE. CAN FEEL IT. SO HUNGRY. MUST EAT... SOMETHING.
CAN'T KEEP FOOD DOWN... ANYTHING I EAT JUST COMES BACK UP.
I CAN SMELL THAT MOUSE. SO SWEET. NEARLY HEAR ITS HEARTBEA HAMMERING AGAINST MY EARS.
SNAP
CAN'T CONTROL MYSELF...CAN'T STOP...MUST...EAT...
TASTES SO...GOOD. SO...FRESH. SO...SWEET.
SLUUUURP
I FEEL...STRONGER AS THOUGH MY ENTIR BODY IS CHARGED WITH SOME SORT O FANTASTIC ENERGY..
ONE MEASLY MOUSE ISN'T ENOUGH. NEED SOMETHING BIGGER. I MUST FIND...
..MOR GUINE PIGS.

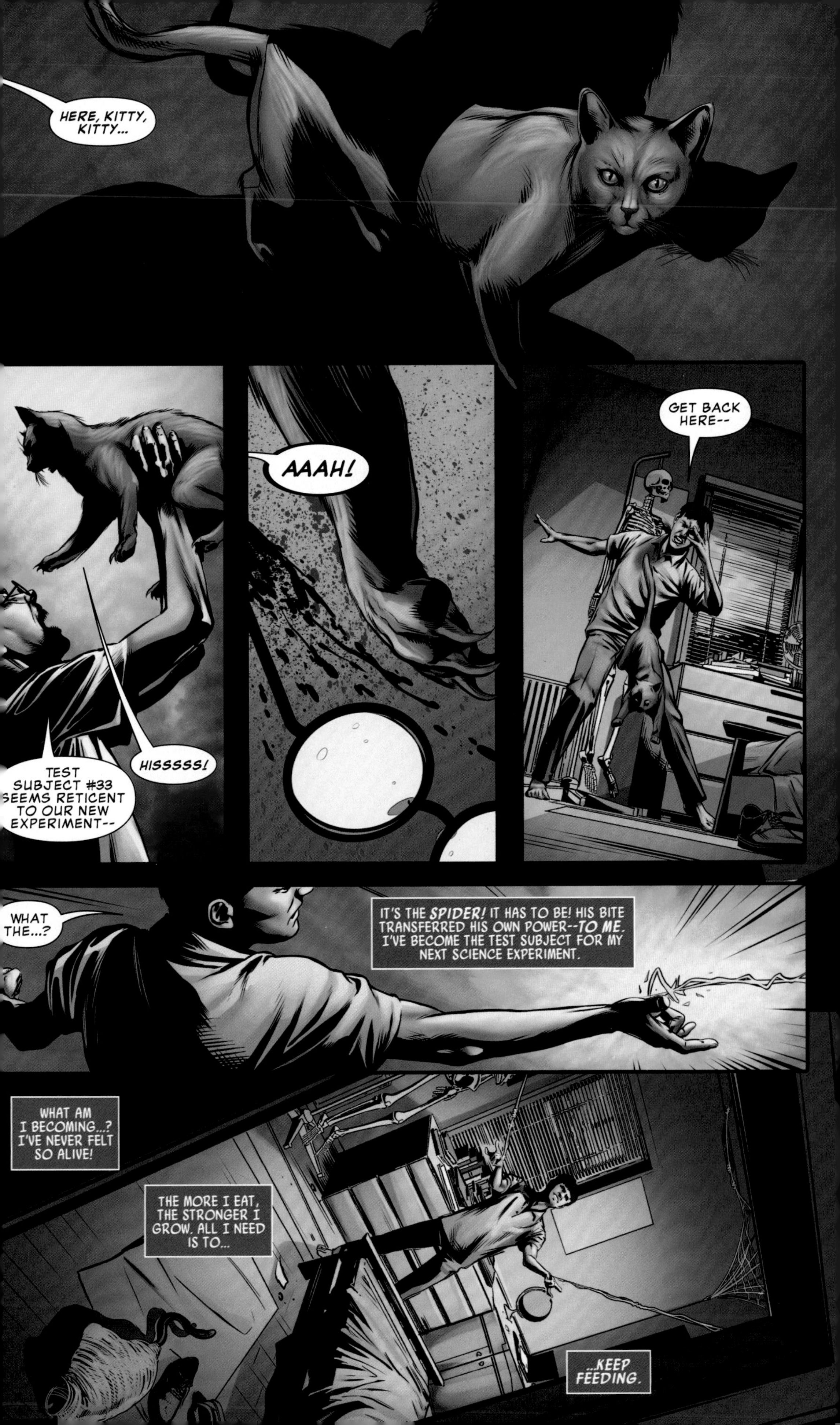
HERE, KITTY, KITTY...
TEST SUBJECT #33 SEEMS RETICENT TO OUR NEW EXPERIMENT--
HISSSSS!
AAAH!
GET BACK HERE--
WHAT THE...?
IT'S THE SPIDER! IT HAS TO BE! HIS BITE TRANSFERRED HIS OWN POWER--TO ME. I'VE BECOME THE TEST SUBJECT FOR MY NEXT SCIENCE EXPERIMENT.
WHAT AM I BECOMING...? I'VE NEVER FELT SO ALIVE!
THE MORE I EAT, THE STRONGER I GROW. ALL I NEED IS TO...
...KEEP FEEDING.

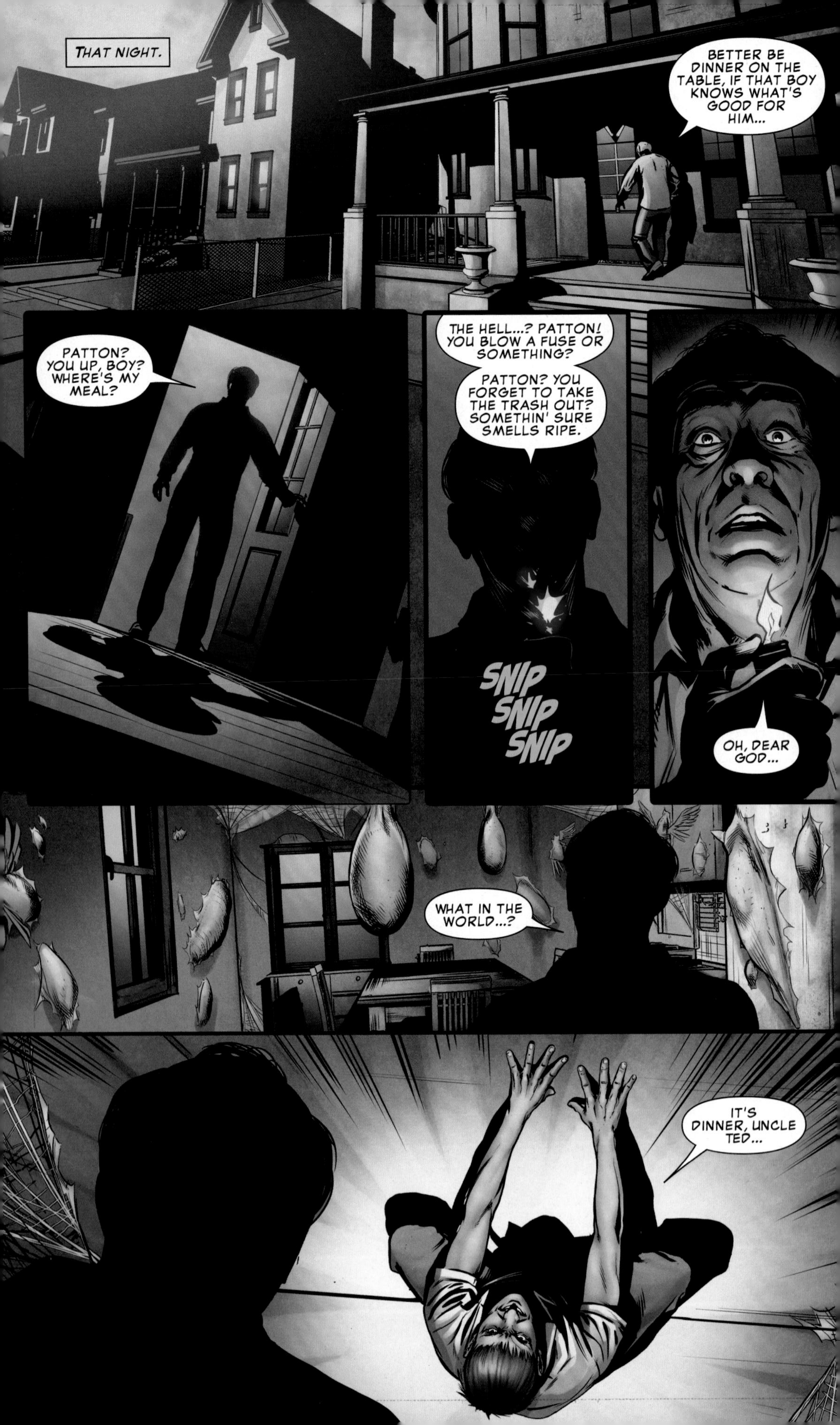
THAT NIGHT.
BETTER BE DINNER ON THE TABLE, IF THAT BOY KNOWS WHAT'S GOOD FOR HIM...
PATTON? YOU UP, BOY? WHERE'S MY MEAL?
THE HELL...? PATTON! YOU BLOW A FUSE OR SOMETHING?
PATTON? YOU FORGET TO TAKE THE TRASH OUT? SOMETHIN' SURE SMELLS RIPE.
SNIP SNIP SNIP
OH, DEAR GOD...
WHAT IN THE WORLD...?
IT'S DINNER, UNCLE TED...

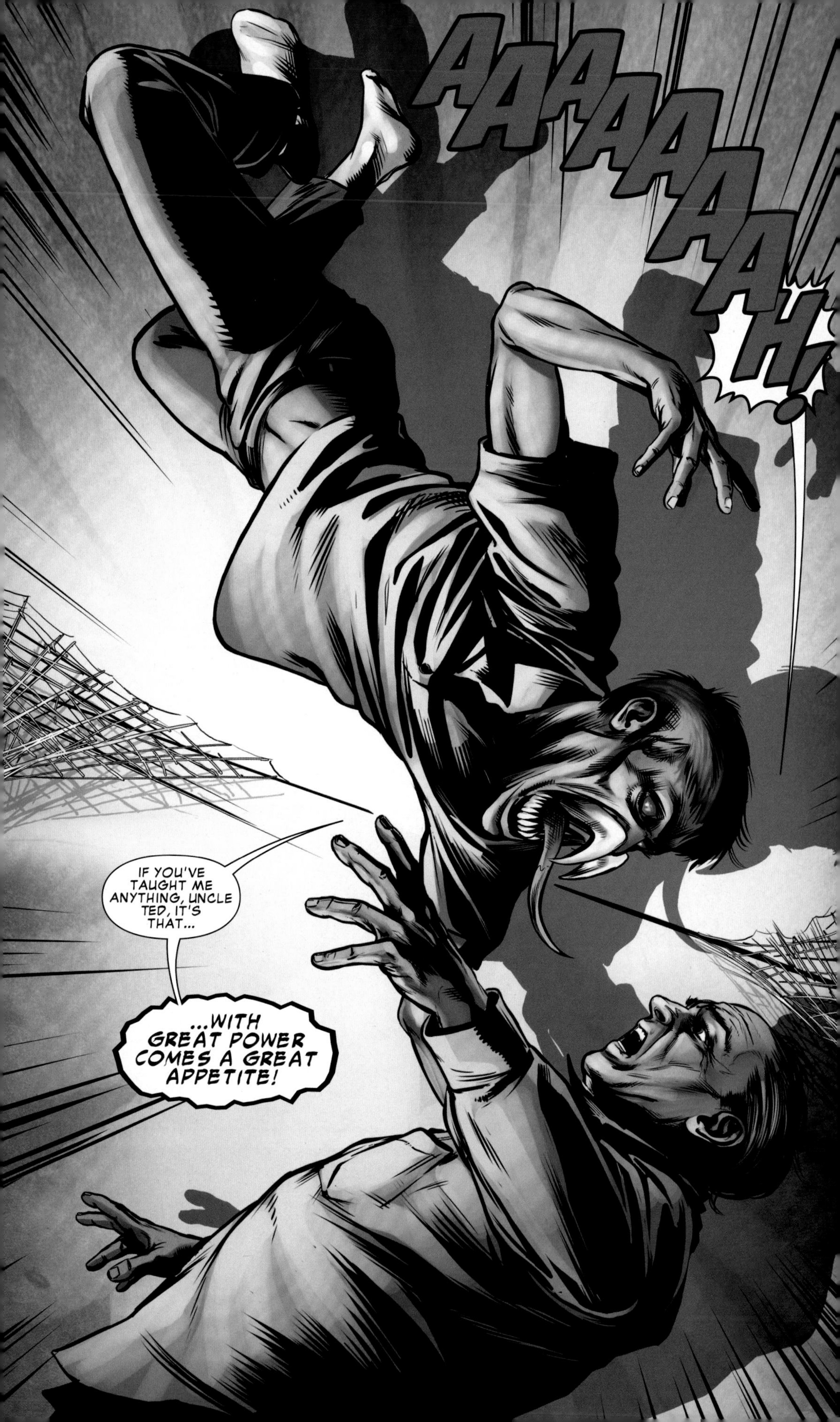
AAAAAAAAH!
IF YOU'VE TAUGHT ME ANYTHING, UNCLE TED, IT'S THAT...
...WITH GREAT POWER COMES A GREAT APPETITE!

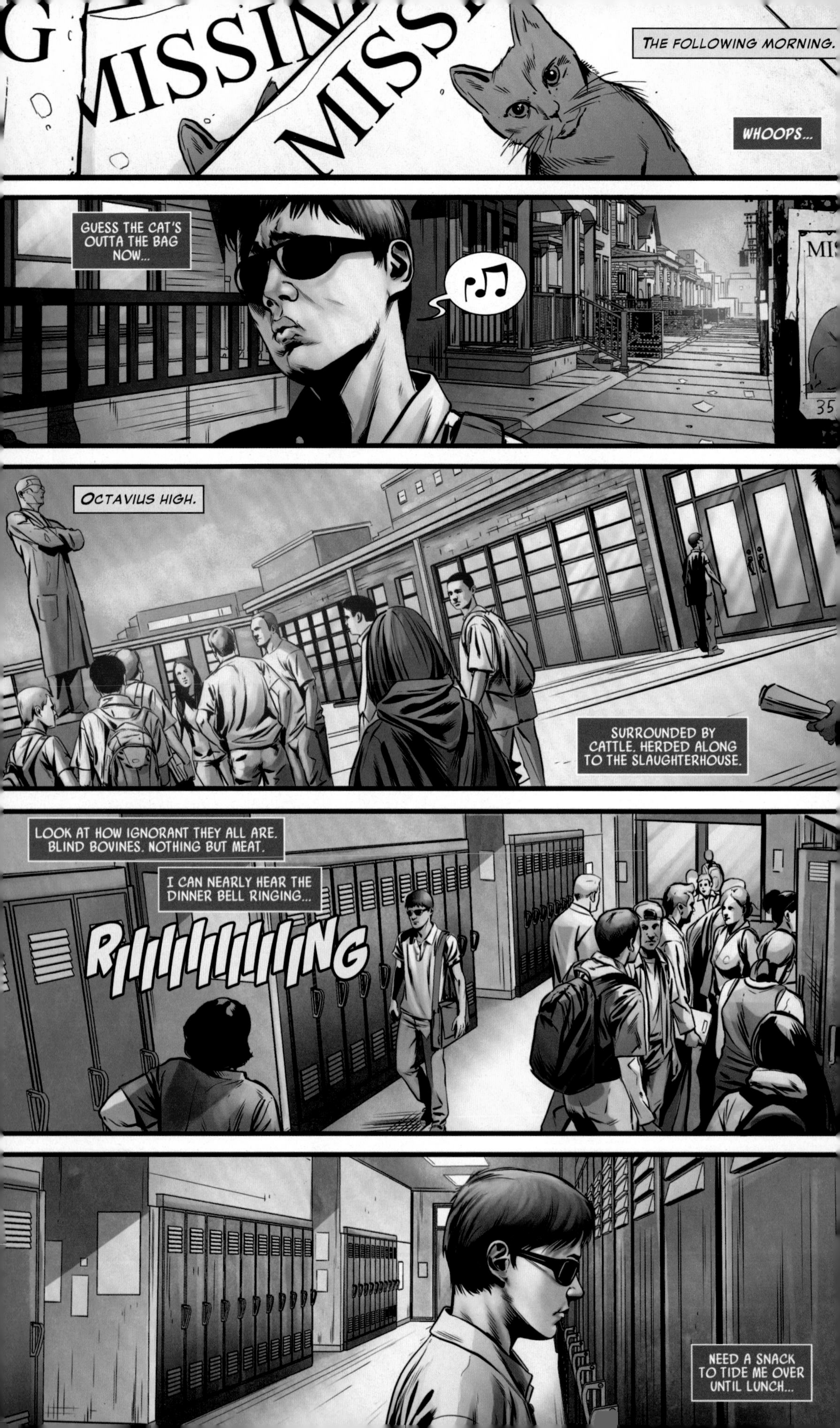
MISSING
MISS
THE FOLLOWING MORNING.
WHOOPS...
GUESS THE CAT'S OUTTA THE BAG NOW...
MI
35
OCTAVIUS HIGH.
SURROUNDED BY CATTLE, HERDED ALONG TO THE SLAUGHTERHOUSE.
LOOK AT HOW IGNORANT THEY ALL ARE. BLIND BOVINES. NOTHING BUT MEAT.
I CAN NEARLY HEAR THE DINNER BELL RINGING...
RIIIIIIIIIIING
NEED A SNACK TO TIDE ME OVER UNTIL LUNCH...

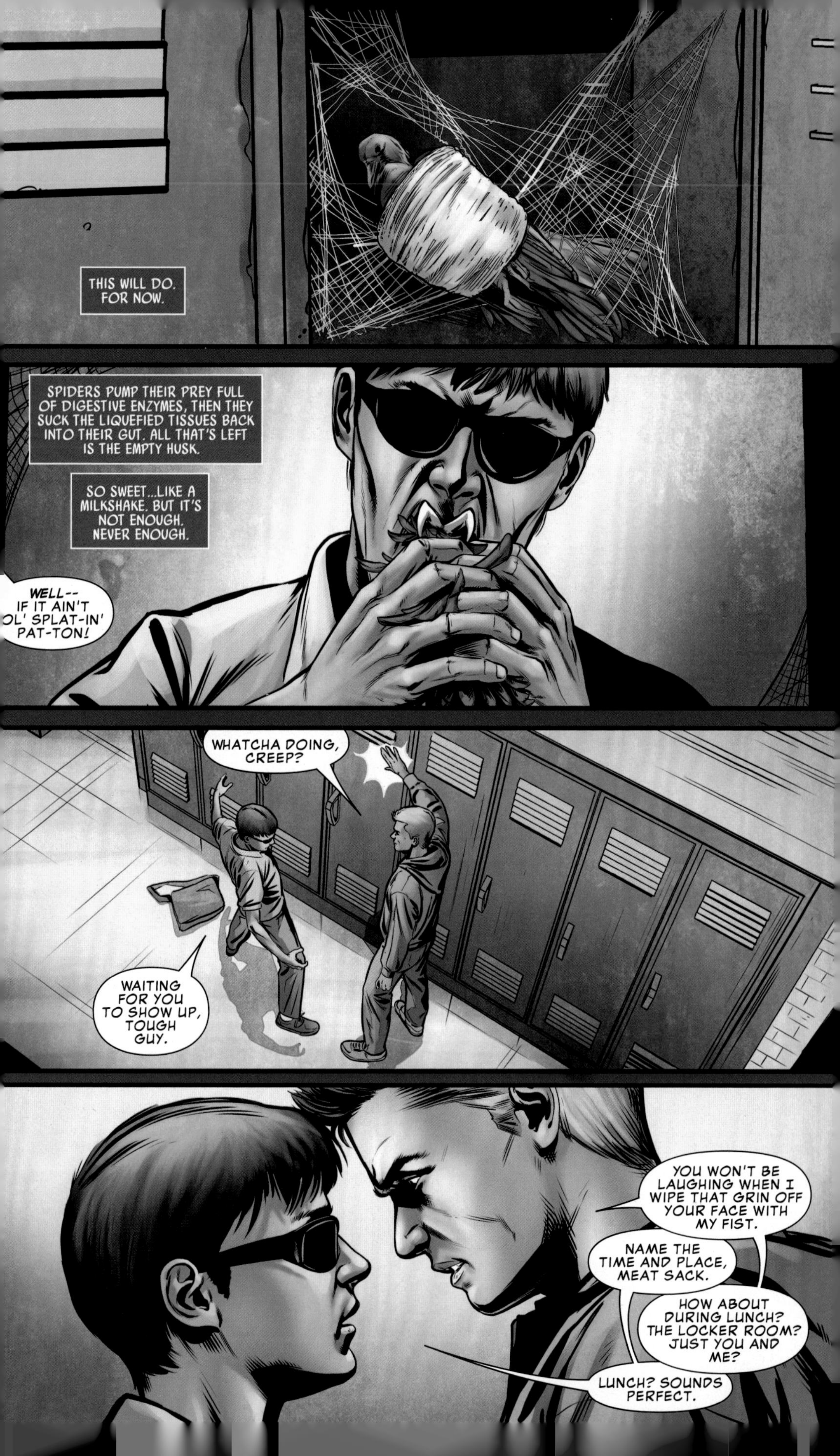
THIS WILL DO. FOR NOW.
SPIDERS PUMP THEIR PREY FULL OF DIGESTIVE ENZYMES, THEN THEY SUCK THE LIQUEFIED TISSUES BACK INTO THEIR GUT. ALL THAT'S LEFT IS THE EMPTY HUSK.
SO SWEET...LIKE A MILKSHAKE. BUT IT'S NOT ENOUGH. NEVER ENOUGH.
WELL-- IF IT AIN'T OL' SPLAT-IN' PAT-TON!
WHATCHA DOING, CREEP?
WAITING FOR YOU TO SHOW UP, TOUGH GUY.
YOU WON'T BE LAUGHING WHEN I WIPE THAT GRIN OFF YOUR FACE WITH MY FIST.
NAME THE TIME AND PLACE, MEAT SACK.
HOW ABOUT DURING LUNCH? THE LOCKER ROOM? JUST YOU AND ME?
LUNCH? SOUNDS PERFECT.

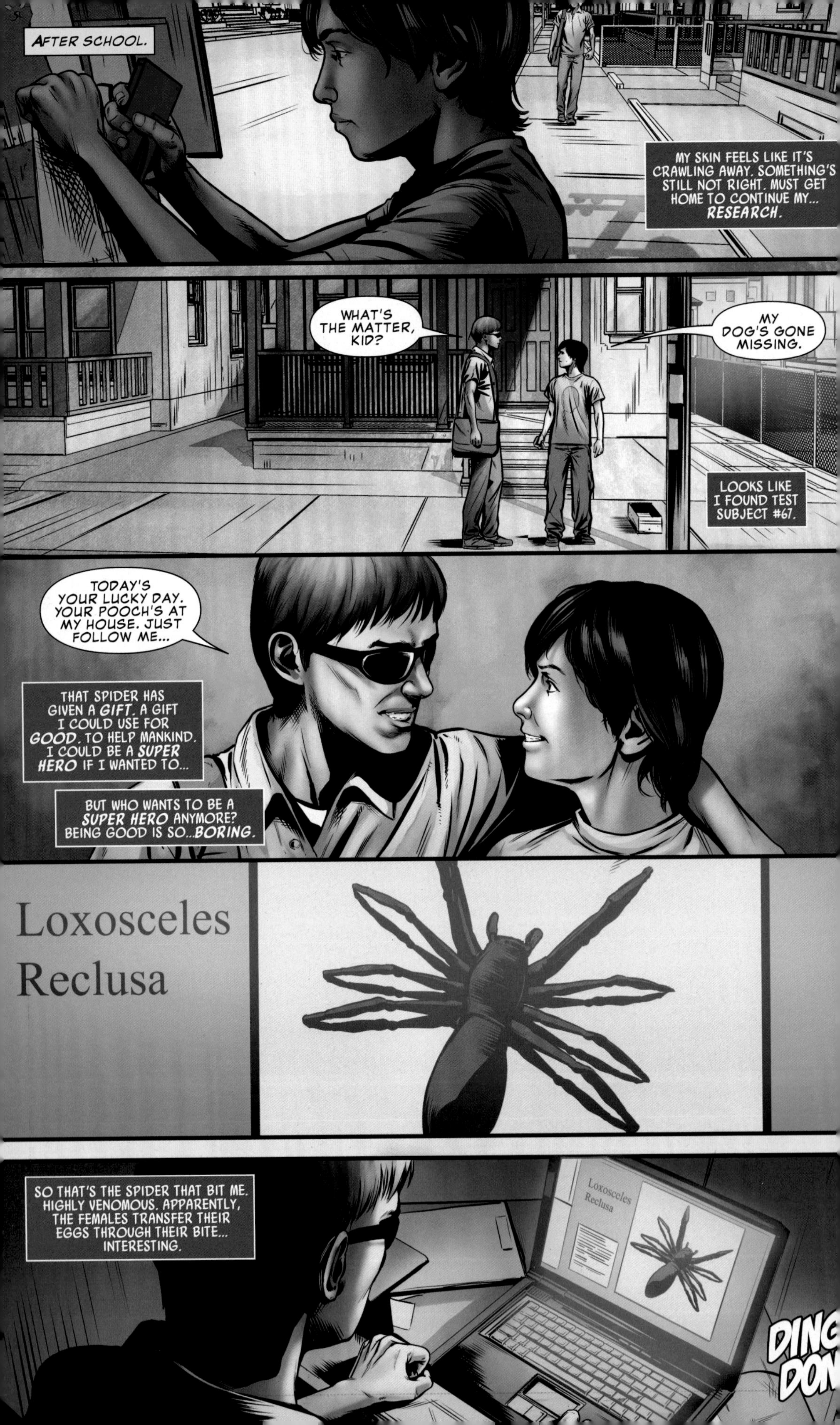
AFTER SCHOOL.
MY SKIN FEELS LIKE IT'S CRAWLING AWAY. SOMETHING'S STILL NOT RIGHT. MUST GET HOME TO CONTINUE MY... RESEARCH.
WHAT'S THE MATTER, KID?
MY DOG'S GONE MISSING.
LOOKS LIKE I FOUND TEST SUBJECT #67.
TODAY'S YOUR LUCKY DAY. YOUR POOCH'S AT MY HOUSE. JUST FOLLOW ME...
THAT SPIDER HAS GIVEN A GIFT. A GIFT I COULD USE FOR GOOD. TO HELP MANKIND. I COULD BE A SUPER HERO IF I WANTED TO...
BUT WHO WANTS TO BE A SUPER HERO ANYMORE? BEING GOOD IS SO...BORING.
Loxosceles Reclusa
SO THAT'S THE SPIDER THAT BIT ME. HIGHLY VENOMOUS. APPARENTLY, THE FEMALES TRANSFER THEIR EGGS THROUGH THEIR BITE... INTERESTING.
Loxosceles Reclusa
DING DON

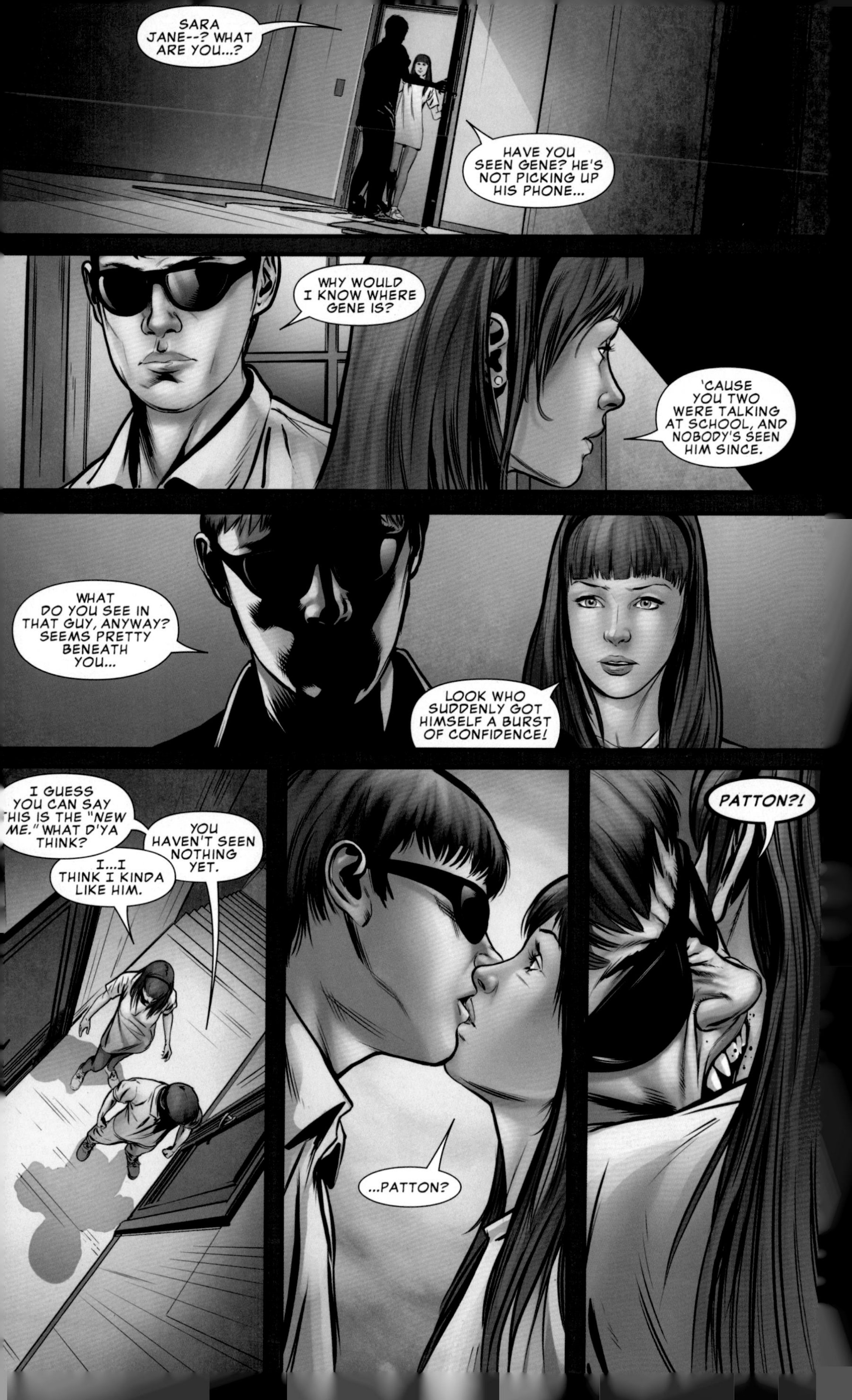
SARA JANE--? WHAT ARE YOU...?
HAVE YOU SEEN GENE? HE'S NOT PICKING UP HIS PHONE...
WHY WOULD I KNOW WHERE GENE IS?
'CAUSE YOU TWO WERE TALKING AT SCHOOL, AND NOBODY'S SEEN HIM SINCE.
WHAT DO YOU SEE IN THAT GUY, ANYWAY? SEEMS PRETTY BENEATH YOU...
LOOK WHO SUDDENLY GOT HIMSELF A BURST OF CONFIDENCE!
I GUESS YOU CAN SAY THIS IS THE "NEW ME." WHAT D'YA THINK?
I...I THINK I KINDA LIKE HIM.
YOU HAVEN'T SEEN NOTHING YET.
...PATTON?
PATTON?!

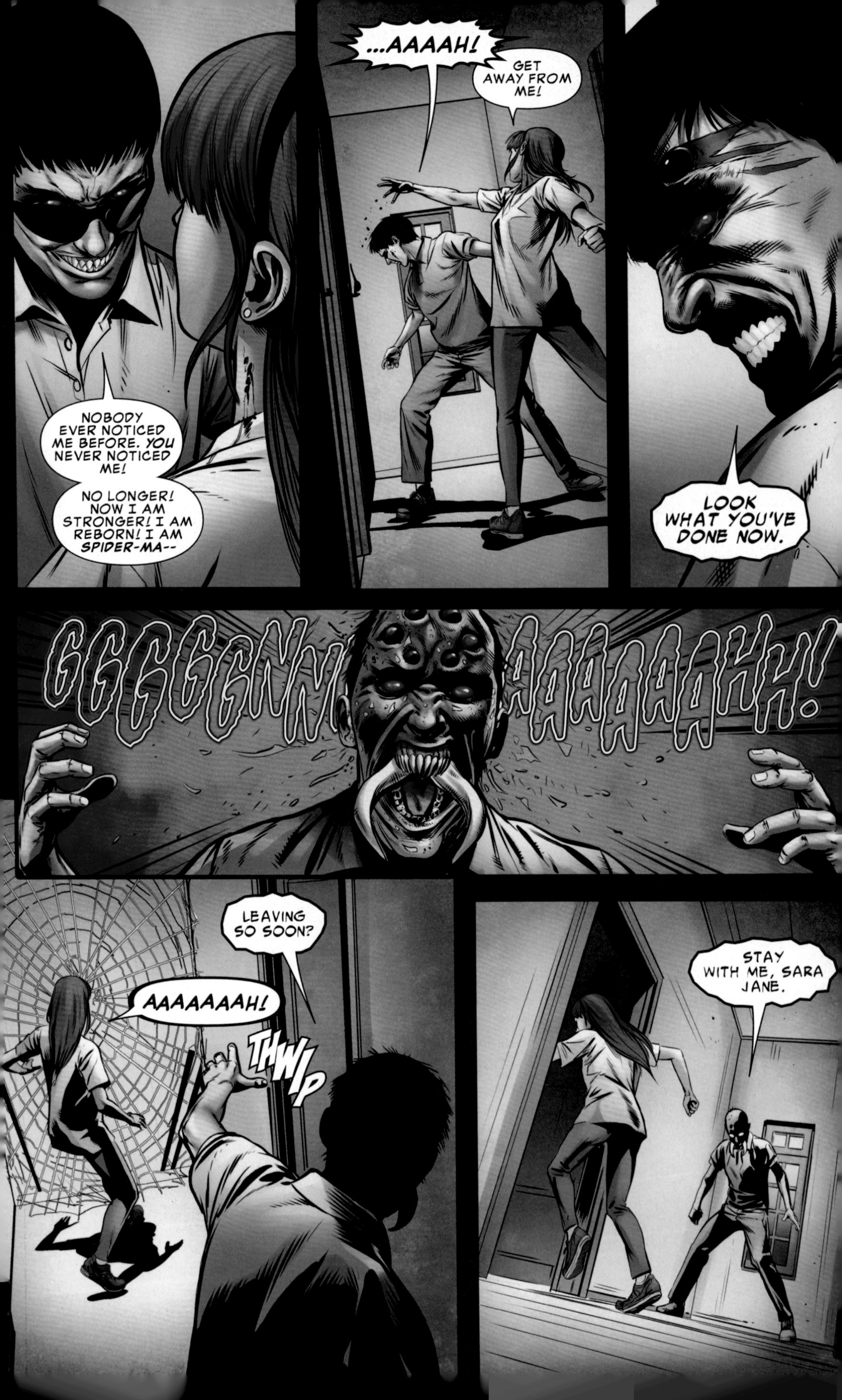
NOBODY EVER NOTICED ME BEFORE. YOU NEVER NOTICED ME!
NO LONGER! NOW I AM STRONGER! I AM REBORN! I AM SPIDER-MA--
...AAAAH!
GET AWAY FROM ME!
LOOK WHAT YOU'VE DONE NOW.
GGGGGNNAAAAAAAAHH!
LEAVING SO SOON?
AAAAAAAH!
THWIP
STAY WITH ME, SARA JANE.

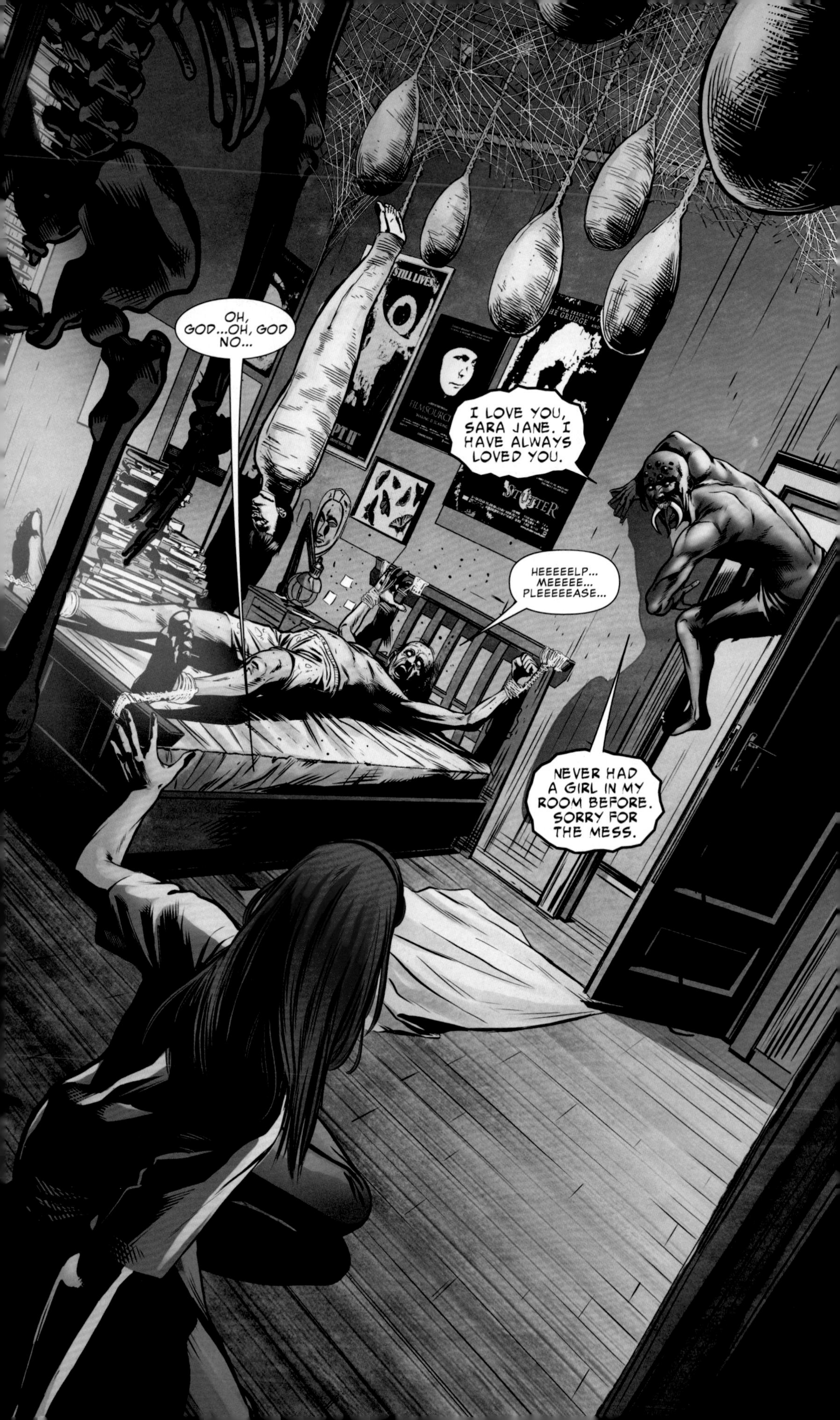
OH, GOD...OH, GOD NO...
I LOVE YOU, SARA JANE. I HAVE ALWAYS LOVED YOU.
HEEEEELP... MEEEEE... PLEEEEEASE...
NEVER HAD A GIRL IN MY ROOM BEFORE. SORRY FOR THE MESS.

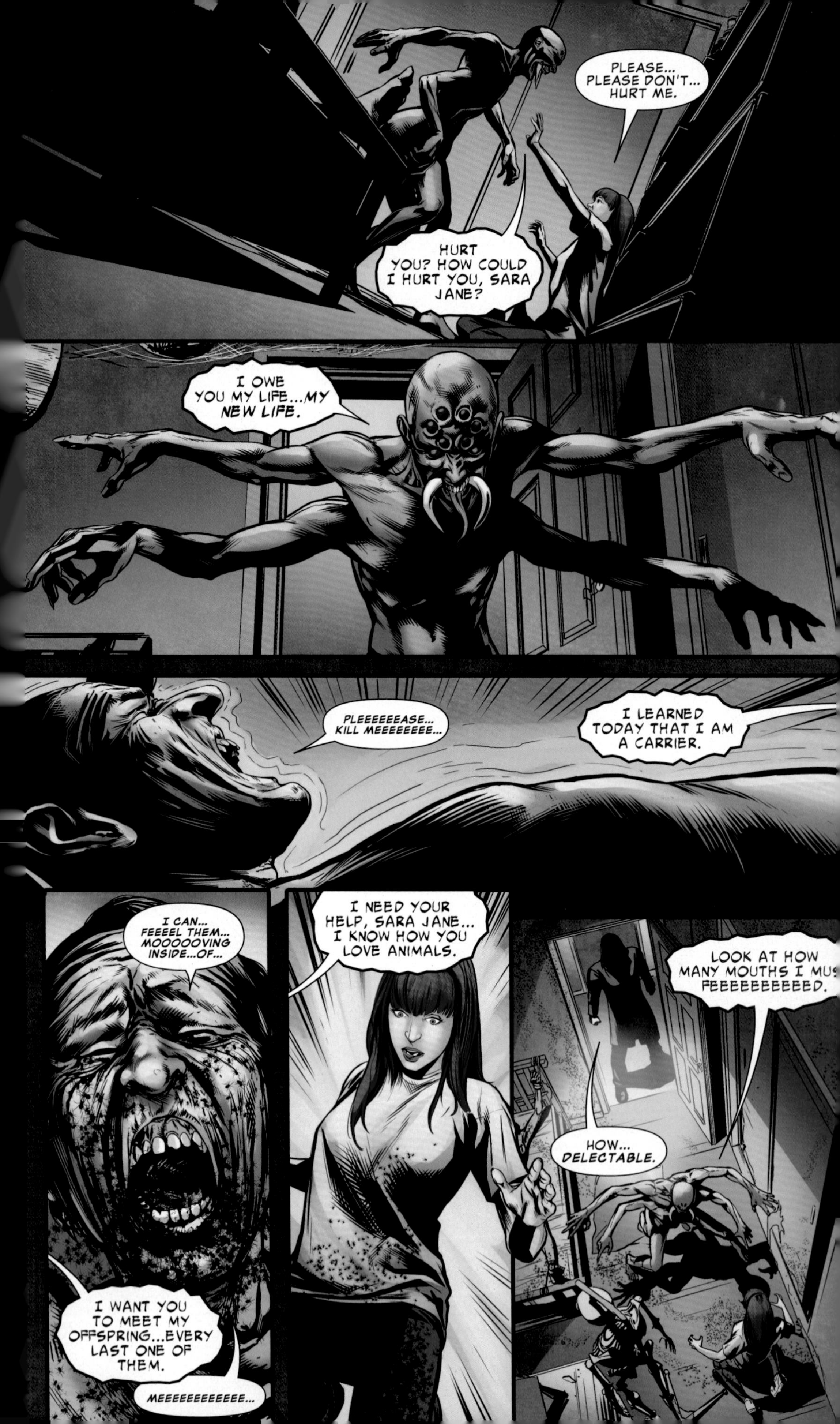
PLEASE... PLEASE DON'T... HURT ME.
HURT YOU? HOW COULD I HURT YOU, SARA JANE?
I OWE YOU MY LIFE...MY NEW LIFE.
PLEEEEEEASE... KILL MEEEEEEEE...
I LEARNED TODAY THAT I AM A CARRIER.
I CAN... FEEEEL THEM... MOOOOOVING INSIDE...OF...
I WANT YOU TO MEET MY OFFSPRING...EVERY LAST ONE OF THEM.
MEEEEEEEEEEEE...
I NEED YOUR HELP, SARA JANE... I KNOW HOW YOU LOVE ANIMALS.
LOOK AT HOW MANY MOUTHS I MUS
FEEEEEEEEEED.
HOW... DELECTABLE.

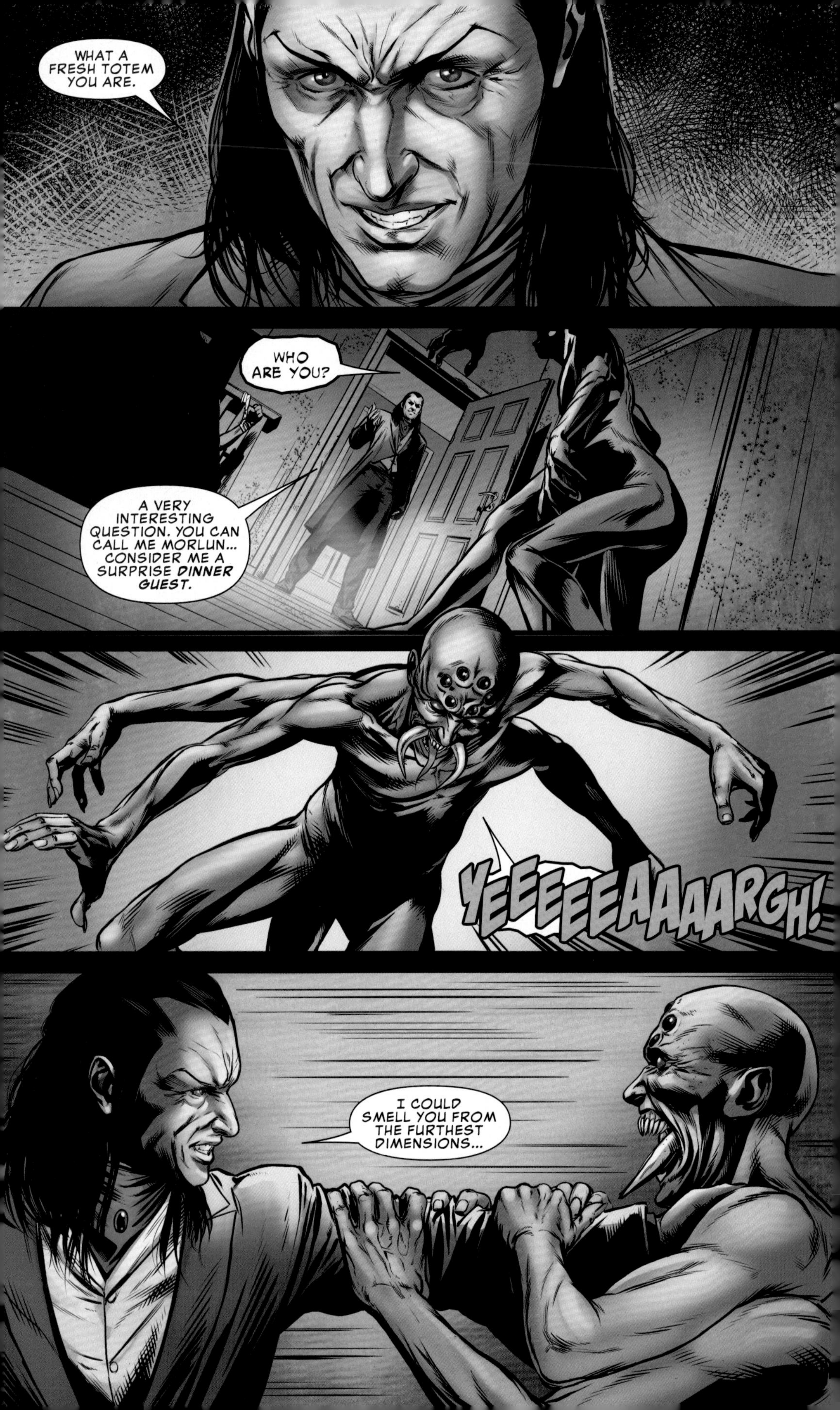
WHAT A FRESH TOTEM YOU ARE.
WHO ARE YOU?
A VERY INTERESTING QUESTION. YOU CAN CALL ME MORLUN... CONSIDER ME A SURPRISE DINNER GUEST.
YEEEEEAAAARGH!
I COULD SMELL YOU FROM THE FURTHEST DIMENSIONS...

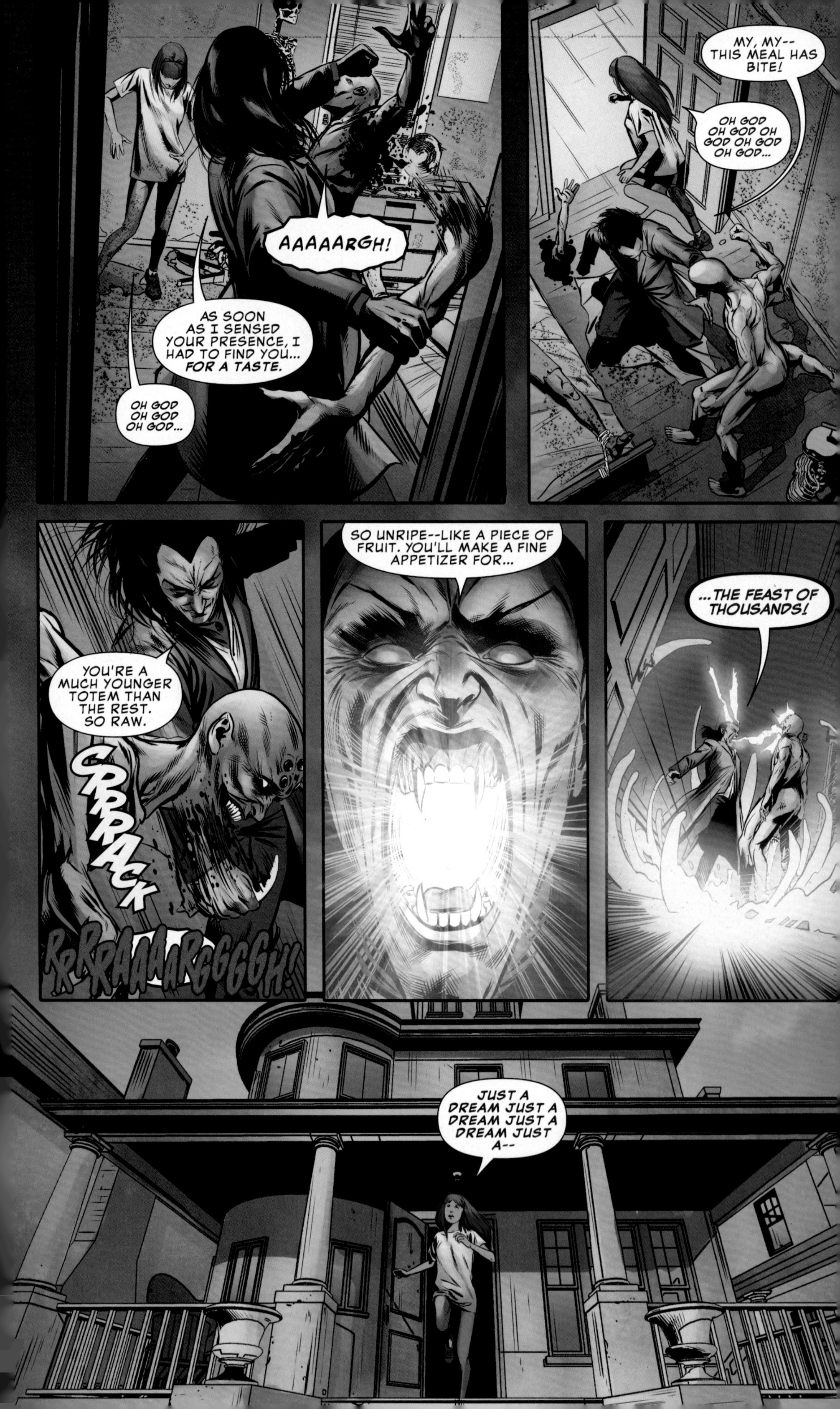
AAAAARGH!
AS SOON AS I SENSED YOUR PRESENCE, I HAD TO FIND YOU... FOR A TASTE.
OH GOD OH GOD OH GOD...
MY, MY-- THIS MEAL HAS BITE!
OH GOD OH GOD OH GOD OH GOD OH GOD OH GOD...
YOU'RE A MUCH YOUNGER TOTEM THAN THE REST. SO RAW.
CRRRACK
RRRRAAAARGGGGH!
SO UNRIPE--LIKE A PIECE OF FRUIT. YOU'LL MAKE A FINE APPETIZER FOR...
...THE FEAST OF THOUSANDS!
JUST A DREAM JUST A DREAM JUST A DREAM JUST A--

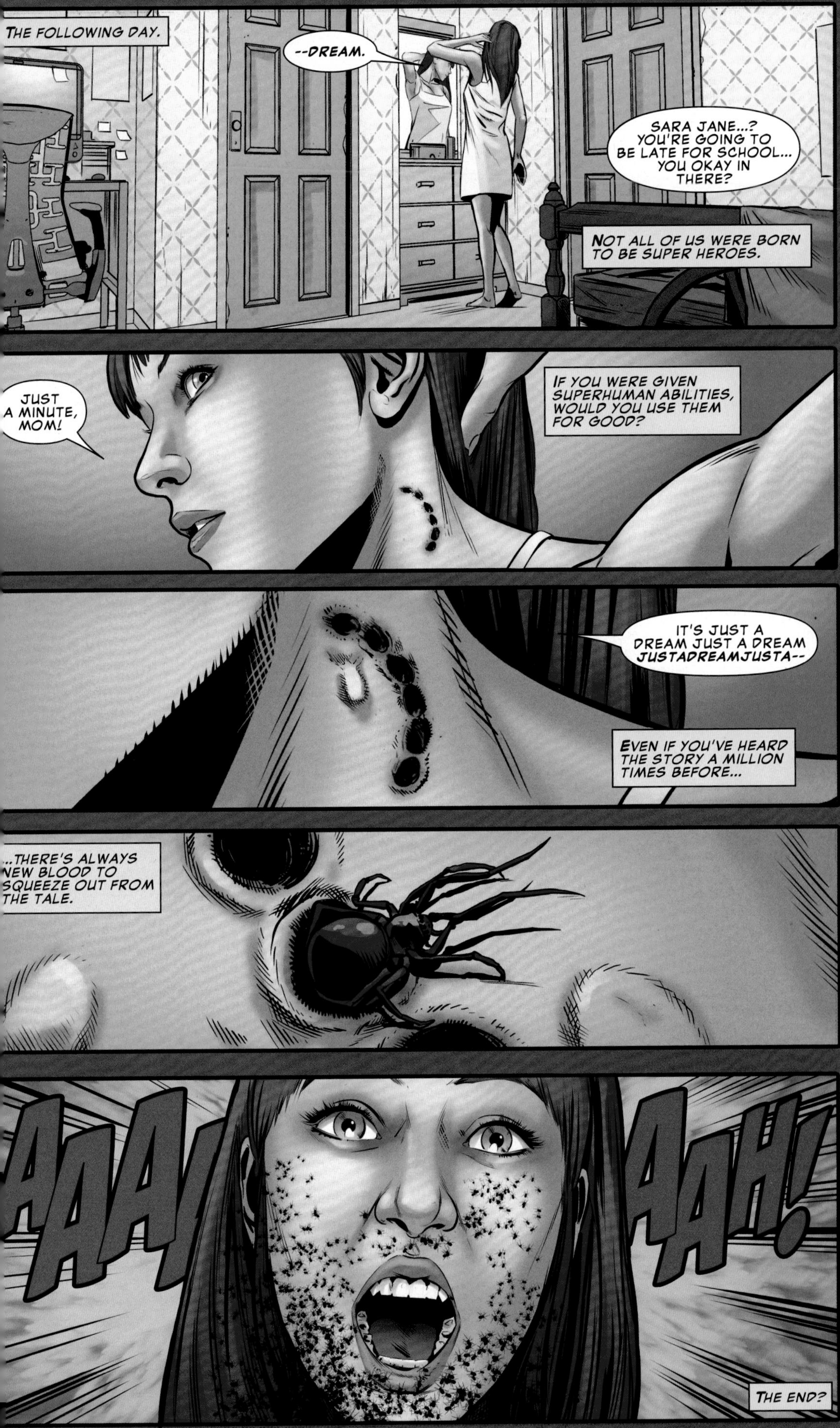
THE FOLLOWING DAY.
--DREAM.
SARA JANE...? YOU'RE GOING TO BE LATE FOR SCHOOL... YOU OKAY IN THERE?
NOT ALL OF US WERE BORN TO BE SUPER HEROES.
JUST A MINUTE, MOM!
IF YOU WERE GIVEN SUPERHUMAN ABILITIES, WOULD YOU USE THEM FOR GOOD?
IT'S JUST A DREAM JUST A DREAM JUSTADREAMJUSTA--
EVEN IF YOU'VE HEARD THE STORY A MILLION TIMES BEFORE...
...THERE'S ALWAYS NEW BLOOD TO SQUEEZE OUT FROM THE TALE.
AAAAAAH!
THE END?

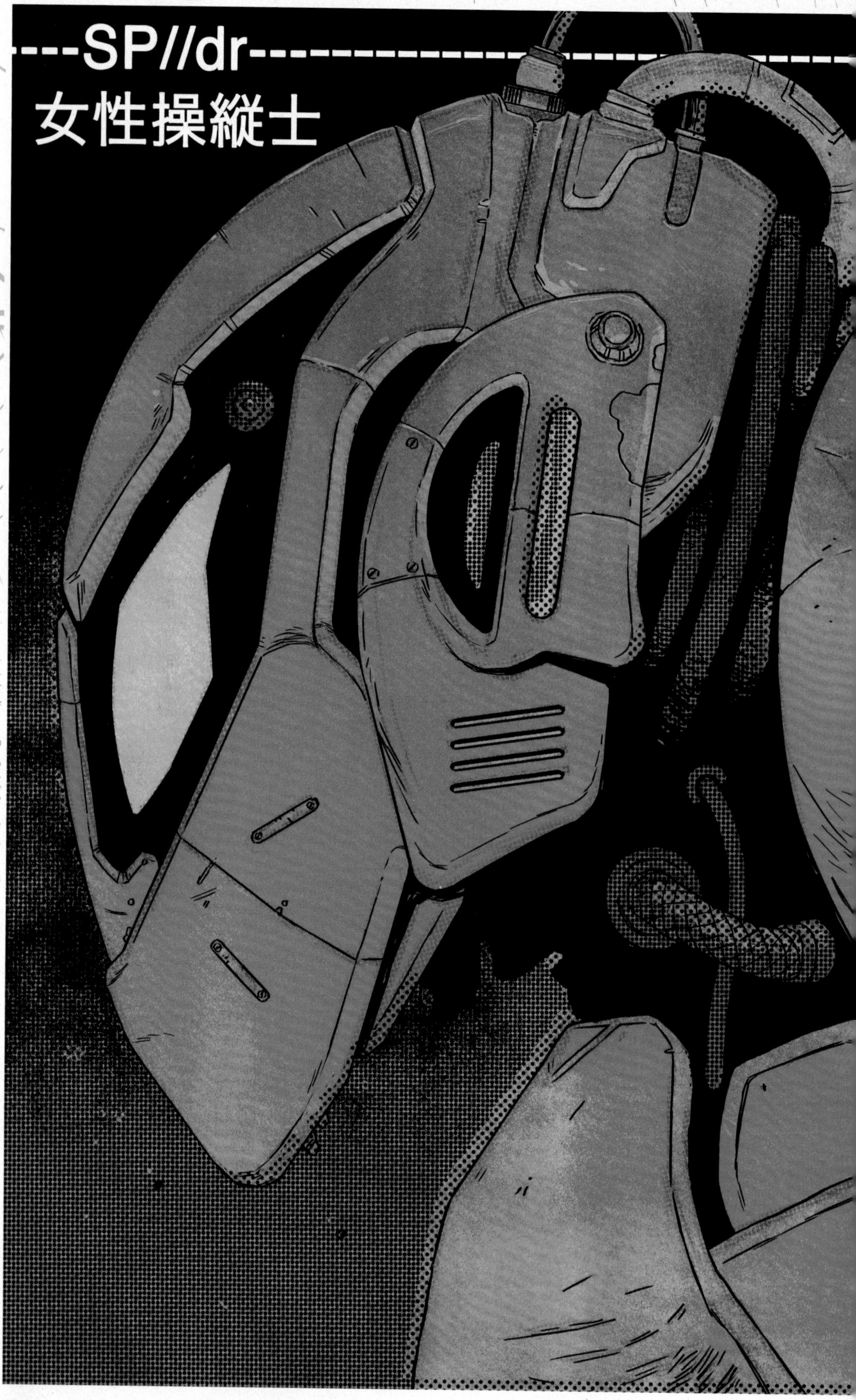
SP//dr
女性操縦士

5

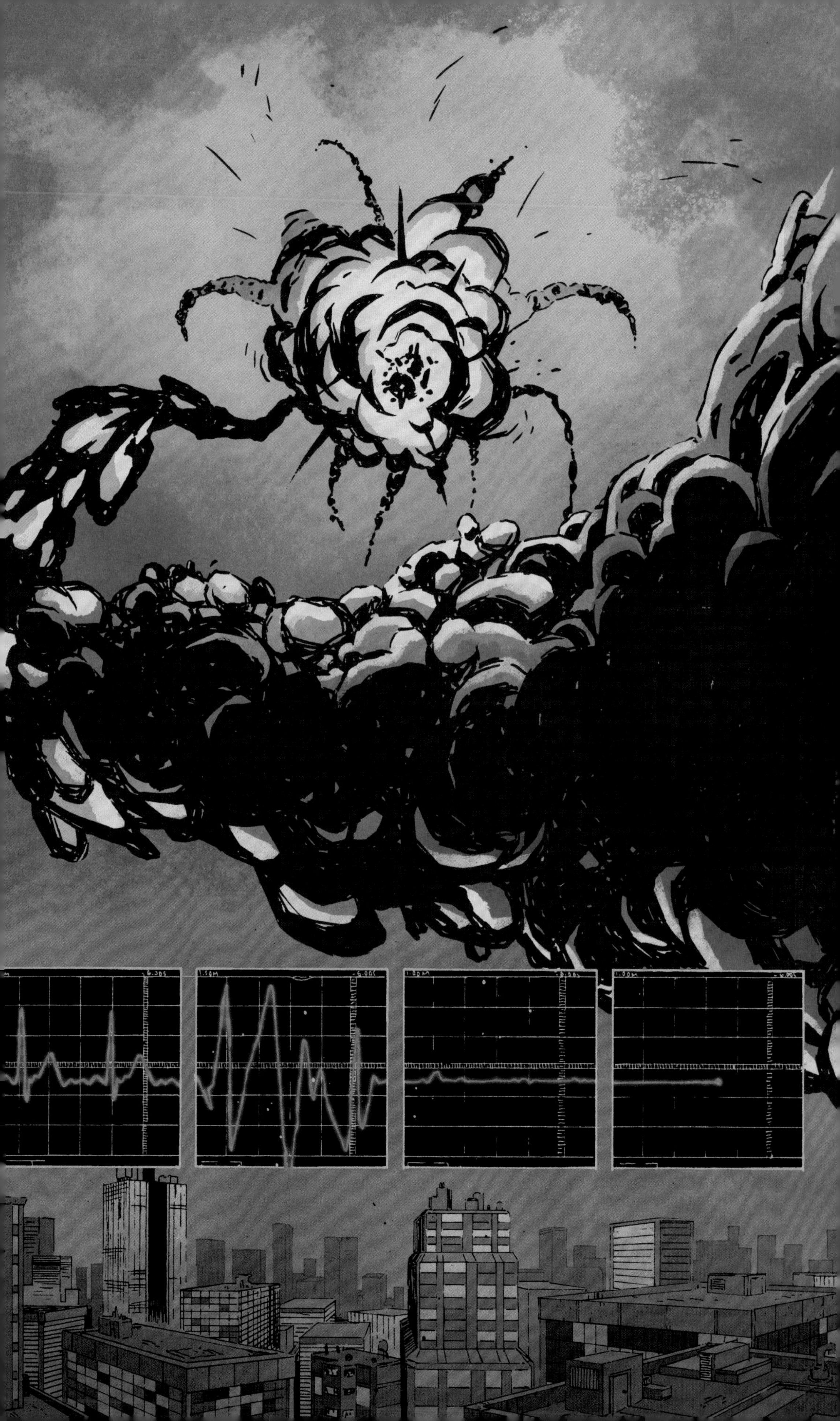

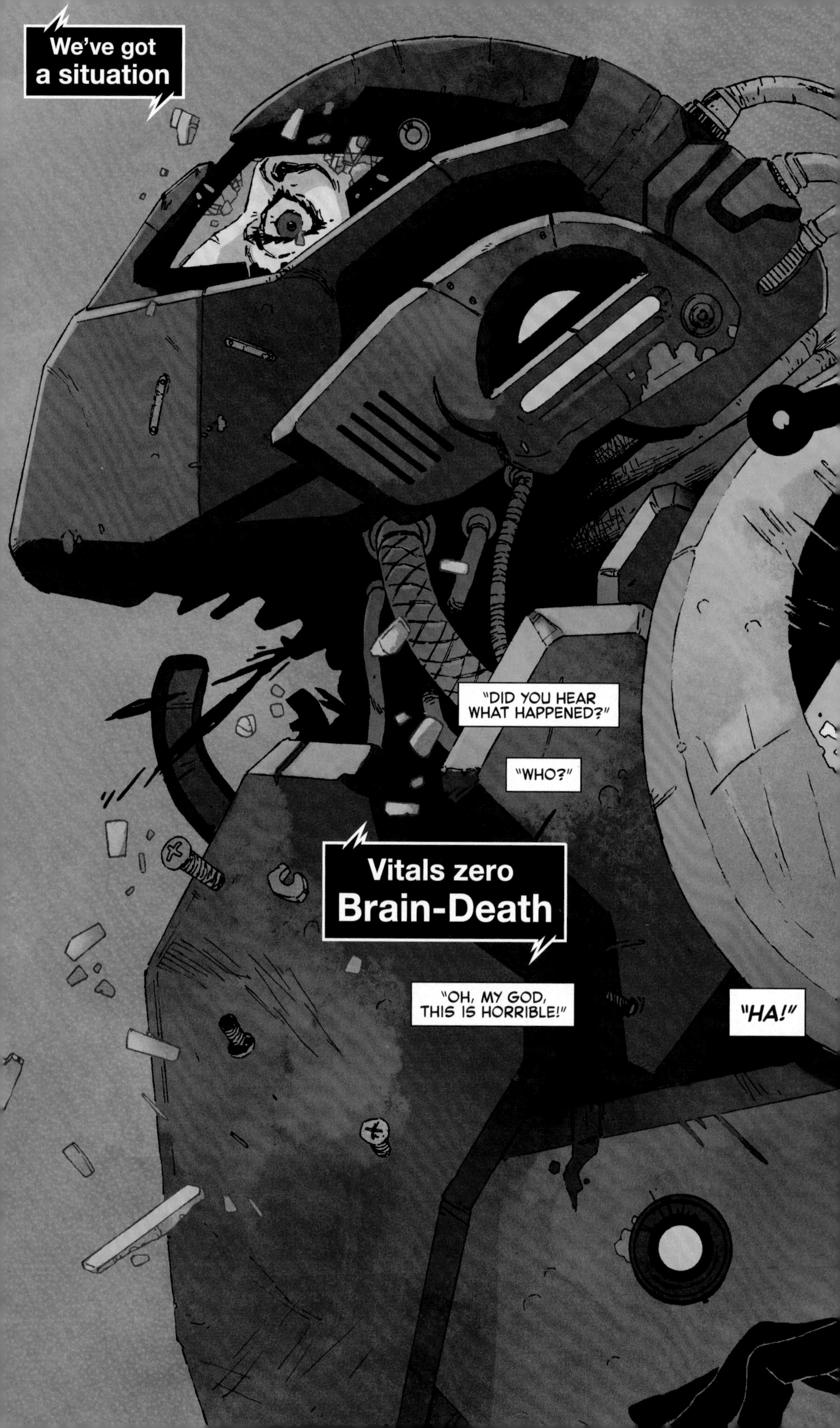
We've got a situation
"DID YOU HEAR WHAT HAPPENED?"
"WHO?"
Vitals zero Brain-Death
"OH, MY GOD, THIS IS HORRIBLE!"
"HA!"

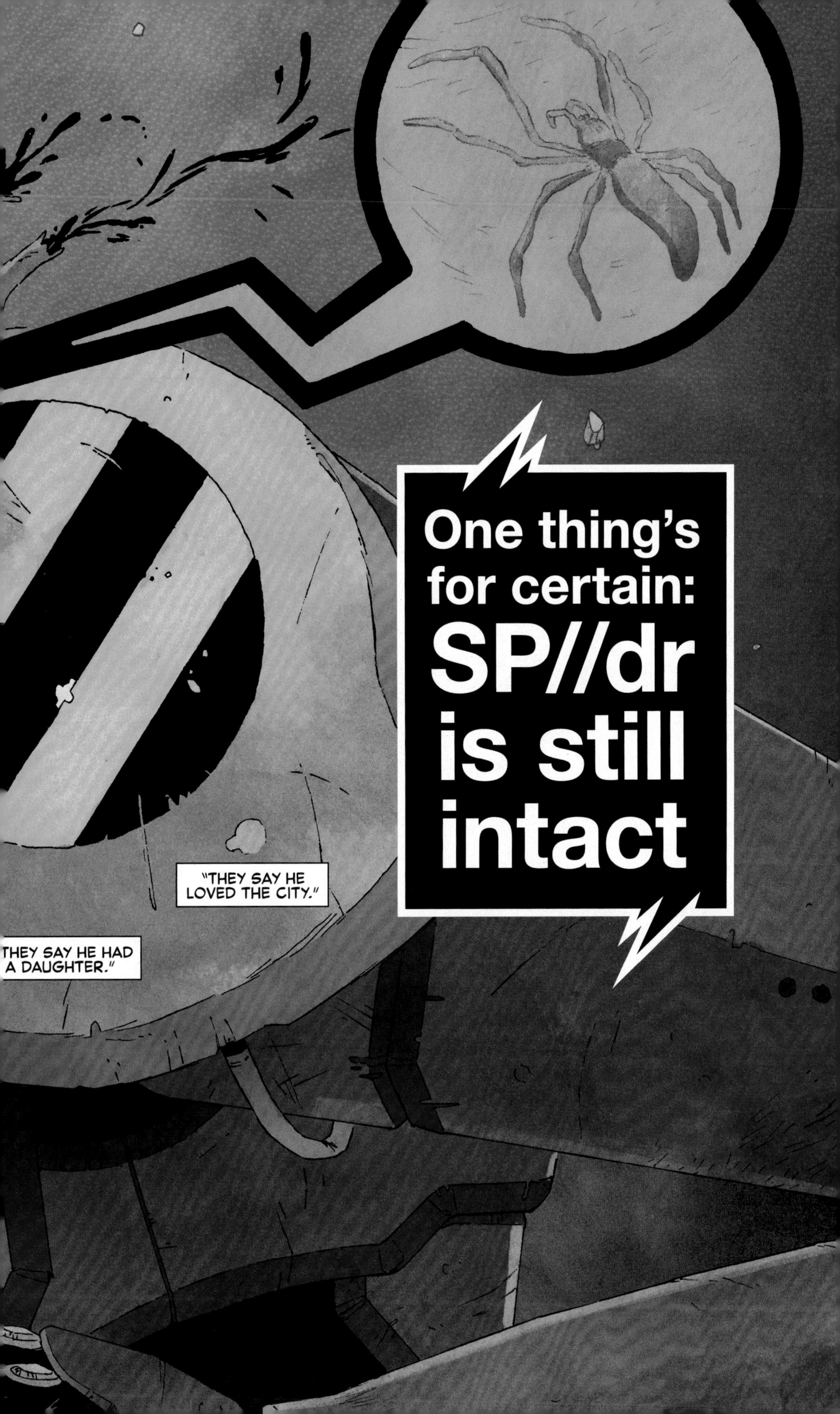
One thing's for certain: SP//dr is still intact
"THEY SAY HE LOVED THE CITY."
THEY SAY HE HAD A DAUGHTER."

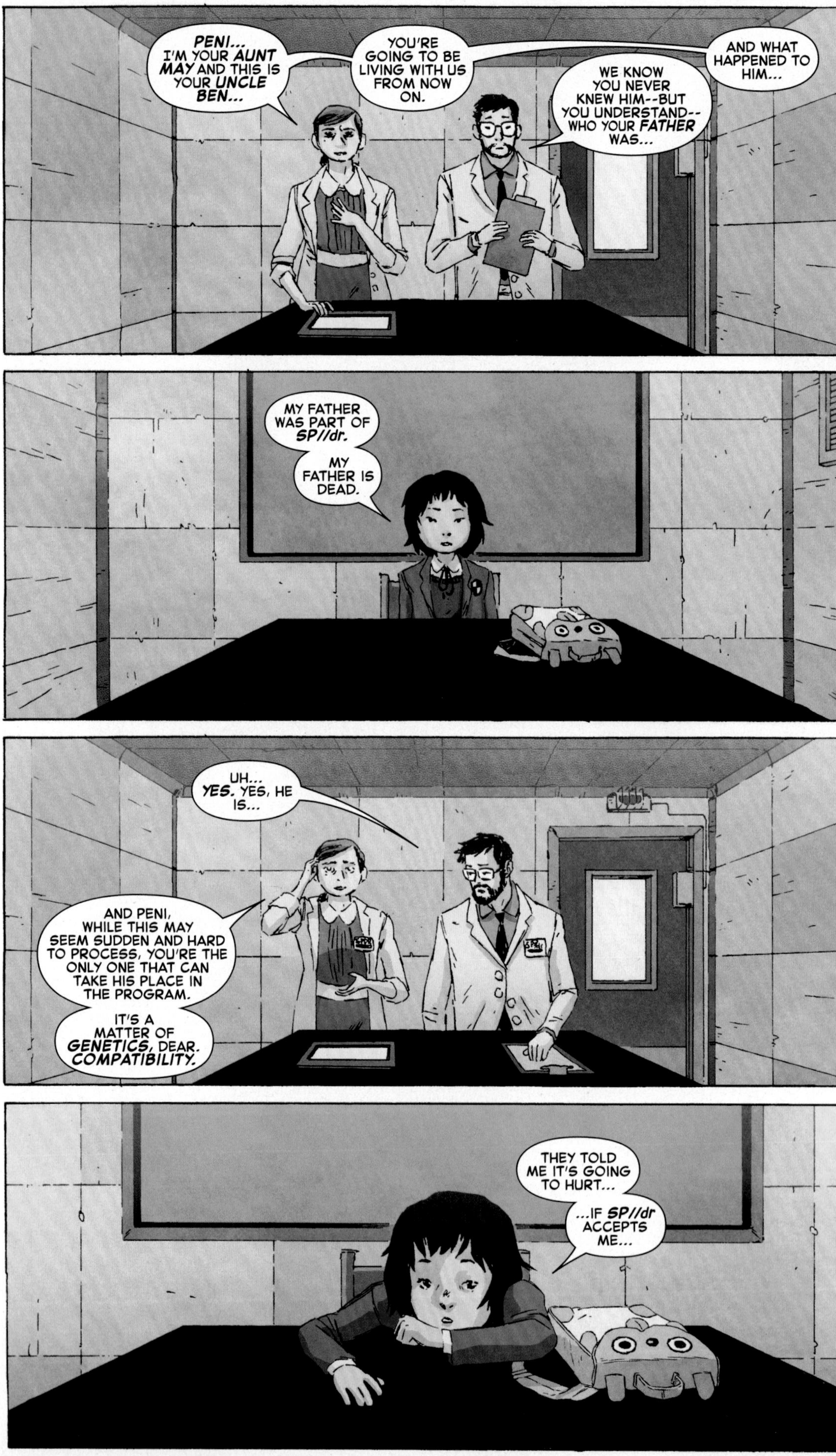
PENI... I'M YOUR AUNT MAY AND THIS IS YOUR UNCLE BEN...
YOU'RE GOING TO BE LIVING WITH US FROM NOW ON.
WE KNOW YOU NEVER KNEW HIM--BUT YOU UNDERSTAND-- WHO YOUR FATHER WAS...
AND WHAT HAPPENED TO HIM...
MY FATHER WAS PART OF SP//dr.
MY FATHER IS DEAD.
UH... YES. YES, HE IS...
AND PENI, WHILE THIS MAY SEEM SUDDEN AND HARD TO PROCESS, YOU'RE THE ONLY ONE THAT CAN TAKE HIS PLACE IN THE PROGRAM.
IT'S A MATTER OF GENETICS, DEAR. COMPATIBILITY.
THEY TOLD ME IT'S GOING TO HURT...
...IF SP//dr ACCEPTS ME...

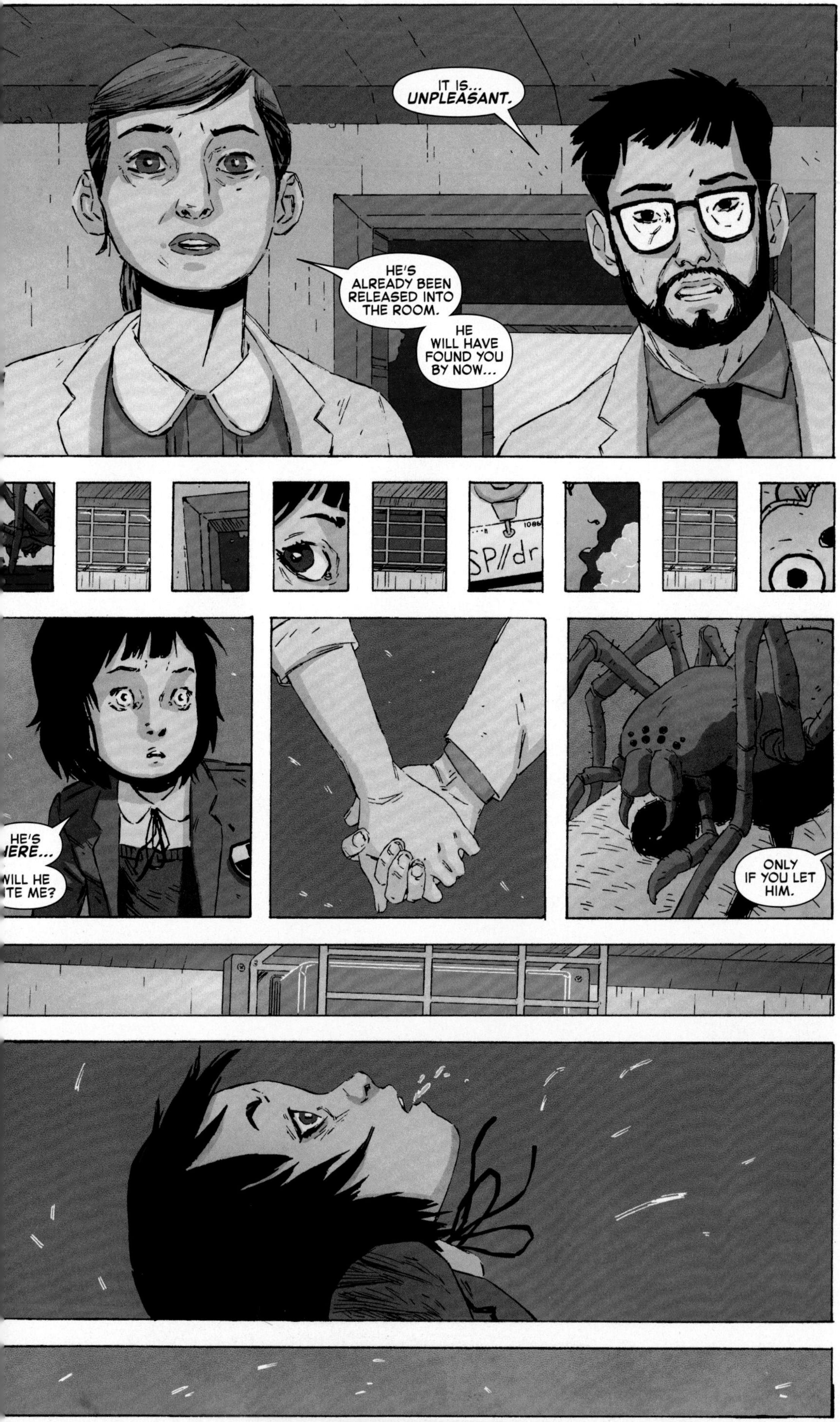
IT IS... UNPLEASANT.
HE'S ALREADY BEEN RELEASED INTO THE ROOM.
HE WILL HAVE FOUND YOU BY NOW...
SP//dr
HE'S
WILL HE
ONLY IF YOU LET HIM.

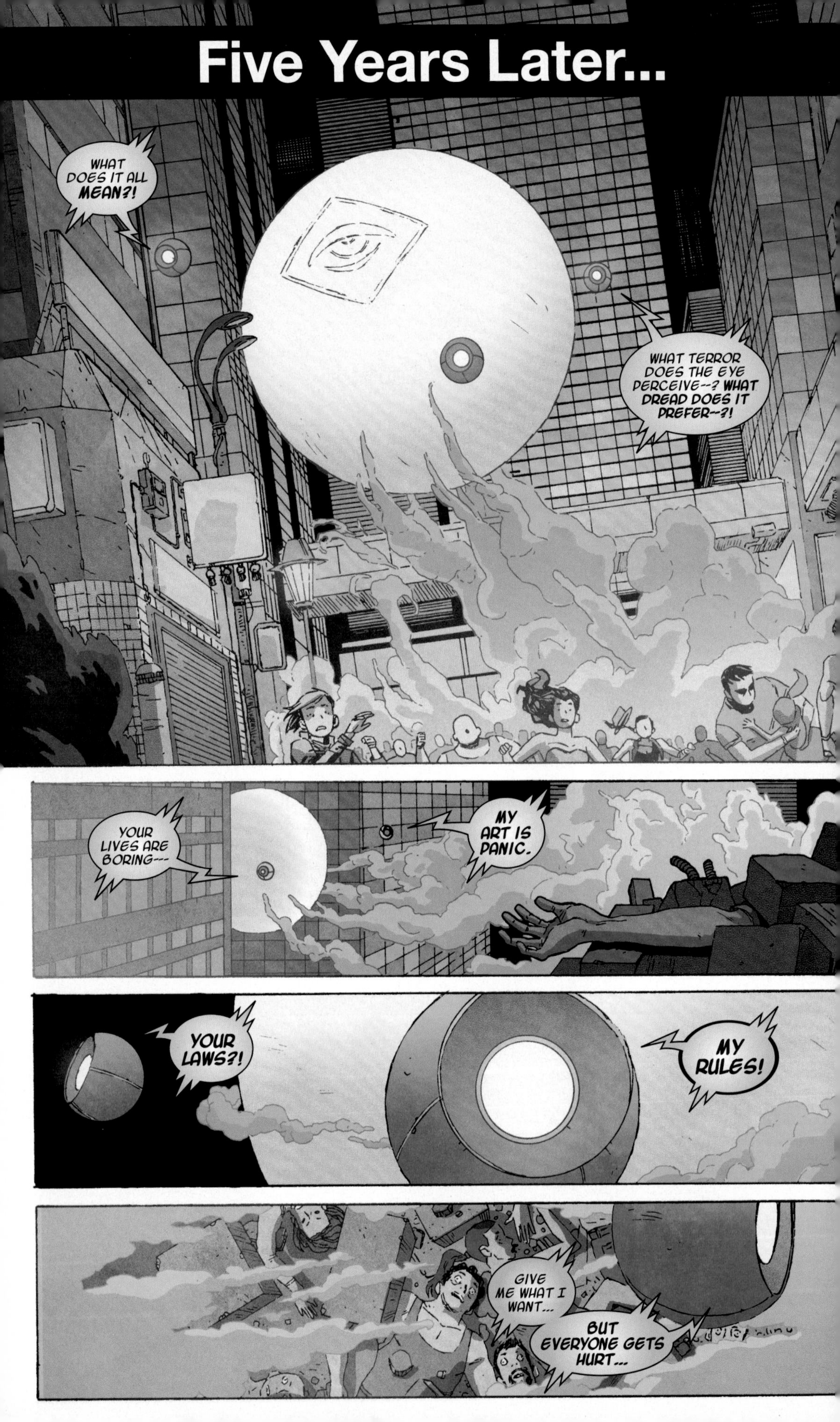
Five Years Later...
WHAT DOES IT ALL MEAN?!
WHAT TERROR DOES THE EYE PERCEIVE--? WHAT DREAD DOES IT PREFER--?!
YOUR LIVES ARE BORING---
MY ART IS PANIC.
YOUR LAWS?!
MY RULES!
GIVE ME WHAT I WANT...
BUT EVERYONE GETS HURT...

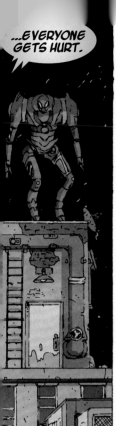

...EVERYONE GETS HURT.

PENI, YOUR UNCLE HAS REQUESTED THAT I REMIND YOU TO BE EXTREMELY CAUTIOUS OUT THERE--

THIS ONE ISN'T LIKE THE OTHERS.

THIS ONE TALKS A LOT.

HIS NAME IS MYSTERIO-- AND HE'S USING SOME SORT OF NERVE GAS WITH HALLUCINOGENIC PROPERTIES.

FILTERS?

THEY SHOULD PROTECT YOU, BUT KEEP AN EYE ON YOUR TOXICITY LEVELS.

CAN WE LISTEN TO MUSIC?

IT HELPS US FOCUS.

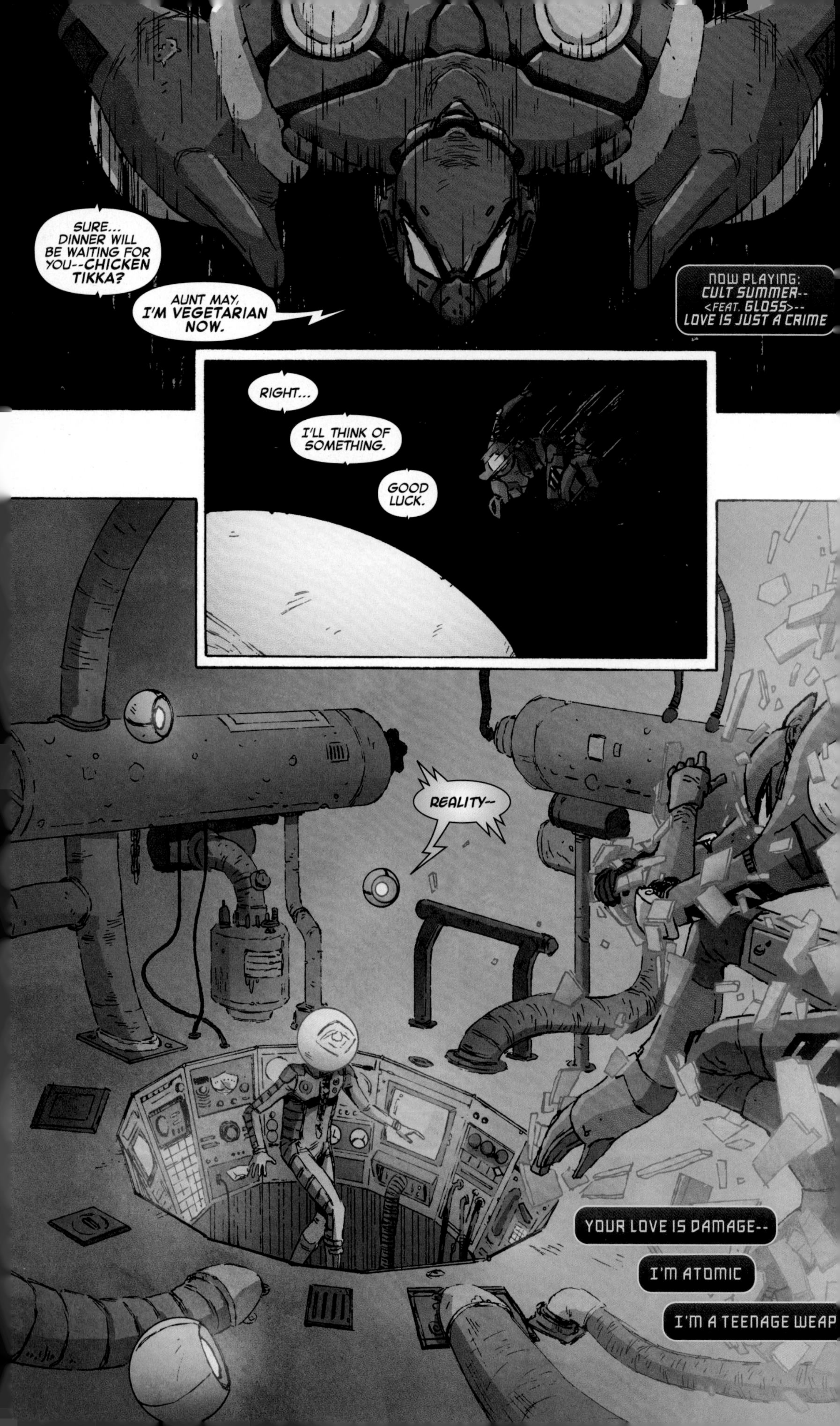
SURE... DINNER WILL BE WAITING FOR YOU--CHICKEN TIKKA?
AUNT MAY, I'M VEGETARIAN NOW.
NOW PLAYING: CULT SUMMER-- <FEAT. GLOSS>-- LOVE IS JUST A CRIME
RIGHT...
I'LL THINK OF SOMETHING.
GOOD LUCK.
REALITY--
YOUR LOVE IS DAMAGE--
I'M ATOMIC
I'M A TEENAGE WEAP

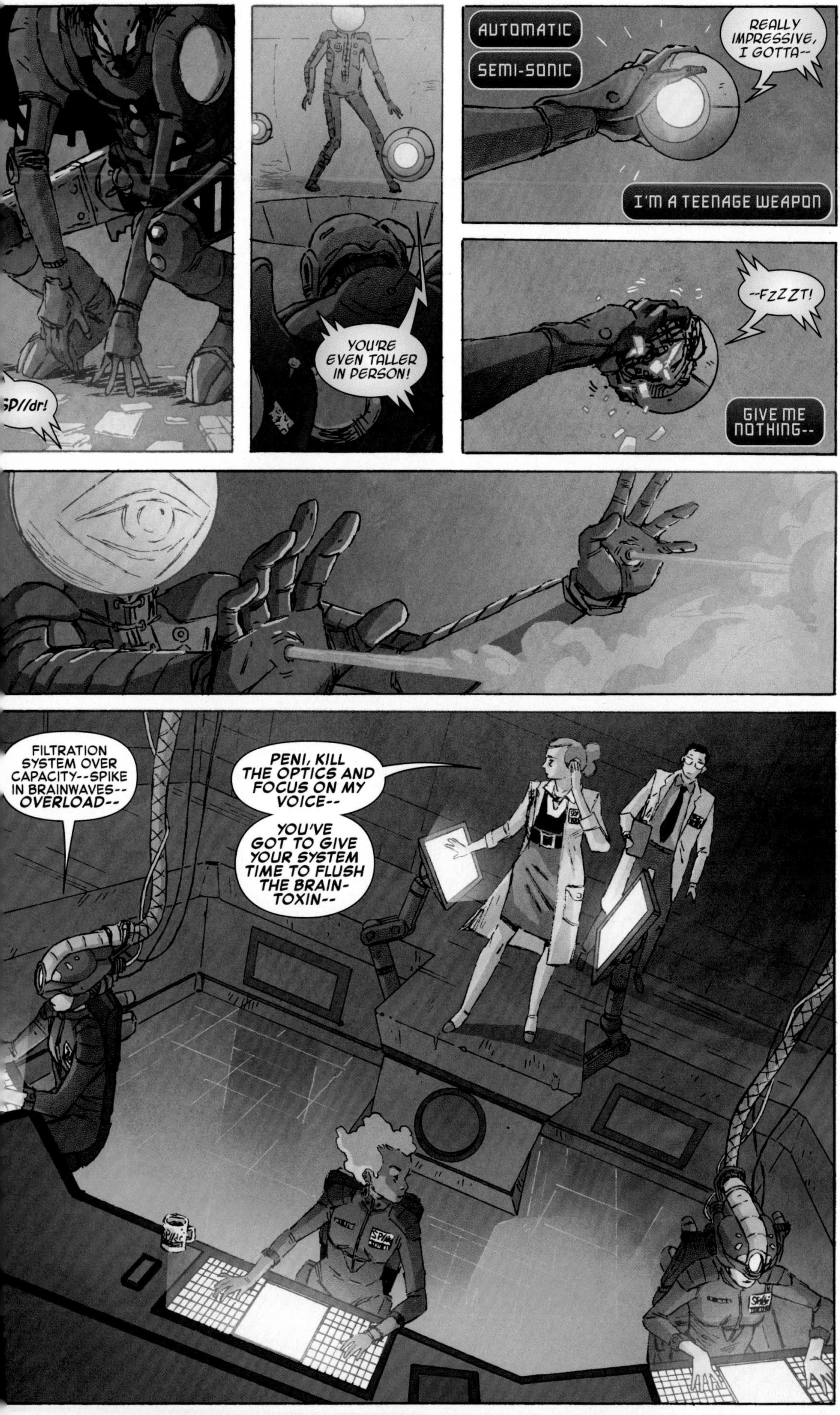

SP//dr!
YOU'RE EVEN TALLER IN PERSON!
AUTOMATIC
SEMI-SONIC
REALLY IMPRESSIVE, I GOTTA--
I'M A TEENAGE WEAPON
--FZZZT!
GIVE ME NOTHING--
FILTRATION SYSTEM OVER CAPACITY--SPIKE IN BRAINWAVES--OVERLOAD--
PENI, KILL THE OPTICS AND FOCUS ON MY VOICE--
YOU'VE GOT TO GIVE YOUR SYSTEM TIME TO FLUSH THE BRAIN-TOXIN--

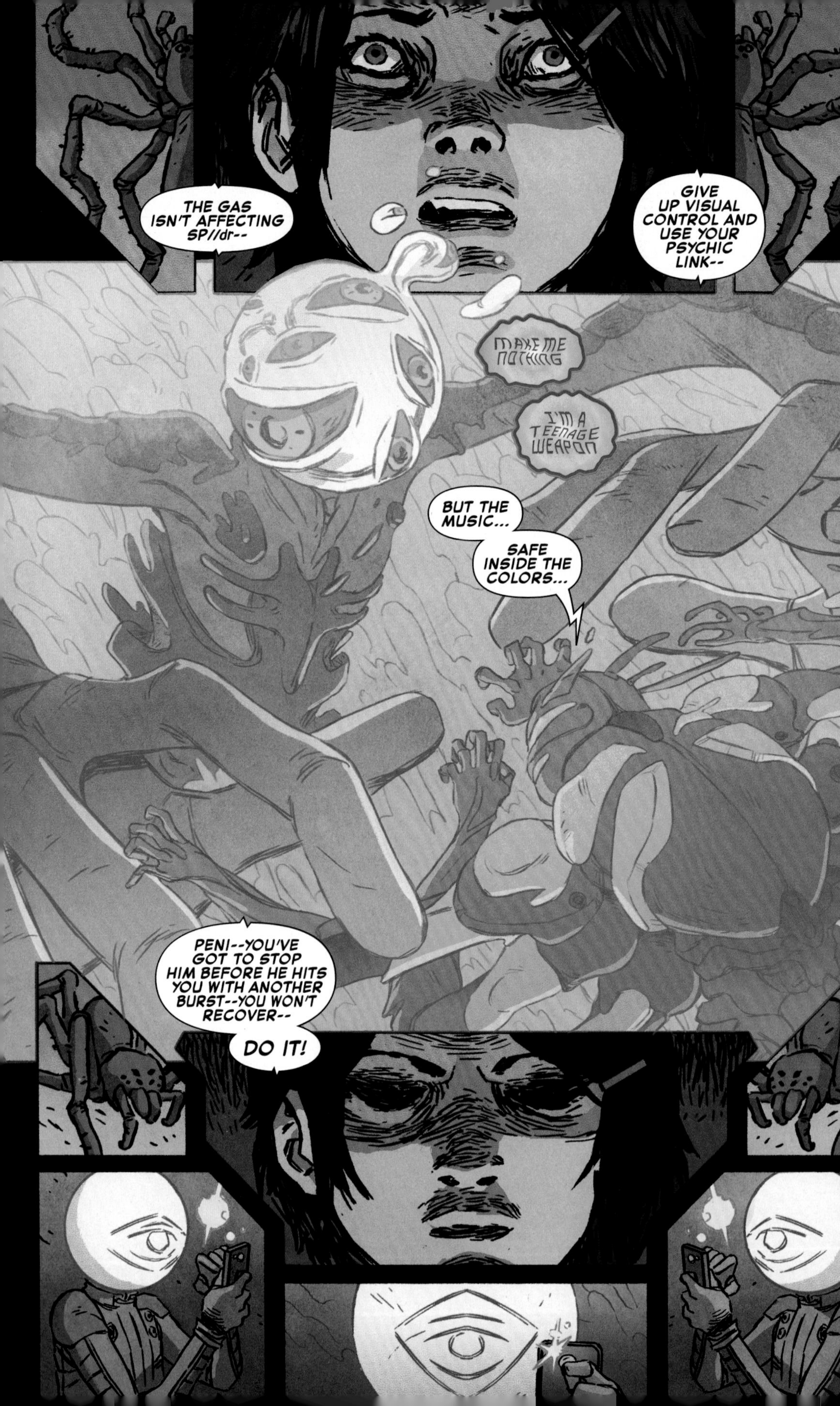
THE GAS ISN'T AFFECTING SP//dr--
GIVE UP VISUAL CONTROL AND USE YOUR PSYCHIC LINK--
MAKE ME NOTHING
I'M A TEENAGE WEAPON
BUT THE MUSIC...
SAFE INSIDE THE COLORS...
PENI--YOU'VE GOT TO STOP HIM BEFORE HE HITS YOU WITH ANOTHER BURST--YOU WON'T RECOVER--
DO IT!

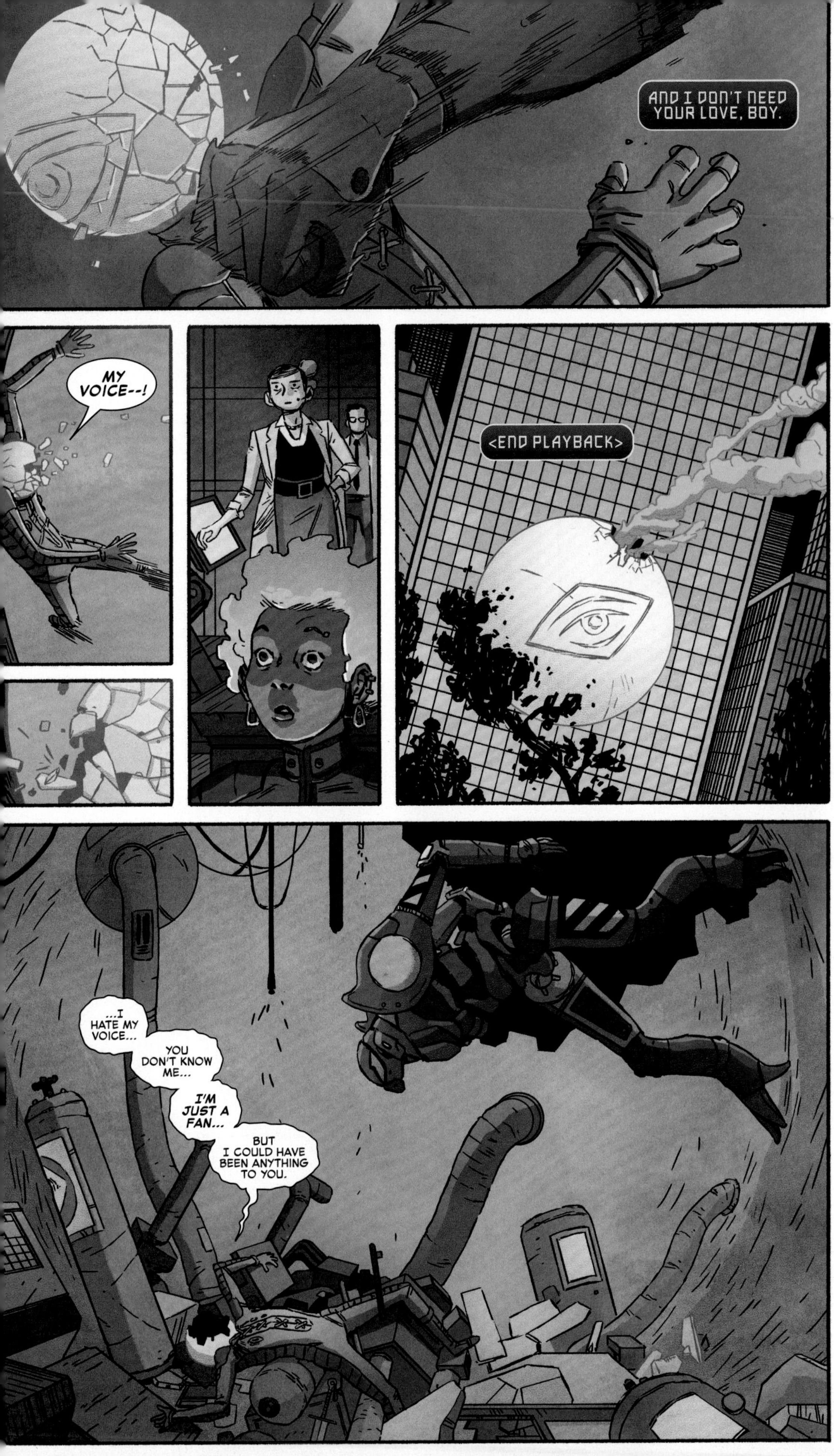
AND I DON'T NEED YOUR LOVE, BOY.
MY VOICE--!
<END PLAYBACK>
...I HATE MY VOICE...
YOU DON'T KNOW ME...
I'M JUST A FAN...
BUT I COULD HAVE BEEN ANYTHING TO YOU.

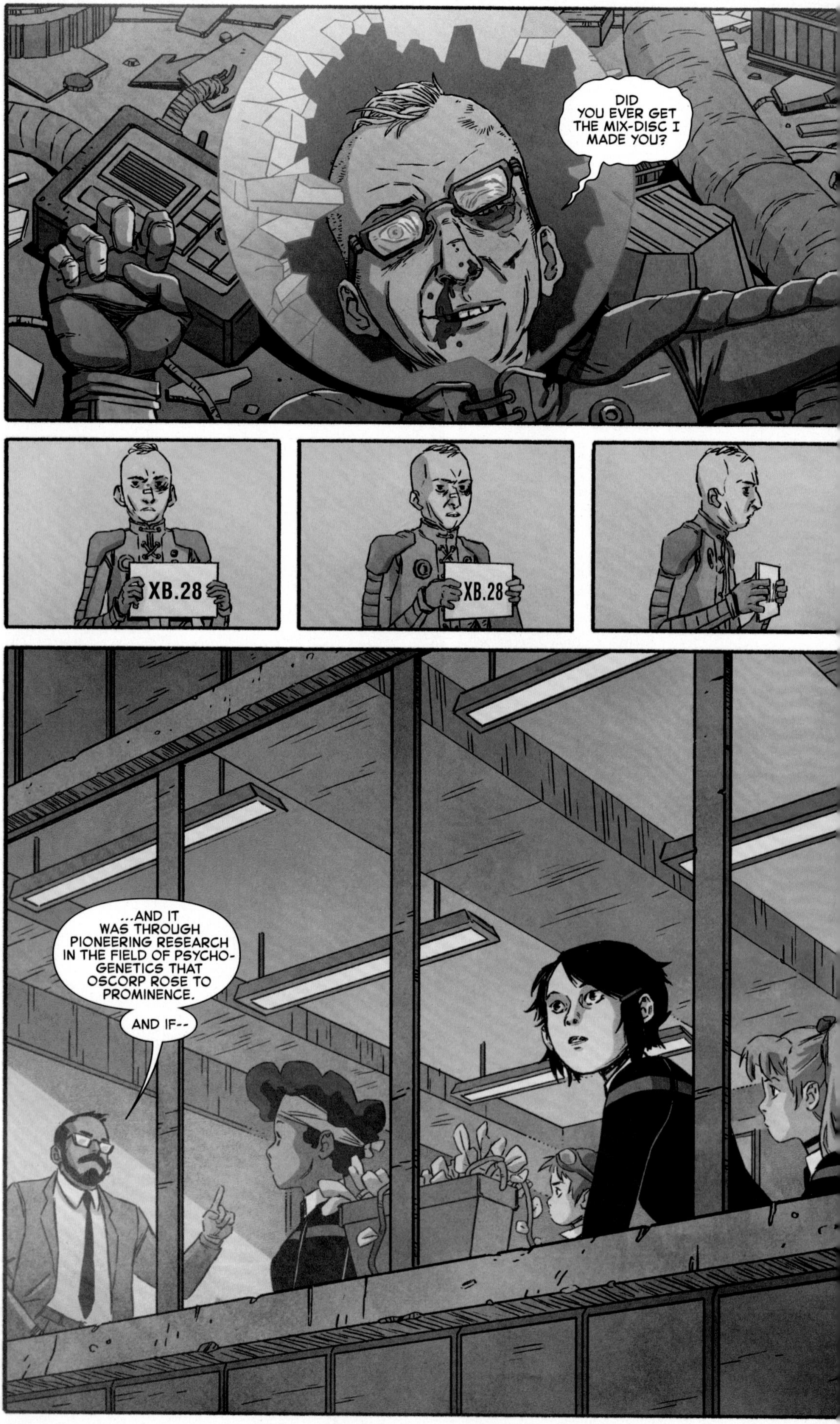
DID YOU EVER GET THE MIX-DISC I MADE YOU?
XB.28
XB.28
...AND IT WAS THROUGH PIONEERING RESEARCH IN THE FIELD OF PSYCHO-GENETICS THAT OSCORP ROSE TO PROMINENCE.
AND IF--

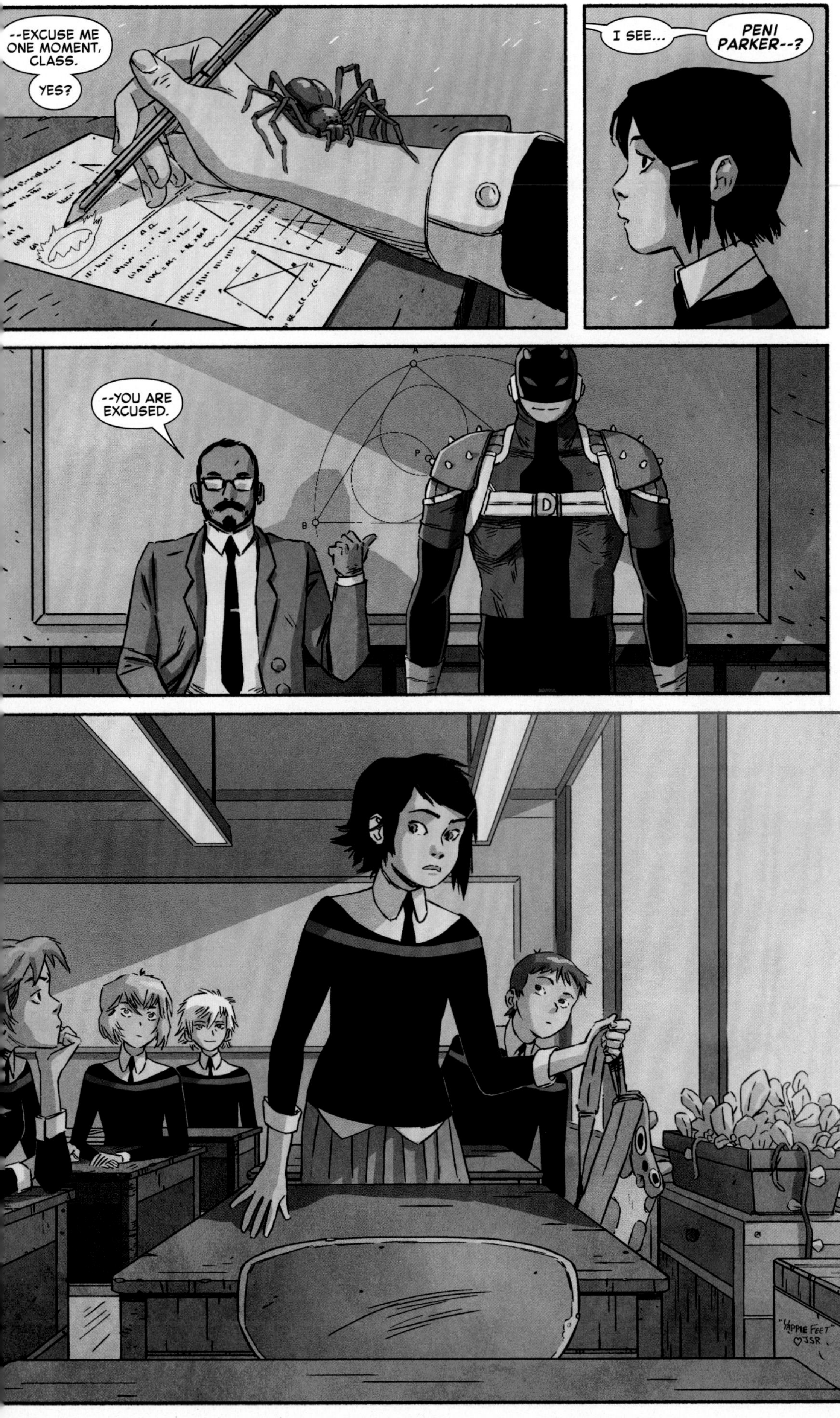
--EXCUSE ME ONE MOMENT, CLASS.
YES?
I SEE...
PENI PARKER--?
--YOU ARE EXCUSED.
"YAPPIE FEET"
♡JSR

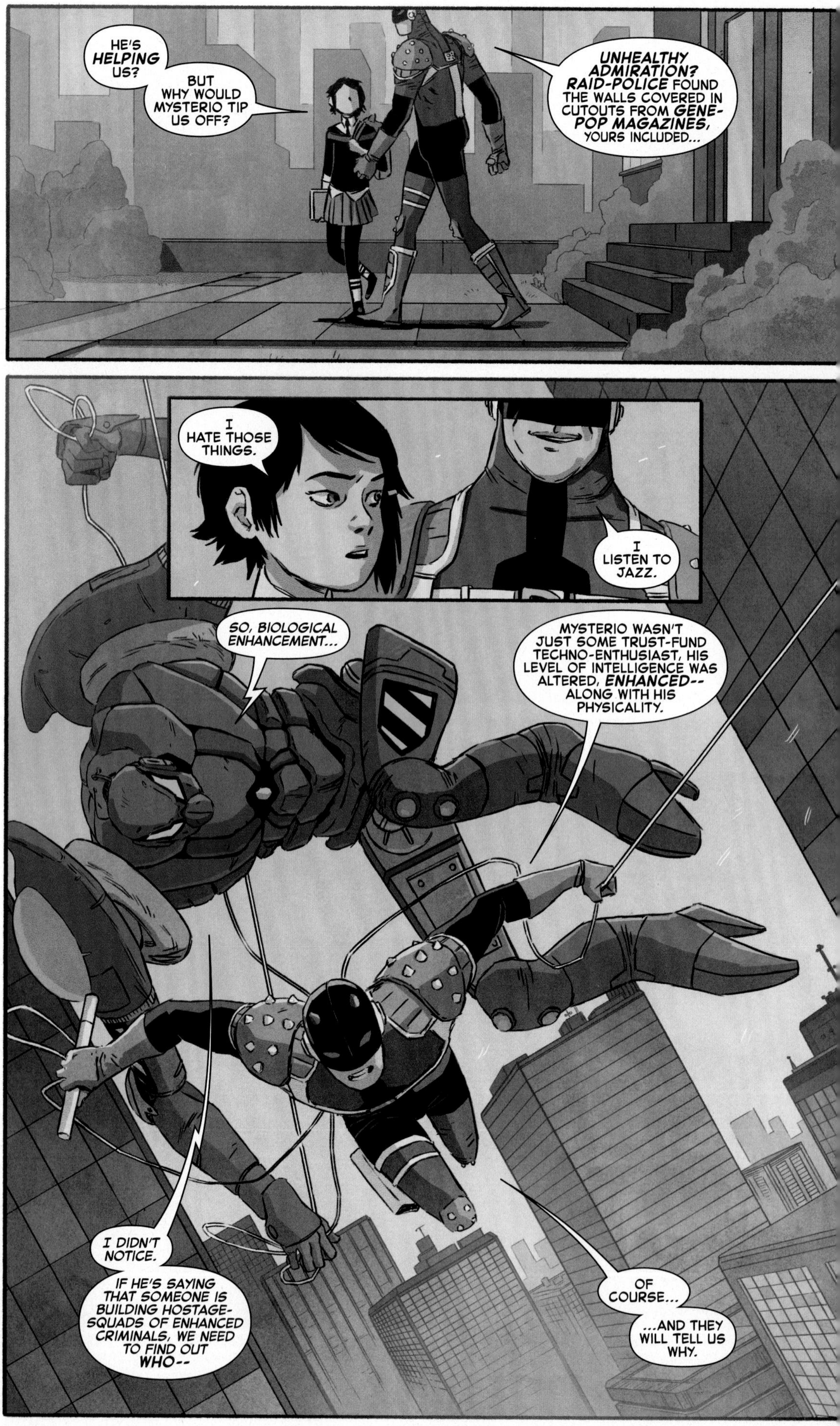

HE'S HELPING US?
BUT WHY WOULD MYSTERIO TIP US OFF?
UNHEALTHY ADMIRATION? RAID-POLICE FOUND THE WALLS COVERED IN CUTOUTS FROM GENE-POP MAGAZINES, YOURS INCLUDED...
I HATE THOSE THINGS.
I LISTEN TO JAZZ.
SO, BIOLOGICAL ENHANCEMENT...
MYSTERIO WASN'T JUST SOME TRUST-FUND TECHNO-ENTHUSIAST, HIS LEVEL OF INTELLIGENCE WAS ALTERED, ENHANCED-- ALONG WITH HIS PHYSICALITY.
I DIDN'T NOTICE.
IF HE'S SAYING THAT SOMEONE IS BUILDING HOSTAGE-SQUADS OF ENHANCED CRIMINALS, WE NEED TO FIND OUT WHO--
OF COURSE...
...AND THEY WILL TELL US WHY.

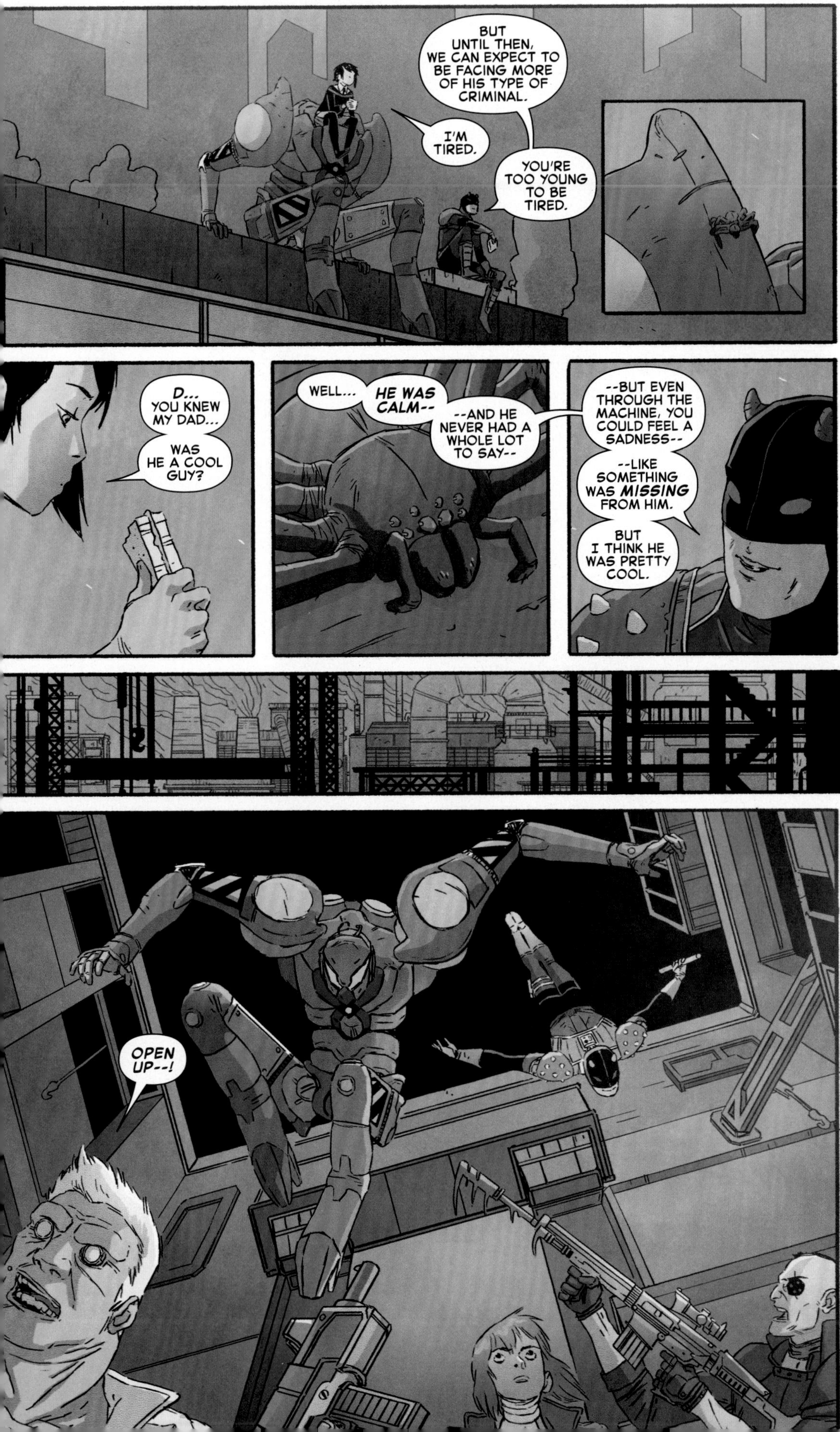

BUT UNTIL THEN, WE CAN EXPECT TO BE FACING MORE OF HIS TYPE OF CRIMINAL.
I'M TIRED.
YOU'RE TOO YOUNG TO BE TIRED.
D... YOU KNEW MY DAD...
WAS HE A COOL GUY?
WELL...
HE WAS CALM--
--AND HE NEVER HAD A WHOLE LOT TO SAY--
--BUT EVEN THROUGH THE MACHINE, YOU COULD FEEL A SADNESS--
--LIKE SOMETHING WAS MISSING FROM HIM.
BUT I THINK HE WAS PRETTY COOL.
OPEN UP--!

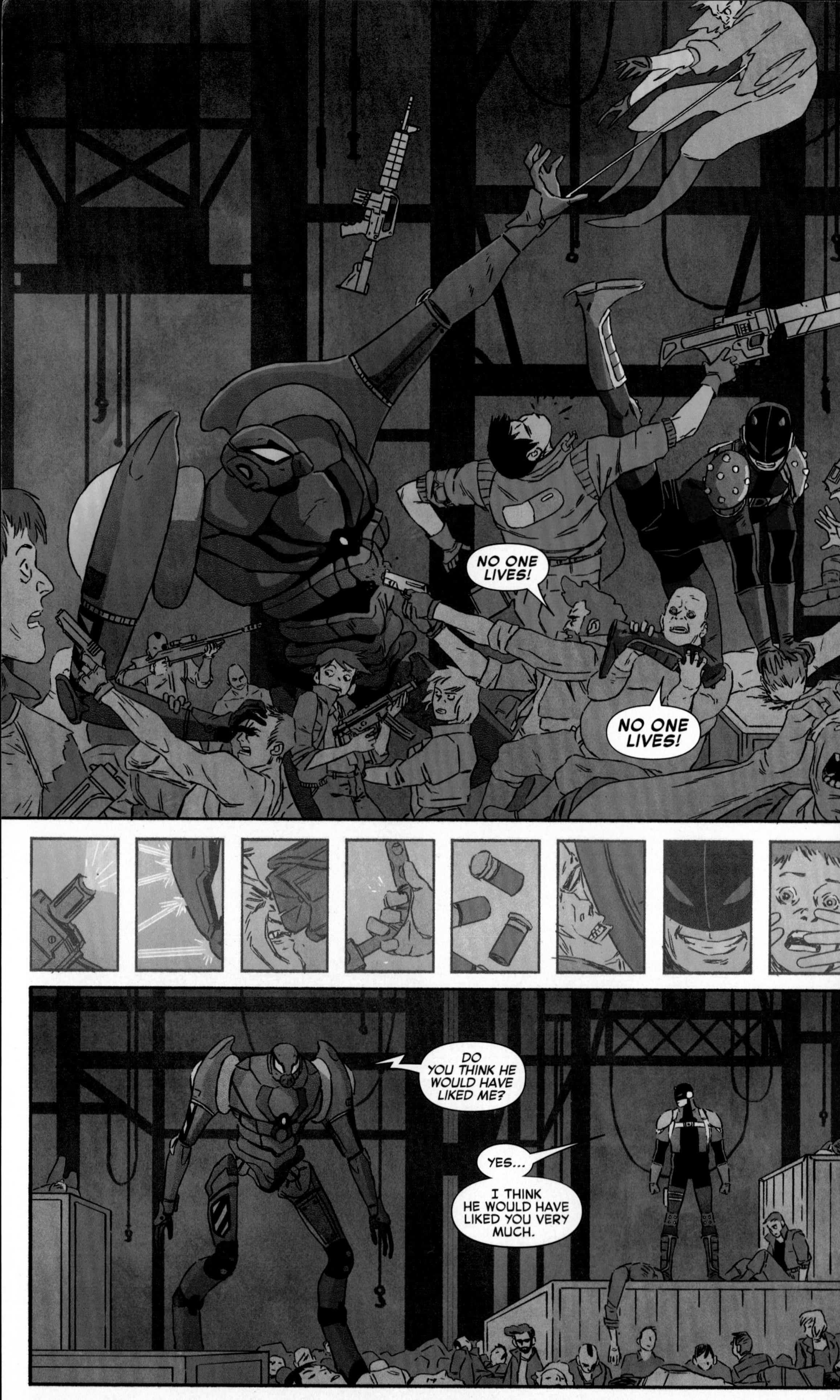
NO ONE LIVES!
NO ONE LIVES!
DO YOU THINK HE WOULD HAVE LIKED ME?
YES...
I THINK HE WOULD HAVE LIKED YOU VERY MUCH.

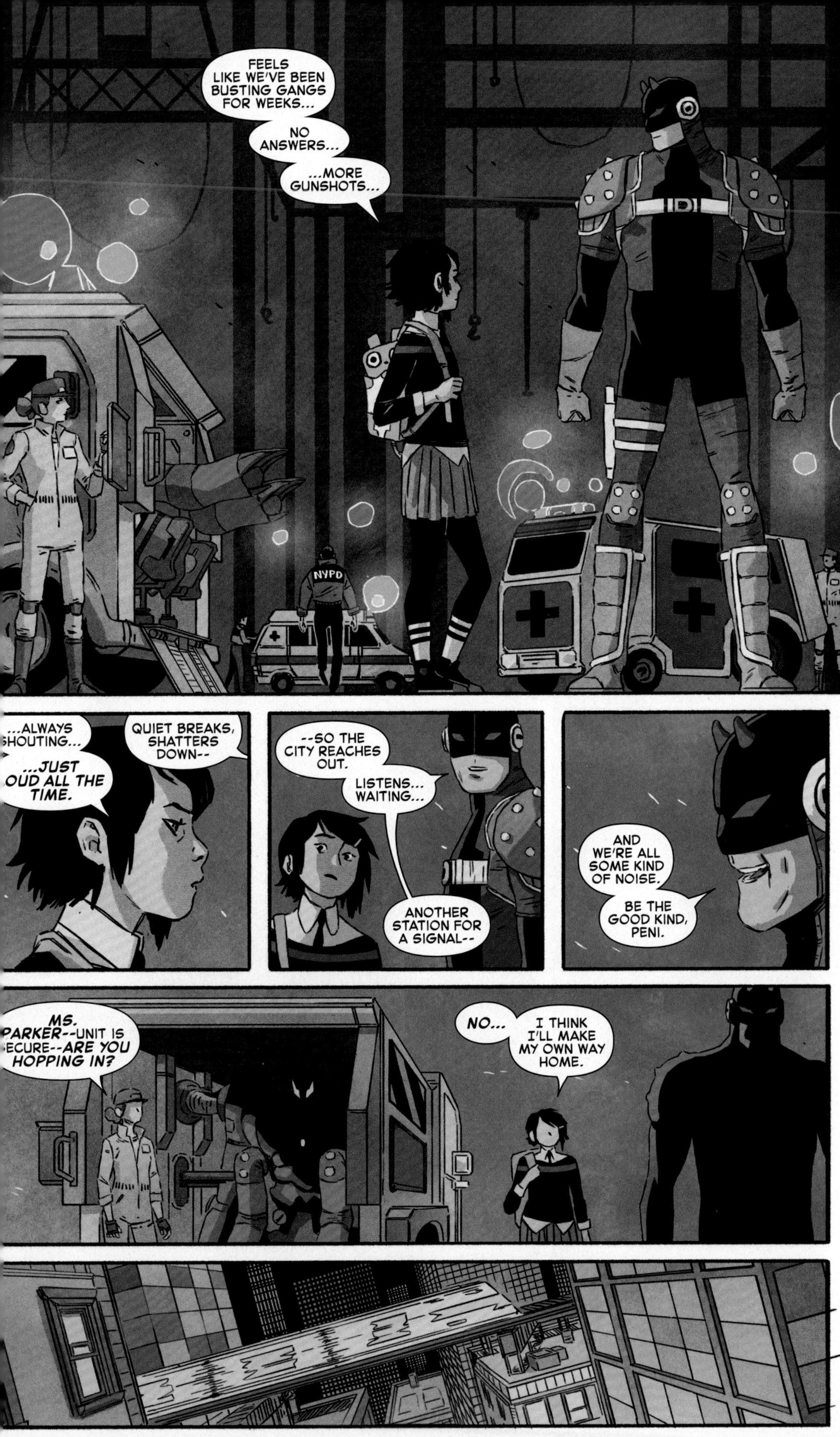
FEELS LIKE WE'VE BEEN BUSTING GANGS FOR WEEKS...
NO ANSWERS...
...MORE GUNSHOTS...
NYPD
...ALWAYS SHOUTING...
...JUST LOUD ALL THE TIME.
QUIET BREAKS, SHATTERS DOWN--
--SO THE CITY REACHES OUT.
LISTENS... WAITING...
ANOTHER STATION FOR A SIGNAL--
AND WE'RE ALL SOME KIND OF NOISE.
BE THE GOOD KIND, PENI.
MS. PARKER--UNIT IS SECURE--ARE YOU HOPPING IN?
NO...
I THINK I'LL MAKE MY OWN WAY HOME.

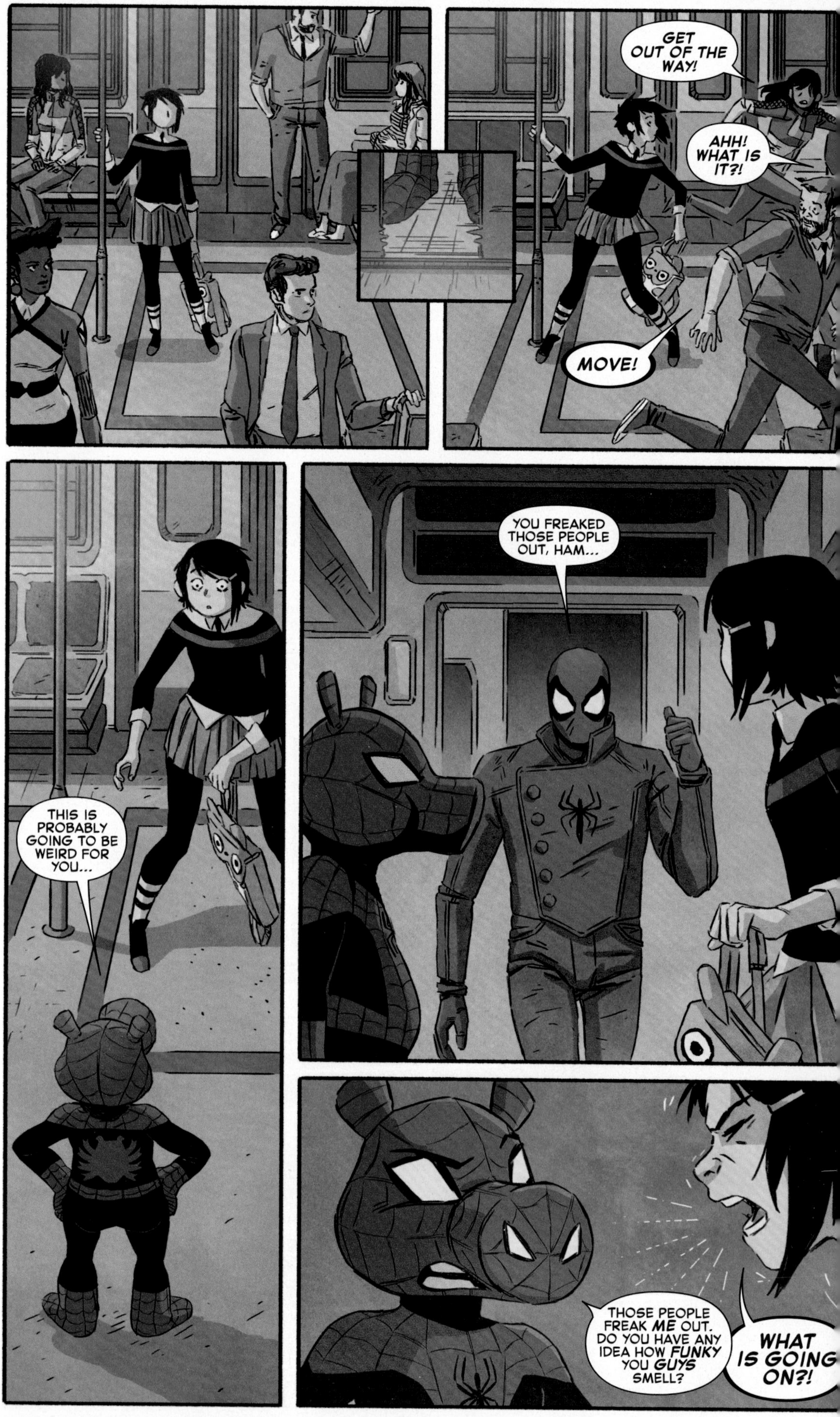
GET OUT OF THE WAY!
AHH! WHAT IS IT?!
MOVE!
YOU FREAKED THOSE PEOPLE OUT, HAM...
THIS IS PROBABLY GOING TO BE WEIRD FOR YOU...
THOSE PEOPLE FREAK ME OUT. DO YOU HAVE ANY IDEA HOW FUNKY YOU GUYS SMELL?
WHAT IS GOING ON?!